Applied Computing

Springer

London
Berlin
Heidelberg
New York
Barcelona
Hong Kong
Milan
Paris
Santa Clara
Singapore
Tokyo

The Springer-Verlag Series on Applied Computing is an advanced series of innovative textbooks that span the full range of topics in applied computing technology.

Books in the series provide a grounding in theoretical concepts in computer science alongside real-world examples of how those concepts can be applied in the development of effective computer systems.

The series should be essential reading for advanced undergraduate and postgraduate students in computing and information systems.

Books in this series are contributed by international specialist researchers and educators in applied computing who draw together the full range of issues in their specialist area into one concise authoritative textbook.

Titles already available:

Deryn Graham and Anthony Barrett
Knowledge-Based Image processing Systems
3-540-76027-X

Linda Macaulay
Requirements Engineering
3-540-76006-7

Derrick Morris, Gareth Evans, Peter Green, Colin Theaker
Object Orientated Computer Systems Engineering
3-540-76020-2

John Hunt
Java and Object Orientation: An Introduction
3-540-76148-9

David Gray
Introduction to the Formal Design of Real-Time Systems
3-540-76140-3

Mike Holcombe and Florentin Ipate
Correct Systems: Building A Business Process Solution
3-540-76246-9

Available in the Advanced Perspectives in Applied Computing series:

Sarah Douglas and Anant Mithal
The Ergonomics of Computer Pointing Devices
3-540-19986-1

Jan Noyes and Chris Baber

User-Centred Design of Systems

Springer

Jan Noyes, BSc PhD, Cert.Ed
Department of Psychology, University of Bristol,
8 Woodland Road, Bristol. BS8 1TN, UK

Chris Baber, BSc PhD
School of Manufacturing and Mechanical Engineering,
University of Birmingham, Edgbaston, Birmingham. B15 2TT, UK

Series Editors
Professor Ray J. Paul, BSc MSc PhD
Department of Information Systems and Computing, Brunel University,
Uxbridge, Middlesex UB8 3PH, UK

Professor Peter J. Thomas, BA PhD MIEE MErgS MBCS CEng FRSA
Centre for Personal Information Management, University of the West of England,
Frenchay Campus, Bristol BS16 1QY, UK

Dr Jasna Kuljis, PhD MS Dipl Ing
Department of Mathematical and Computing Sciences, Goldsmiths College,
University of London, New Cross, London SE14 6NW, UK

ISBN 3-540-76007-5 Springer-Verlag Berlin Heidelberg New York

British Library Cataloguing in Publication Data
A catalogue record for this book is available from the British Library.

Library of Congress Cataloging-in-Publication Data
Noyes, Janet M.
    User-centered design of systems / Jan Noyes and Chris Baber.
        p. cm. (Applied computing)
    Includes bibliographical references and index.
    ISBN 3-540-76007-5 (alk. paper)
    1. System design. 2. Human-computer interaction. I. Baber,
Christopher, 1964- . II. Title. III. Series.
QA76.9.S88N69 1999   99-17688
004.2'1—dc21   CIP

Typeset by Gray Publishing, Tunbridge Wells, Kent
Printed and bound at the Athenæum Press Ltd., Gateshead, Tyne & Wear
34/3830-543210 Printed on acid-free paper SPIN 10504860

Contents

Preface

System design has conventionally been the province of engineers, and the approaches taken to the design of systems have conventionally led to formal specification of the system. The past decade or two has seen the rise of another approach, that of human–computer interaction (HCI). Given the number of incidents and accidents which are attributed to 'human error', it is sensible to develop an approach to system design which views humans as an essential element in the system. Thus, an important aspect of designing systems is the study of the interaction between humans and the technology that they use. In terms of bringing computers and computing to a wide audience, the 1980s were the boom years. The first personal computer (PC) was launched onto the market in February 1978, and since then, PCs have become a common-place feature of our homes, offices, schools, retail outlets, hospitals, banks, etc. Within Western society today, there are very few organisations that have not been infiltrated by computer technology, and few individuals who have not had experience of computers. However, the increase in use of computers has not been matched with a corresponding spread of training of users; much of the human–computer interaction research has sought to design systems which do not require special training, i.e. which people can simply walk up to and use. Not surprisingly, this has resulted in a number of difficulties; some of which have yet to be satisfactorily resolved.

USER-CENTRED DESIGN

From the *human* perspective taken in this book, the principle purpose in studying and comprehending the many human–technology interactions is to ensure that the system is designed to support the user, minimise error and promote productivity and performance gains. Hence, the stance taken is to design systems with the focus primarily on the user; changes and modifications being made wherever possible to the technology in order to harmonise interactions. This approach has been described as 'user-centred design' (Norman and Draper, 1986), and is often depicted graphically with the human at the centre of a series of ever-increasing circles, representing, for example, the interface, the technology, the workplace and the environment. This is shown in the Figure 0.1.

This diagrammatic representation has a number of important features: (i) it places the human in the centre of the design process; (ii) it indicates that you cannot consider human–computer interaction on its own; it must extend to encompass the many other influences on HCI, namely, the workplace, the environment and the organisation; (iii) it demonstrates the need for a generic term to cover 'computers, technology, systems, etc.' Although the approach taken in this book is human-centred, we focus primarily on human–machine interactions (i.e. HCI), and do not cover the 'other interfaces' of human–workplace, human–environment, human–organisation, in any detail. This would be a book in itself. However, despite the stance adopted here, the importance of the influence of these other interfaces on HCI can be considerable. For example, HCIs could be severely degraded in hostile environmental conditions.

Eason (1995) pursued the precise meaning of user-centred design in an interesting debate about whether this type of design was primarily *for* the users or *by* the users. Design by users, e.g. using the opinions and expectations as the basis for design, is problematic for a number of reasons. For example, users may not be aware of alternatives to current technology, and may expect the new system to be simply an improved version of the old one. Users may not be able to step back from their work practices to see how technology can change the way they work, and/or they might not be familiar with the design methods used or the technology, and may simply feel over-awed by the design process (which leads to them feeling unqualified to comment). This last point is neatly illustrated in the following scenario, where a team of highly qualified engineers was briefed on the design of a new control room system. The designers' presentation consisted entirely of data flow diagrams and formal systems analysis, which the engineers were unable to follow, and subsequent discussion was based on interpreting the diagrams, rather than discussion of the system. This suggests that involving users in design requires more than simply presenting design solutions for their ratification; it requires consultation with users in their own language and terms.

Design for users can have a number of interpretations. It might mean design for the capabilities of the users (both in terms of human physical and cognitive capabilities), or design of the work that the users will be performing. The first meaning refers to the traditional domain of ergonomics, and the second meaning has been termed 'user-centred design' by Carroll (1985). In this book, we assume that the definition of 'user-centred design' can change during the design process, from soliciting user opinion, to designing to accommodate work activities, to designing to accommodate the capabilities of people who are going to use the system. Hence, we will cover an amalgam of interpretations, including both ergonomic and traditional HCI approaches.

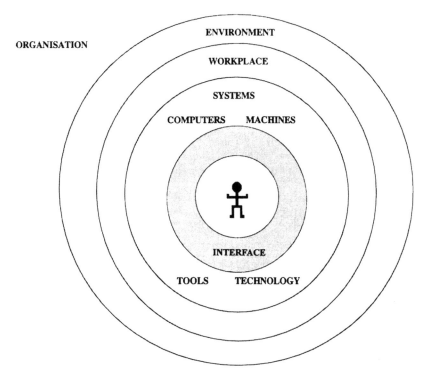

FIG. 0.1 Diagrammatic representation of user-centred design.

DESIGN AS A MULTI-DISCIPLINARY ACTIVITY

The design of systems is a multi-disciplinary activity. The optimum situation must be where a team of professionals work together, each representing the interests of the various parties, e.g. engineers designing the hardware, computer scientists developing the software, and human factors psychologists focusing on the humans who will have roles in the development, operation and maintenance of the system. There is also no need to delimit contributions from only science and engineering. As Johnson (1992) has pointed out, as the discipline of HCI has progressed, contributions have been made from the disciplines of mathematics, graphic art, sociology and artificial intelligence. He also stated that there was much to be gained from linguistics, philosophy, anthropology, and the creative and performing arts. However, it could be argued that having such a varied and rich source of disciplines able to make a contribution is in itself problematic, since it presupposes that the expertise will be available to co-ordinate and integrate the relevant activities into the system design process. As mentioned, in this book we place the interaction between human and technology centre stage, thus taking a human-centred approach. Such an approach requires frequent excursions into a wide spectrum of different research domains, methodologies and theories. In the domain of computer science and engineering, there are specialists involved in hardware design and specialists involved in software design. In the domain of human–computer interaction, specialists are involved in designing the manner in which humans can use the hardware and the software, and in this book, we aim to extend this latter aspect of design.

The focus on human–technology interaction in the design of systems raises a number of difficult questions. This book will examine these questions and demonstrate a range of potential solutions within a framework of user-centred design. Having supplied the tools and concepts for this work, we hope that the reader will be sufficiently armed to undertake the adventure of designing systems with which humans interact with good result.

Acknowledgements

The authors thank the publishers for their patience and help in the delivery of this text.

They also acknowledge the kind permission given by Cheltenham and Gloucester College of Higher Education to use some of the headings from the book *Display Design for Human–Computer Interaction* by Jan Noyes and Stella Mills (Cheltenham and Gloucester College of Higher Education, 1998, ISBN 1-86174-037-9).

Part 1
Defining Systems

1   What Is a System?

OBJECTIVES OF CHAPTER:

- To introduce the definition of system used in this book
- To consider the role of humans in system activity
- To relate the notion of system to processes of design

HAVING READ THIS CHAPTER, THE READER WILL BE ABLE:

- To specify the components of a system
- To define the mission of a system
- To consider the allocation of function to system components

---

1.1   SYSTEMS

Each approach to the design of systems has its own notion of what a system is, how it works, how to improve it, etc. As an example, people with a background in computer science will probably think of a system in quite different terms to people with a background in organisational psychology. In this section, our aim is to produce a working definition of systems which will be followed throughout this book, and which will draw upon ideas familiar to people from a variety of backgrounds.

Planes, Trains and Cars

In order to appreciate the approach taken to systems in this book, we will first consider the domain of transport systems. This is, of course, a large step away from the computer and the advanced technological systems to be discussed in the rest of the book, but it does allow us to draw analogies between types of systems. Consider the automobile: at one level of analysis, the system comprises the physical components that make up the car. Designing the system at this level of analysis requires the knowledge and expertise to select the appropriate components (having ensured that the performance of each component has been optimised), and fitting the components together into an efficient system. Let us call this the 'physical' level of system description. It should be clear that the physical level of system description can be applied to different types of transport systems (planes, trains and cars), and comprises a significant area of engineering. However, this is not the only level of description.

In order to operate, the physical system needs to have certain materials added to it. For the car, for example, these materials will be petrol, oil, water, brake/clutch fluid, etc. which will provide fuel, coolant and lubrication to the physical system, without which it will not operate to its design potential. This represents the 'operational' level of system description.

The physical and operational system is placed in an environment. For the car, this environment comprises roads, other vehicles, traffic lights and signs, petrol stations, etc. For the train, the environment comprises rails, signals, stations, other trains, etc. Likewise, for the aeroplane, the environment comprises airports, other aircraft, air traffic control systems, etc. (One might assume that planes do not have roads or rails, but in effect they do, as they will fly along specified flight paths.) This third level of description will be the 'environmental' level.

The three levels of description are thus physical, operational and environmental. As the transport systems described exist to perform specific missions of moving people and objects, we can add a fourth level of system description – the 'social' level. This will contain the various rules of operation (relating to signs and signals, laws and law enforcement, air traffic control procedures, etc.) and to the social dimensions of system use, e.g. time-tables, reasons for travel, etc.

The central question for this book is where to site humans in these different levels of description. Humans could simply be seen as orthogonal to all the levels of description, which makes the incorporation of humans into system design difficult (or, put another way, makes it easy to leave humans out of system design). However, working 'backwards' through the four levels (social, environmental, operational, physical), it is apparent that humans play key roles at each level. For example, at the social level of system description, the role of humans is both to define and police the manner in which the system is used, i.e. transport systems operate because humans desire to move themselves or their property from place to place. Humans will perform a significant safety function, in conjunction with other system components. This point can be illustrated when other components fail, e.g. when traffic lights on a busy intersection fail, it is the role of humans in the system to minimise the likelihood of cars crashing. This raises the interaction between humans and system components at the environmental level. For example, in order to operate efficiently, it is essential that the environmental components of the system interface with the operational components, e.g. when a traffic light turns red, vehicles approaching it should stop. At present, this interfacing is almost entirely performed by humans (although ongoing research could lead to cars that 'automatically' stop at red lights, i.e. where the interface between environmental and operational system components does not require human intervention). In order for the human to interface between the other system components, particular skills and abilities are required (which will be discussed in subsequent chapters). At the operational level, the role of the human is to ensure that the required materials are maintained in the system, and that the system is operating efficiently. In cars, this requires a further interface between the operational and environmental system components, e.g. to ensure that there is sufficient petrol to complete a journey, the car must be taken to a petrol station. This also requires consideration of the social level description, in that the person needs to plan a journey to the petrol station, or modify a current journey. In order for the human to perform this role efficiently, the system needs to ensure that its status is clear, e.g. through the use of fuel gauges. In large systems, such as trains and aircraft, the interface between operational and environmental components can be performed by a number of different people. The final level of description, the physical level, often requires special knowledge and skills to allow interaction; in order to provide an operational interface to the car, humans require training in the use of the controls (and to have a social obligation to demonstrate competence in driving by passing a driving test). At a lower level of interaction with the physical system, humans require more specific knowledge and skills, e.g. in order to maintain and repair the automobile.

Having outlined a four-level description of systems (physical, operational, environmental, social), we need to apply these points to advanced technology, and, in particular, computer systems. We propose that the physical level of description of computer systems will comprise the hardware of the computer, and will extend from the board circuitry of the microprocessor chips, to the display screen, to various input devices used to drive the computer. The operational level will primarily consist of the software used to run the computer, and will extend from machine code, to compilers, to the programming languages used. The social level will comprise the various goals that users will have for using the computer, while the environmental level will compose the workplace in which the computer is used. The reader might feel that this definition has missed a significant part of the computer system – namely the interface. However, there are interfaces between each level of system description, and the particular 'interface' we speak of in human-computer interaction links the operational level of the system to the human. (Indeed, one could suggest that the human, in this system, is another operational component.) The removal of one level of the system can compromise the efficiency and performance of the system as a whole, which means that the design of the system ought to operate across all levels. Finally, the key point in this argument is that humans are inextricably linked with all levels of the systems considered in this book; attempts to remove the human, through increasing automation, may solve problems on one level, but will create problems at others.

1.2   LEVELS OF SYSTEMS

In this section, we present a synthesis of ideas from general systems theory, which has a history of some 50 years (von Bertalanffy, 1950). Our aim is not to provide a complete review of general systems theory, so much as to reinforce the points made in Section 1.1. Figure 1.1 presents a simple notion of a system, which is discussed below.

A System is Made Up of Many Parts . . .

The first section of our definition of a system is simply the fact that a system is made up of many parts. This obvious statement has equally obvious consequences; in particular, one problem for the system designer is what parts 'belong' to the system. If we take a motor car as an example, it is obvious that parts such as engine, drive shaft, wheels, tyres, seats,

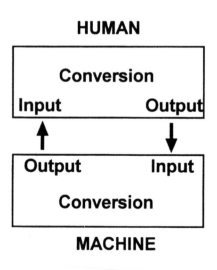

FIG. 1.1   Schematic of simple notion of a system.

steering wheel, etc. 'belong' to the system. However, is it obvious that parts such as road surface, traffic lights, petrol stations also belong to the system? The consequences of not including the parts in the second list are that the car would not be able to function effectively, i.e. without roads it might not be able to travel, without traffic lights it might not be able to move without collision, without petrol stations it might not be able to obtain fuel. A system should be considered not simply as the 'nuts and bolts' parts which make up the object, but also as those parts which enable the object to function effectively. We suggest that it is not plausible to have a system consisting solely of physical parts (which can be acted upon) without also having 'operational/environmental/social' parts. As an example, consider an automated teller machine (ATM) as a system. The 'physical' parts of the system consist of those parts that are acted upon, i.e. the machine (with screen, keypad, card reader, cash dispenser, etc.) cash and the card. The 'operational' parts of the system are those parts that support the action, i.e. the software driving the ATM, and the humans using the machine. Furthermore, the majority of ATMs are connected to one of a number of computer networks, with information concerning transactions being sent to host computers. Thus, for example, it is not possible to exceed a withdrawal limit simply by performing transactions on several machines. The computer network forms the 'environmental' part of the system, together with the placement of the ATM, e.g. whether the ATM is in the high street or in a bank lobby. Finally, the social components consist of the various goals that people have for using ATMs, or that banks have for providing ATMs.

The Output From Some Parts Acts as Input to Other Parts ...

Given that a system has many parts, there will be interfaces between the parts. In a human–computer system, the human–computer interface will consist of the specific devices used by the human to enter data, commands, etc. into the computer, and the devices used by the computer to display feedback to the user. Within the computer, there will be interfaces between hardware and software parts, which lie beyond the scope of this book. For the human, there will be interfaces between the person and the workplace, the environment and the organisation in which they are working. At each interface, information is exchanged. System design is about ensuring that the right information is exchanged at the right time, at each interface.

The Parts in a System Change in Response to Input to Them ...

When information is passed across an interface, the part receiving the information will be changed. For example, entering a personal identification number (PIN) on an ATM involves pressing a key on a keyboard – this leads to a key being moved (change 1). Movement of the key is recognised by the software (change 2), where it is converted to a machine code (change 3). The machine code is passed to another part of the software (change 4), which leads to a number appearing on the display screen (change 5). Notice that some of the changes also occur within parts. This process is termed 'conversion', and is shown in Figure 1.1.

The Changes in System Parts Lead to Changes in System Output . . .

As the parts in the system change, so the output of the system as a whole changes. Some of the changes might be so small that they are negligible, until they combine to facilitate a large change. For example, assume that the system being considered is an ATM. When a person presses a number key, the main change (gaining access to an account) only occurs when a complete PIN has been entered. Each key-press has a change associated with a PIN register (storing the digits as a string) and with the screen (presenting an asterisk * as feedback to each key press), but the system does not change until the PIN has been entered. Once a complete PIN has been entered, the system either 'moves forward' to the next step or (should the PIN not match the card) 'moves back' to the PIN entry step.

Systems Are Only Complete During Their Operation . . .

This final statement may seem a little odd at first; after all, the hardware of an ATM does not simply disappear when it is not being used. However, remember the levels of description given above. When an ATM is not being used, the system will only comprise the physical components (and some part of the operational and environmental components). It is only when operational, environmental and social components are called upon, i.e. when a person uses the machine, that the system becomes complete. This is an important consideration in system design, as there is much greater effort directed at design decisions concerning physical and operational components than at other components. The reason for this difference in emphasis lies in the ability of formal specification techniques to describe the discrete relationships between physical and operational components, rather than the less easily defined relationships between environmental and social components. For instance, it is possible to define the architecture of a computer, the manner in which inputs will be handled and processed, and the way in which output will be presented. In contrast, it appears to be more difficult to follow the same process to describe all the possible ways in which a person could use the machine.

1.3 LEVELS OF DESIGN

Having briefly introduced a notion of a system, the next question is what level of analysis should be used when examining 'system design'? In this book, we view design very much as the initial phase of developing ideas for a system, rather than the development process. Often writers imply that 'design' and 'development' are synonymous, e.g. the often-reported 'waterfall' model of design is more accurately described as a model of development, with the phases of the model leading to a working system (see Chapter 5). Our concern is with the notion of design as a process of arriving at the idea for the system. This means that the level of analysis will almost certainly exclude those parts relating to the hardware, and will probably exclude many of the parts relating to the software. These parts will be treated as black boxes, and it will be sufficient to be able to state what the inputs and outputs of these parts should be, rather than the process of conversion they will employ. Conversion of the physical parts is a matter for the development phase of the project. On the other hand, the book is concerned with those operational, social and environmental system components that involve people, and will consider the conversions that they make. It will also provide comment on the design of completed systems in the operational and maintenance phases of the life cycle.

1.4 PARADOXICAL TECHNOLOGY

A common problem in system design projects is the lack of consideration for the activity of humans as system parts (Landauer, 1995). Specification of the physical and operational parts are given priority (not least because, of themselves, these are highly complex), with attention given to the operational parts which directly act upon the physical parts, e.g. for computers this will be the software. In designing computer systems, attention is being given to the operational level, with around 50% of software writing time comprising writing of the user interface (Myers and Rosson, 1992). However, the failures of systems can often be traced to problems in the design of physical parts, and in particular to the problems at the interface between humans and hardware/software. Some writers have suggested that these problems occur as a direct result of focus on operational design, with humans being given those tasks which cannot be performed by the operational parts, i.e. the 'left-over' tasks (Bainbridge, 1983; Rasmussen, 1986). What makes this state of affairs a paradox is that the role of humans is to intervene when things go wrong. However, as the humans have not been 'designed into the system', it is not possible for them to follow the functioning of the operational parts, so that when things do go wrong, humans are not in a position to make appropriate corrections and remedial actions. From our systems' model, paradoxical technology results from lack of information exchange across the human–machine interface, leading to an inability of conversion in the (human) physical part of the system. Clearly, if such problems occur in another physical part of the system (e.g. software), the system would be expected to malfunction or crash. Thus, designs should ensure adequate interfacing across operational and physical parts of a system, and should support conversion within each part of the system.

1.5 ALLOCATION OF FUNCTION

In the human factors engineering literature, there has been considerable interest in how best to allocate activities to machines and people. Given the discussion of paradoxical technology, it is clear that simply assigning activity to operational components without consideration of the role of physical components can lead to problems in system operation. One somewhat simplistic approach to this aspect of the design problem is to list those activities where the performance of humans or machines is superior (see Table 1.1).

This 'Fitts list' approach (Fitts, 1951) can be useful in initial design discussions. However, there are several problems with it. Chapanis (1965a) argued that the distinctions drawn between humans and machines rely on over-simplifications of the ability of both. For example, machines evolve faster than the lists can be drawn, and human performance can be modified through training and experience, although of course, there are still limits to human capabilities. More importantly, just because a machine can do something does not mean that it must be used. One approach to allocating function, beyond simply listing capabilities, is to define different versions of the system, for example,

Table 1.1 Example of a Fitt's list

Characteristic	Human	Machine
Speed	Moderate, tires	Fast, constant
Power	Moderate, tires	High, constant
Repeatability	Variable	Excellent
Memory	Limited	Large storage
Decision-making	Heuristic	Rule-based
Calculation	Slow	Fast
Intelligence	Flexible	Limited
Dexterity	Flexible	Limited

Table 1.2 Meister's allocation of function

Mainly human	Human–Machine	Mainly machine
Operator detects target, examines features of target, and reports likely type of target.	Operator detects target. Computer also detects target, and looks up target in database.	Signal exceeds threshold and is identified as target. Target looked up in database.
Computer suggests likely type.	Likely target displayed to operator.	
Operator determines likely type on basis of computer advice and own judgement, and reports.	Operator reports target.	

(From *Human Factors, Theory and Practice* by D. Meister, © 1971. Reprinted by permission of John Wiley & Sons, Inc.)

one which has a mixture of operational and physical components, one which is predominantly operational, etc. The following example, taken from Meister (1971) illustrates how this might work.

While the 'mainly machine' design has definable advantages in terms of operator training, operator workload and reduced human error, it also has a number of problems, e.g. if several signals of equal probability can be identified, how to determine the most likely, solely on the basis of the available information. Humans are very good at adding additional information to aid interpretation of information (which can also lead to human error or bias). If the human is removed from the loop, then the paradoxical technology situation will arise. This means that, before allocating functions to components, it is sensible to define the mission of the system, and the activities that need to be performed. One useful technique at this stage of design is to draw flow diagrams.

1.6 MISSION ANALYSIS

When systems are operating, they produce definable output. This output can be considered in terms of the mission of the system, i.e. a social component of the system. The mission of the system can be defined by the actions it has been designed to perform. We can define the actions of physical components in terms of discrete factors, such as their mechanical properties. Defining the actions of physical components can be more difficult. For example, given the role of software as a physical component in the system, there is the possibility of actions arising which have not been planned, i.e. emergent behaviour. Such emergent behaviour can arise from 'bugs' in the software, or from complex interactions between different parts of code that had not previously been considered. A great deal of effort is put into ensuring that software is reliable for the task at hand (although there are still many debates as to whether emergent behaviours can be eradicated). Assuming that emergent behaviour is a characteristic of physical components of a system, it is probable that humans will introduce yet more emergent behaviours into the system.

In order to define the unfolding mission of a system, one can draw a physical flow diagram. For this, it is necessary to define the activities (functions) which will be performed by the system, and to understand the sequence in which activities will occur. This means that, in addition to listing the activities, you must decide which activities need to be completed before others can be started, so that the output of one system component, for example, can be fed into the next component. Figure 1.2 shows an example of a function flow diagram. Each block in the diagram represents a specific activity that can be undertaken by a system component. Notice that there is no distinction between physical and operational components at this stage. The aim is to produce a description that defines the mission of the system. Ideally, these diagrams will evolve through a number of iterations. It is often useful to write each activity on a 'Post-it' note to enable activities to be moved around during design discussions.

In order to generate the physical flow diagram, there are several stages that need to have occurred, the main one being to define the mission of the system. To a large extent, defining a system's mission is either provided by a client or another outside body. However, in product development, there is a need to define novel products, and it is at this

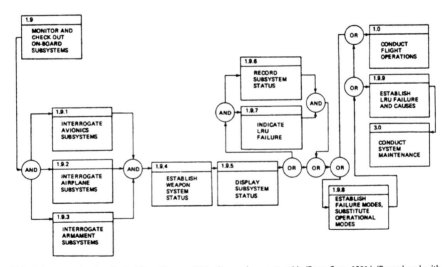

FIG. 1.2 Example of a physical flow diagram (LRU = line replacement unit). (From Geer, 1981.) (Reproduced with permission of the McGraw-Hill Companies.)

stage that other techniques might be required to define initial concepts. This topic is discussed in more detail in Chapter 7.

Notice that the diagram not only indicates the sequence of activities but also the relationship between them, in the form of Boolean logic. The use of *and* and *or* gates can allow decisions to be made as to whether activities should, in fact, be performed together, e.g. it might be possible for activities 1.9.1–1.9.3 to be combined into a single display. The question is whether such a combined display would be intelligible to the person reading it. In other words, the operational components could combine information in a parallel fashion (i.e. a single display), but the physical components (i.e. human operator) might need to deal with the information in a serial fashion. Furthermore, the relationship between the information sources will need to be determined before display decisions are made, e.g. if the aircraft and avionics subsystems are always checked together, they need to be placed adjacently. This is the basic principle of layout analysis.

1.7 CONCLUSIONS

In this chapter, we have introduced the notion of a system comprising many components. We have suggested that humans constitute a significant component of many systems, and that system design should consider this aspect. By marginalising human requirements, the risk of producing paradoxical technology is heightened. This can lead to a major cause in system failure – namely, human error. By describing the mission of a system, and seeing the process of describing a mission as an iterative process, it is possible to develop a core understanding of the activities the system needs to perform, and these can be represented in the form of physical flow diagrams. Clearly, an objection to this approach may be that it will detract from the real business of making something, and there has been a trend towards using rapid prototyping (see Chapter 5). However, rapid prototyping requires commitment to design principles (embodied in the initial design) which may not be appropriate to the final system. It is obviously more cost-effective to make changes to earlier designs than to later versions, when not only design decisions, but also production and other decisions, will have been finalised.

1.8   EXERCISE 1

Exercise 1 Mission Analysis

Task:

You have been asked to produce a ticket-vending machine for use on a small underground rail network. There are, at present, six stations in the network (although there are plans for more stations). The ticket-vending machine should be able to accept all forms of payment (coin, notes, credit cards), and should dispense adult and child, single, return, and full-day tickets.

a) What is the mission of the system?
b) What are the 'physical' parts of the system?
c) What are the 'operational' parts of the system?
d) What are the 'environmental' parts of the system?
e) What are the 'social' parts of the system?
f) What information exchanges are likely to occur between operational parts?

Model Answer:

Mission:

To vend tickets to passengers that are valid for specific journeys, and to allow all forms of payment.

Physical parts:

Hardware of machine/buttons/display/dispensing mechanism/money and card mechanisms/tickets/money/card.

Operational parts:

Users.

Environmental parts:

Station concourse.

Social parts:

Other passengers.

Information exchanges between operational parts:

Status display, instructions, feedback, labels on buttons, prompts.
Ticket request, payment insertion (coins, notes, cards).

1.9 SELECTED REFERENCES

David Meister, *Human Factors Testing and Evaluation*, Elsevier, New York, 1986. A discussion of the discipline of human factors by one of its leading exponents, with detailed consideration of the methods used by human factors practitioners, and the reasons for choosing different methods.

Donald Norman, *The Psychology of Everyday Things*, Basic Books, New York, 1988. A book that considers the difficulties of operating everyday objects (doors that are difficult to open, microwaves that are difficult to use, light switches that confuse), and poses various suggestions for how to make products more usable.

T. Morris Fraser, *The Worker at Work*, Taylor and Francis, London, 1989. Chapter 2, 'A Systems Viewpoint', provides a good and relevant overview of a system within the context of different environments.

2

Who Will Use the System?

OBJECTIVES OF CHAPTER:

- To introduce ideas from psychology to system designers
- To consider the role of knowledge, skills and abilities of users
- To introduce basic knowledge elicitation techniques

HAVING READ THIS CHAPTER, THE READER WILL BE ABLE:

- To apply the seven stage model of human action to describe human–computer interaction
- To use simple knowledge elicitation techniques
- To categorise users

2.1 USERS

When designing systems, the human component is commonly referred to as the 'user' or 'end-user'. The emphasis on the human means that psychologists, and specifically human factor psychologists, or ergonomists,[1] have a role to play in designing systems. In order to facilitate

---

[1]Ergonomics (from the Greek *ergon* meaning work, and *nomos* meaning natural laws) is a term used to refer to the study of human interactions with machines in the workplace. Its usage originated in the UK at a meeting on 16th February 1950, although the term was not new, and was reported in use in 1857 (Oborne, 1995). It is more commonly used in Europe than in the USA, which favours the term 'human factors'; this is generally interpreted as having a wider definition than ergonomics, the latter often used specifically to refer to the physical design of the interface, i.e. the design of 'knobs and dials' on tools, machines, and the like. This difference in terminology is reflected in the two professional bodies: the Ergonomics Society in the UK, and the Human Factors Society in the USA, although the latter has recently adopted the term 'ergonomics' in its title. For further discussion, see De Montmollin and Bainbridge (1985).

smooth interactions between the human and the technology, an understanding of how the human behaves is paramount.

Psychology provides this information, directly through human factors, where specific studies focus on aspects of the user interaction, e.g. evaluating help systems with groups of users in order to make recommendations with regard to the design of computer systems in the future, and indirectly, by applying the findings from psychology. As a discipline, psychology encompasses a wide range of topics (from social, developmental, clinical, physiological, cognitive, to organisational aspects, to name but a few). However, the commonality across these topics is that they attempt to study and explain various aspects of human behaviour using the so-called scientific method, i.e. the application of rigorous experimental techniques and methodologies before any deductions or conclusions concerning human behaviour can be made.

2.2 DEFINING USERS

Sometimes users are referred to as 'end-users', to differentiate between those who use the system during the various stages of its development, and those who use the finished product, at the end of the life cycle. In comparison to the users, the end-users are therefore more likely to have direct contact with (a final version of) the technology on a day-to-day basis. However, we have encountered a confusing situation, in which the 'end-users' were the purchasers of the technology, i.e. the budget holders responsible for commissioning the technology, who would not be using the technology. In this book, we will employ the term 'user' to denote a person who actually uses the technology.

In the Health and Safety Executive Regulations on the use of display screen equipment, users are defined according to a number of criteria (Health and Safety Executive, 1992). Basically, a user of a computer system is someone who relies on the computer for their work (and who will have no alternative means of performing the job). However, the regulations also assume that the computer user will interact with other artefacts, both technological, e.g. telephones, facsimile machines, photocopiers, etc., and non-technological, e.g. filing cabinets, paper work, etc. Human–computer interaction often misses the importance of these other components, by focusing on the use of the computer. It is important, in thinking about systems, to consider these other components, and how interaction with them has an impact on the work the person performs. An excellent example of this is given by Gray, John and Atwood (1993). In a study of computer-support for telephone operators, a new computer system was designed and installed. However, subsequent study suggested that the new computer system had not resulted in the anticipated throughput of calls. It appeared that the use of the computer to retrieve information did not lie on the operators' 'critical path', i.e. speeding up this task had no overall effect on performance time, whereas the various tasks of handling the telephone conversation did lie on the critical path. In this example, the emphasis had initially been placed on the operational interface between human and computer, whereas the important system components came from the social and operational interfaces between humans.

Employment of the scientific approach inherent in psychological studies necessitates defining the user population. Users, like humans, come in a variety of shapes and sizes, with differing expectations, attitudes and cognitive skills, and in the majority of situations it is unrealistic to work with all (potential) users during product life cycles. It is therefore necessary to:

1. define the characteristics of the user population, and
2. work with a representative sample of the user group.

Some individuals have attempted to categorise user populations in terms of their experience with technology. For example, Sutcliffe (1988) distinguished four main categories of users:

1. Naïve – individuals having no experience of the technology (although one could argue that, paradoxically, they should not even be referred to as users!);
2. Novice – beginners who have some experience of computers, but are new to a particular type of technology;
3. Skilled – users who have gained considerable experience with using the technology, and are competent and proficient operators;
4. Expert – people who are not only experienced users, but have an understanding and knowledge of the internal system structure and how the technology works, to the point where they would be quite at ease taking components apart in order to inspect or modify them.

Hackos (1994) modified Sutcliffe's categorisation to end up with five categories: (1) novice; (2) occasional; (3) transfer; (4) rote; (5) expert. Transfer users were defined as those individuals who already knew about using one system and were transferring to learn about a new one, while rote users include those people who follow instructions, but do not understand what is happening behind the computer interface.

There are always difficulties inherent in making a classification, primarily due to blurred boundaries, which make distinctions problematic, e.g. at what point do users move from being novice to expert? Moreover, some users may be novice at certain tasks, but experienced at others, so are difficult to categorise. If we define people solely in terms of their experience of the technology, we are at risk of focusing simply on the physical system components; the particular group of users may have high levels of knowledge and understanding of the social components of the system, i.e. they will be well-practised in the day-to-day management of their work activities. If we consider only their experience of technology, we will probably miss a great deal of valuable information, and lose many of the users' key skills. For example, the archiving department of an audio-visual library used to rely on tapes of television programmes. Recently, a new system was introduced to play the recordings digitally. The skilled operators of the old equipment were unable to adapt to the new equipment; when searching for a particular clip, the operators were able to use the changes in sound from fast-forwarded videotape to identify segments. This information was not present on the digital tape. The designers of the digital system had assumed one model of information search (type in relevant location and jump straight to it), rather than the model of information search employed by the operators (cue to a place near the segment and then find it). Apparently, the digital system has now been modified to provide tape noise to support the previous search method. This example is interesting for a number of reasons:

1. The system needed to be modified to allow operators to employ their old skills.
2. It might be the case that, within a decade, new operators will search using the 'digital' method of typing in identifiers, rather than the 'analogue' method of scanning the tape.

There is also a problem in locating naïve users, since it is often near impossible to find people who are totally unfamiliar with a certain technology, or aspects of it. For example, much research has been conducted into computer keyboard layouts, and many researchers have attempted to compare new keyboards with the well-established QWERTY keyboard, which has been recognised as the *de facto* standard for several decades (Alden *et al.*, 1972). From a methodological viewpoint, this type of experimental research is problematic, since it is extremely difficult to locate people who are naïve users of the ubiquitous QWERTY keyboard. Subsequently, this confounds experimental comparisons of a new keyboard (where naïve users are readily located) with one which is well-known and established. The issue of 'naïvety' is further exacerbated by the fact that the majority of people in Western countries will have encountered the QWERTY keyboard, even if they are not proficient typists, and any alternative designs (such as the split keyboards currently on the market) could be rejected purely because they 'look' different (Noyes, 1983).

2.3   HUMANS AS SYSTEMS

In Chapter 1, a four-level description of systems was presented: physical, operational, environmental and social. In this section, these levels will be applied to the human component of the system.

Physical Level Description

The human body can be thought of as a mechanical system which obeys physical laws (Bridger, 1995). Like any mechanical system, the body may be stable or unstable, and the role of the designer is to ensure that the physical demands placed on the human when interacting with technology do not cause instability leading to discomfort, stress, disease, or in extreme cases, death.

Anthropometry provides information about body measurements, usually taken when the human is in a static position. Tables covering all imaginable dimensions of the body have been compiled over the decades, using large samples of the population, in order to allow means and standard deviations to be calculated (see Pheasant, 1996). These data can then be applied to design workspaces, e.g. arm reaches and leg lengths for both sexes could be used in the design of vehicle cabs. There are many difficulties associated with designing to accommodate a range of human sizes, especially if the equipment/technology is intended for use by the infamous 'Joe Public'.

Over the years, a number of approaches have evolved: one is to design for the mythical 'Mr/Ms Average', as has happened with a number of supermarket checkouts. The main problem with this approach is that this person is indeed mythical, and there are very few individuals, if any, who are 'average' on all dimensions. It cannot be assumed that short people have short legs! A more successful approach is to design working on the parameters generated from consideration of the 5th and 95th percentile of the population. For example, the distance of car dashboard controls from the driver would be determined from anthropometric data concerning the arm reach distances of male and female adults. Therefore, controls should be placed within the reach envelope of the 5th percentile female, in order to accommodate the majority of the population. Likewise, if the maximum height of doorways was set at the 95th percentile of the height of the adult population, the majority would be accommodated. A further approach has been labelled 'universal design', where you design to meet the needs of disabled individuals on the premise that if this user group can comfortably access the technology, then the requirements of the majority will be met. This, of course, is a generalisation, primarily due to the diversity presented by this population. Nevertheless, it provides an interesting perspective on the design problem. Other means include producing a number of different sizes (assuming the technology is to be used exclusively by one or a few individuals), and the development of adjustable products, which allow the user to customise the technology to meet their personal physical needs. This latter approach will overcome some of the problems associated with designing for different populations. For example, Chapanis (1974) noted that products designed according to USA anthropometric data fitted 90% of Germans, 80% of the French, 65% of Italians, 45% of Japanese, 25% of Thais and 10% of Vietnamese.

Biomechanics and work physiology, on the other hand, provide information about the human body in movement. These dynamic measurements, e.g. when the body is walking or carrying out a manual task, allow analyses of body movements to be carried out. By simulating various tasks and activities, it is possible to find out the type of body postures the human needs to adopt; hence weak body postures likely to impose high postural stress on workers, perhaps even leading to physical damage of the human tissues, can be avoided. For example, comprehension of various body postures in relation to operation of the skeletal, circulatory and nervous systems will help make decisions about how to reduce the incidence of fatigue. Grieco (1986) hypothesised that postures that exert static loads on the body will interfere with the nutritional exchange which takes place among the inter-vertebral discs along the spine, to the detriment of the discs, so hastening their degeneration. Interpretation of this when applied to the workplace suggests that maintaining a sitting posture for long periods of time, as people do when driving or working at a computer, may hasten degeneration of the discs, and is best avoided.

Operational Level Description

In addition to ensuring that technology is designed to meet our physical characteristics, it must suit and be responsive to our cognitive needs. One approach taken by psychologists to this design problem has been to view humans as information processors, i.e. information from the external world is received by the senses, 'processed' by the brain, resulting in responses being selected and executed. In general, all information processing models are based on the assumption that humans handle information in a number of stages, beginning with input via the senses, and terminating in output, usually in the form of execution of actions. Norman (1988) has proposed a seven-stage action model which incorporates these features of human information processing.

In order to appreciate Norman's model, consider the mundane task of extracting money from an ATM (automated teller machine). The initial goal of the person is to obtain money. This goal can be satisfied in a number of ways, some less legal than others. The first intention to act must take account of legal alternatives. Assume that this results in an

Table 2.1 Seven-stage action model of 'accessing an ATM'. (Note: read one column at a time)

	I	II	III
1. **Form goal**	Access ATM	Obtain cash	Obtain £20
2. **Form intention**	Gain access	Select from menu	Select from menu
3. **Specify action**	Use card and PIN	Select 'cash'	Select £20
4. **Execute action**	Insert card/enter PIN	Press key	Press key
5. **Perceive results**	Access granted	Menu changes	Screen changes
6. **Interpret results**	Read menu	Read amount menu	'Other service?'
7. **Evaluate outcome**	Decide how to get cash	How much cash?	Decide 'no'

intention to withdraw money from an ATM. This will lead to the action 'use ATM'. However, evaluation of the 'world' (i.e. the immediate surroundings of the individual) reveals no ATM. This means that a further goal needs to be developed, i.e. to find an ATM. This leads to a further intention, i.e. to find a working ATM of an appropriate bank within walking distance, and then the action is executed. Once the ATM is reached, the original goal is reintroduced, i.e. to withdraw cash. The 'world' consists mainly of the ATM interface, and the user will progress through the various steps of interpreting machine state, forming intentions and acting, to move towards the goal.

This information-processing model encapsulates many areas of cognitive psychology: attention, perception, memory, decision-making. Psychological research, leading to improving our understanding of how humans function cognitively, is of direct relevance to the design of systems. Each area of cognitive psychology has much to offer to ensure that systems are designed and tailored to meet the cognitive attributes of the user. Some of these will be briefly covered here.

Visual Perception

Words, written communication in the form of text, pictures, graphs, diagrams, icons, all make up information that is transmitted visually. Detailed description of the human visual system and the mechanisms by which we view and interpret information is beyond the scope of this book (see, Gregory and Colman, 1995, for an introductory text on this topic). Briefly, the human visual system consists of two eyes connected via the optic nerves to the visual cortex of the brain. In the first instance, the eye views the visual world, responding to the fractions of electromagnetic energy that we call light. This information is transmitted to the photoreceptors situated on the retina, which turn it into neural impulses, to be passed along the optic nerve to the primary visual cortex of the brain. It is here that perceptual processing begins, which will eventually result in integration and organisation of the image. The human eye has been likened to a camera; the pupil lets in light that falls on the retina at the back of the eye, and it is this image which is then transmitted to the brain for interpretation.

Viewing written information, for example, is an active process, whereby the eyes continually scan the text. Closer examination of the eye movements during reading has indicated that individuals exhibit fast jerky movements (known as saccades) punctuated by stationary periods (described as fixations). The eyes will also move back over the text (known as regressions), and if the information is difficult to process, more regressions will be evident. It is thought that perception occurs during the fixation periods, which take up most of the time spent reading. Given the speed with which people can read, and the relatively brief durations of fixations (i.e. a few hundred milliseconds), it is accepted that people must be able to process information *before* they read it. This rather odd statement simply refers to the processes by which people infer what will come next, and how they use these inferences to guide the reading process. Thus, if presented with the sentence 'The cat sat on the ...', the reader will be able to supply a suitable word, e.g. mat, chair, window-sill. This process of inference appears to be so strong that it can lead to human error, e.g. in the task of proof reading (particularly reading one's own work), it is highly likely that spelling mistakes or other typographical errors will be missed. Further, while we can rely on the computer to remove some of these errors, experience of reading undergraduate essays shows that the 'spell checker' does not capture all errors. Thus, we can compound human error by technological support. The processes which underlie inference can also lead to other problems of interpretation. Consider examples of so-called 'visual illusions'. Inference means that information design must be carefully considered in order to reduce the possibility of misinterpretation, and to ensure appropriate response. To illustrate how unexpected outcomes may arise as a result of inadequate consideration of the processes of inference, consider the following: one of the authors helped to develop a speech recognition system, in which the user would speak words to fill a short form. Once the form was complete it could be 'sent' to the computer. We assumed that the user would check the form prior to sending it. However, on a significant number of occasions, users interpreted form completion as a cue to send it (irrespective of whether or not the contents of the form were correct). In this case, we had inadvertently created a situation in which the user could infer that a complete form was a correct form, and proceeded to send it.

The question for system design is how can we use what we know about human vision and perception in the design of technology. For example, it has been suggested that our peripheral vision works better in low illumination levels. This is due to the properties of the photoreceptors located at the back of the retina – the rods and cones – as it is these neurones which are responsible for converting the light energy to neural energy. The rods function better at low illumination levels, unlike the cones, which are active at higher illumination levels, e.g. daylight, or in artificial light. It is known that the rods are positioned towards the periphery of the retina, whereas the cones are found towards the centre of the retina. When applying this information about peripheral vision to design issues, it might be appropriate to consider placing information at the limits of our visual field, if it needs to be viewed in low illumination, or involves dimly lit displays. Although this sounds counter-intuitive, it is supported by our knowledge and understanding of the visual system.

Auditory Perception

In humans, the outer ear (the pinna) intercepts sound waves; these vibrations of air travel along the auditory canal to the cochlea, where they are transformed into nerve impulses, and finally, move along the auditory nerve to the brain. The higher order processing of these signals begins in the auditory cortex, in the temporal lobes of the cerebral hemispheres. Various characteristics of the sound result in different combinations of neurone activity, which enables the brain to interpret information being presented via the auditory channel.

Our hearing is sensitive to a number of parameters, e.g. the frequency, amplitude, and timbre of the sound. The frequency of the sound results in the pitch: a low frequency produces a low pitch, while a high frequency generates a high pitch. The amplitude of the sound is perceived as its loudness. Timbre relates to the quality of sound: sounds may have the same pitch and amplitude, but different timbres. This may be because they were generated from different sources, e.g. different musical instruments.

Auditory sensitivity is greatest between 1000 and 4000 hertz (or cycles per second). This is the frequency band in which human speech is transmitted, although we can hear frequencies from about 20 hertz to around 20 000 hertz. Below the 15 hertz threshold, it is possible for humans to distinguish sounds, but we are less accurate at doing this at low frequencies when compared to high frequencies. In contrast, sound with frequencies above the range of hearing, known as ultrasound, has no similar influences on the human body, as far as it is currently known.

The human auditory system is sensitive to hearing a wide range of sound of differing loudness. Zimbardo et al. (1995) quoted the example of hearing the tick of a watch at six metres, compared with a jet aircraft taking off 90 metres away, which can be so loud as to result in painful sensations in our ears. It is concluded that the absolute threshold has to be determined by our physiology, in that if our hearing became any more sensitive, we could, for example, literally hear the blood rushing through our ears. However, inaudible sound does exist. Very low frequencies, e.g. less than 20 hertz, can be perceived if they are sufficiently intense; this type of sound is called infra-sound. Research has shown that infra-sound, which is very intense, e.g. sound levels over 100 dB at frequencies under 10 hertz can give rise to headaches and tiredness (Brüel and Kjaer, 1982). Loudness, as measured by the physical intensities of sound, is usually expressed in ratios, rather than absolute amounts, e.g. in units called decibels. Figure 2.1 shows a variety of sounds given in decibel units.

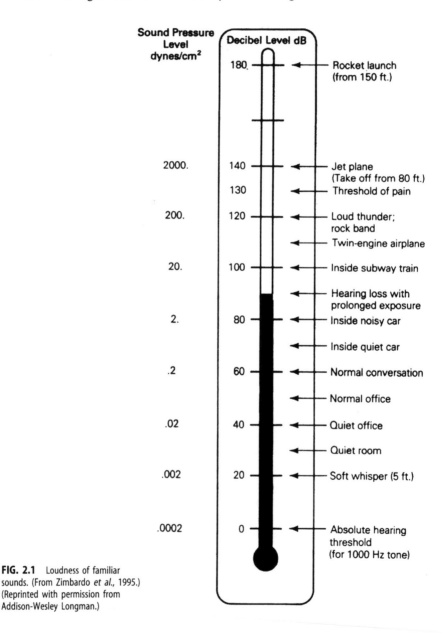

FIG. 2.1 Loudness of familiar sounds. (From Zimbardo et al., 1995.) (Reprinted with permission from Addison-Wesley Longman.)

There are two aspects to the role of auditory information in human interaction with technology. First, understanding how humans hear and perceive sounds has implications for systems design, e.g. when designing alarms for a process control application, the information conveyed by different types of sounds has implications for the design of auditory warnings. Second, given that most human work depends on verbal communication and concentration, the ability of humans to handle information and communicate in environments where noise is a characteristic has to be considered in the design of systems. Noise is an area of study within its own right (see Davies and Jones, 1982): we know that noise affects humans physically, psychologically and socially, and can damage hearing, interfere with communication, be a source of annoyance, cause tiredness and reduce efficiency.

Other Types of Perception

Although the visual perception (followed by the auditory) is the most dominant when considering design issues, there are other senses, e.g. tactile and proprioceptive, which need to be taken into account in systems' design.

Touch, or haptic perception, is generally viewed as being less important than our visual and auditory senses, and in this respect it is of less interest in the design of technological systems. The haptic interface refers directly to the use of the hands; the word 'haptic' originates from the Greek meaning 'able to lay hold of' (Gibson, 1966, p. 97). Haptic perception is primarily a combination of tactile and kinaesthetic feedback. Tactile feedback arises from the taction of an object, i.e. the extent to which features of an object can be discerned – shape, size, solidity, surface texture, composition, while the active touching of an object takes taction/tactile feedback a stage further. The exploration of an object tends to give us more feedback – the so-called kinaesthetic feedback (England, 1995). However, it is common practice to use the expressions 'tactile feedback' and 'kinaesthetic feedback' together. When considering kinaesthetic information, the receptors are found in the joints, muscles and tendons. The receptors which are located in the joints respond to pressure changes which accompany different positions of the body, while the receptors which are found in the muscles and tendons respond to changes in tension, which accompany muscle shortening and lengthening.

The haptic interface is concerned with using the hands to 'communicate' with technology. Although it is not as dominant in human–computer interaction as our visual and auditory senses, it cannot be ignored, and kinaesthetic feedback is particularly important when considering the design of manual input devices for human–computer interactions, e.g. keyboards for high-speed data entry tasks. Here, information about the positioning of the fingers, hands, wrists, arms and shoulders, as well as the feedback received from hitting the keys, will contribute to the user's overall perception of comfort, as well as their efficiency at carrying out the keying task.

Kinaesthetic feedback is especially important in the field of robotics: one such example is the use of Minimal Access Surgery (MAS) (Taylor *et al.*, 1996). MAS techniques allow surgeons to carry out surgical procedures and operations using a tool that they manoeuvre through small apertures in the tissues of the patient's body. Despite the number of acknowledged advantages of MAS (relating to faster recovery times, less post-operative discomfort, shorter hospital stays, etc.), there are still difficulties to be resolved, relating primarily to the design of the surgeon's tools, which are small and awkward to use, with poor controllability. The primary reason given for this relates to the low level of tactile feedback when using these devices. Ideally, the surgeon should have a good 'feel' for what is happening at the tool tip, i.e. what sort of tissue is being penetrated, whether the tool is passing through or slipping off tissue, etc. To date, the quality of the haptic feedback in this application has been seriously lacking, and research is currently being undertaken at Bristol to address this. Furthermore, for individuals whose visual and auditory channels are compromised, touch may assume a greater importance. For example, visually impaired users may rely on touch as the primary source of information in their interactions with technology, if they are using a concept or braille keyboard.

In terms of the physical location of the touch receptors, one major difference between these and the other senses is that they are not localised in one part of the body, but are found across the skin. Briefly, the skin contains three types of sensory receptors: mechanoreceptors, which respond to pressure; thermoreceptors, which respond to thermal aspects such as heat and cold; and nociceptors, which respond to intense pressure (Carpenter, 1987). In terms of human–computer interaction, it is the mechanoreceptors which are of primary interest (Baber, 1997). Interactive devices which involve manual input need to be designed to match the characteristics of the mechanoreceptors in the skin, e.g. the pressure required to hit keys on a keyboard should be sufficient to be used easily by the majority – too much, and users will be unable to operate the keyboard, while too little is likely to result in a higher number of miskeying errors. As already established, haptic perception also includes kinaesthesis, which involves the individual's ability to perceive where the various parts of their body are positioned in space. The proprioceptive senses that enable the human to do this are found in two separate systems: the vestibular system and the kinaesthetic system. The receptors which handle the vestibular information are located in the inner ear, and inform us about how our body is oriented in space, and the speed, acceleration and direction with which we are moving. Any conflict between the information being received by the visual and vestibular systems can result in the person feeling nauseous. For example, motion sickness when using simulators or VR (virtual reality) systems is thought to be due primarily to the mismatch between information received via the visual system which suggests motion, and information from the vestibular system that the individual is not moving (Hettinger and Riccio, 1991).

Whereas the information supplied by the vestibular system is primarily concerned with maintaining the body's posture, it is the kinaesthetic system that provides constant sensory feedback about the body's positioning. Much of the development of our complex motor skills depends upon the kinaesthetic system. However, it should be noted that in order to enable skilled behaviour to develop, sensory systems have to operate in conjunction with each other. As a skill is learned, the visual system will gradually be replaced by the kinaesthetic system as the primary system for monitoring body movements (Norman and Fisher, 1982).

A final comment is to state that there are many influences on human information processing that have not been mentioned here, e.g. workload, stress, and fatigue. These will all have an effect on cognitive functioning, and hence affect the design of the technology. For instance, humans are poor at vigilance tasks, especially when checking for low frequency events (Davies and Parasurman, 1980). This became particularly evident during the Second World War in the context of radar screen operators, who were monitoring displays for 8-hour shifts. After the first 20–30 minutes, the number of errors became substantial, as the operators grew increasingly unable to sustain their attention for any period of time.

Environmental and Social Level Descriptions

The design of systems does not consider only human physical and cognitive attributes, but extends to include environmental and social issues. Humans usually operate systems in environments and workplaces, with characteristics such as available space, noise, temperature, lighting level, etc. These will influence system performance, e.g. entering data into a portable computer in cramped, noisy conditions will be significantly different to performing the same task in a quiet office. The workplace also contains other people, and yet little attention has been given to the influence of social environmental parameters on performance, safety or comfort (Oborne, 1995).

The social aspects of the environment could have indirect effects on the design of systems; again, the system could be well-designed from the user viewpoint, but not used, because of factors arising from outside of the system. For example, in the 1980s Lloyd's Registry considered the use of voice recognition in a CAD (computer-aided design) application

(Henderson *et al.*, 1984). The technology and the CAD system worked extremely well, but the workers disliked using the system. There were a number of reasons for this. One concerned the embarrassment caused from 'talking' to a machine; this was accompanied by disparaging comments from colleagues, who thought it amusing for individuals to talk aloud (apparently to oneself) in an open-plan office. In this example, it was irrelevant how well the interface for the CAD system had been designed to meet their needs and requirements, as extraneous factors were preventing them from using the system effectively (Noyes and Frankish, 1988).

2.4 ELICITING USER KNOWLEDGE

To help ensure that the requirements of the user population are eventually met in the final product, it is recommended that users should be involved throughout the design process (Berry, 1994). Indeed, it has been suggested by Monk *et al.* (1993) that close involvement with users is the only way to ascertain sufficient initial requirements to produce a good user–interface specification. Conversely, the highest risk approach occurs when a system is produced in a design process that has had no input from the intended users (Weisberg and Lanzetta, 1991). It is therefore thought essential to involve the users; initially, rather than during or after the development of a system, is preferable. However, one of the problems in working with users during the design of a system (or product) concerns getting users to tell us exactly what they do, i.e. how do we elicit the required knowledge from people who are experts in their domain of work?

Knowledge elicitation can be defined loosely as 'the term used to refer to any of the methods employed to gather data regarding what information people have about a particular system', (Boehm-Davis, 1989), and more specifically as 'the process by which facts, rules, patterns, heuristics, operations, and procedures used by human experts . . . are elicited' (Garg-Janardan and Salvendy, 1988). Some researchers have extended this definition to include analysis and interpretation of the material elicited (see, Cordingley, 1989). Hence, it has been recognised for some time that knowledge elicitation is the critical first step in developing expert and knowledge-based systems, and the extraction of knowledge from human experts poses a significant bottle-neck in the expert system building process. Generally, the elicited knowledge constitutes the basic building blocks of an expert system, and the quality of this information will affect the performance of the system (Noyes, Starr and Frankish, 1996).

Some general reasons taken from knowledge elicitation literature explain why elicitation of the required knowledge is a difficult process to carry out. These are:

1. Level of Operation

Expert users rarely operate at a basic level; they make complex judgements very rapidly, with the 'internal processing and the external results' appearing as automated by the user. The resulting speed of response makes it difficult for experts to provide details of the reasons for their various actions. When skilled at carrying out a task, we tend not to think or be aware of the detailed actions required to obtain successful task completion. For example, if you questioned a professional sports player or musician about why they had performed an action at a particular moment, they would probably be unable to tell you.

2. Articulation

Much of an expert's knowledge is difficult, if not impossible, to articulate, and communication of this expertise is not simple. This could be because the knowledge is:

a) knowledge which the expert does not know s/he has;
b) knowledge which the expert might have presumed to be common knowledge;
c) knowledge which the expert never had and never needed, because details of his/her practices had always successfully avoided the problem.

This problem of articulating knowledge is summed up by the fact that you cannot put what you have learned into words; this means that 'know-how' is not accessible to you in the form of facts and rules, but it is 'facts and rules' from the users that are needed by the designers. Although recognised as very problematic for experts to verbalise their actions when carrying out a task, the end-result is sometimes a dialogue littered with metaphors. This type of information can be impossible to interpret at face value, and Gaines (1987) claimed that 'expressed expertise (has been found) to be incomplete, inaccurate, incorrect or irrelevant'.

3. Overlearning

The reasoning processes and task-related behaviours used by experts are overlearned and overpractised, causing them to regard much of their knowledge as superficial, and not worth reporting. In this context, it can be a more useful approach to look at beginners learning a skill, rather than experts.

4. Dislocation

There is a surprising degree of dislocation between conscious, verbally-expressed behaviour and the tacit knowledge which guides skilled behaviour. Even the use of appropriate knowledge elicitation techniques therefore could not guarantee success in locating the required information.

There are many techniques that could be used. However, we propose three techniques here that are relatively easy to conduct.

Scenario Analysis

From initial interviews with domain experts, try to develop a set of scenarios that represent typical work activities. These scenarios should be kept relatively brief, and should contain some particular difficulty. For example, in developing a database for a library, the following scenario could be used to uncover how people currently categorise entries:

A batch of new compact discs (CDs) arrives on Tuesday morning. The CDs have been forwarded by a branch library that is currently being closed down. How would you enter these into the system?

The librarian might simply say, 'I would type all the details into the database.' However, it is more likely that the librarian will sort the CDs (which will cue the interviewer to ask questions about how the CDs will be sorted, e.g. will they be sorted by music type, alphabetically by artist, etc.). Alternatively, the librarian might check to see which CDs are held by the library; this will cue the interviewer to ask questions about searching for CDs, etc. The skill in using this technique is to arrive at vignettes that the interviewee will find credible. This requires knowledge of typical work activity, as well as deciding when to pursue information at a tangent (it helps to have a set of core topics which are of interest, e.g. in the database example, the topics might be classification scheme and information search). Of course, the question arises as to why people should not simply be asked, 'What classification scheme do you use?' However, the reason this does not always work is that people adopt different work practices for different situations, and while there may be a 'standard' routine, this may not always be used. Given the complexity of systems and the likelihood of emergent features (as discussed in Chapter 1), using scenarios which present a range of activities can be a useful method of finding out how people deal with the unusual. Scenario analysis also allows the interviewer to suggest ways in which the current system could be improved, in order to gauge user reactions. It is worth noting that scenario analysis is not intended to obtain a specific design, i.e. you will not 'walk away' from scenario analysis with the design for the system. However, you will gain insight into how the users work and how to support this work with the new system. As Carroll (1995) pointed out in his book, scenarios provide explicit user and task information, and it is hypothesised that these will better equip the designer to accommodate the rich perspective of what people actually do and experience when they use advanced technologies. For this reason, it is normal to conduct scenario analysis on a number of people in the user group.

Card Sort

A number of systems require knowledge of actions and objects to be grouped together. By interviewing people to find typical actions and typical objects, the analyst can prepare cards with the various items written on them. Interviewees are then asked to sort the cards into piles. This is a simple technique to administer, but can prove particularly useful in the design of systems which use a great deal of information. For example, we have used this technique in a project for a major gas supplier, in order to investigate the design of menus for a portable computer system. The computer system contained details of the jobs to be performed by engineers, and the interface comprised menus and forms. A card sort technique was used to define an optimal menu system. The menu system arrived at through the card sort was quite different to that designed by the software engineers. The differences lay entirely in the different ways the engineers and software engineers thought of the work activities, e.g. while the software engineers thought of all financial transactions as belonging together, the engineers placed different financial transactions with different groups of jobs.

Verbal Protocol

One of the best known of the knowledge elicitation techniques involves sitting with the user and asking them to talk through their work. (This is discussed in further detail in Chapter 9.) The analyst records the user's comments (normally with an audio or video recorder), and transcribes these comments after the interview. It is important for the analyst to be prepared to prompt the user, who might not be willing or able to speak all the time. Difficulties in co-articulation have already been mentioned in this chapter. The type of information obtained will depend on the research questions: for example, are you interested in what someone does, or why they perform actions in a certain order, or how well they understand the system, or how they view their work as relating to other people's work? The analysis will also depend on the level of intrusion that the user is prepared to accept; there are many situations when it is better to videotape the user and then use the videotape for the verbal protocol. This is known as a retrospective verbal protocol, as the user will provide a commentary on the video. One of the main problems with the verbal protocol technique lies in the analysis of the recordings. Analysis can be time-consuming and often extremely difficult – as demonstrated by the discussion in Chapter 9.

2.5 CONCLUSIONS

In summary, the findings from psychology help us to understand more about how we function and behave under certain circumstances, and this information can be used to design products and systems better suited to human use. However, selecting and carrying out the appropriate elicitation procedure is not easy. In the first instance, knowledge of different types of elicitation procedures is needed. Locating the relevant materials is not easy, since information pertaining to knowledge elicitation is scattered across a number of different sources from computing to psychology to management. Secondly, even the use of the appropriate knowledge elicitation technique does not necessarily guarantee success in eliciting the 'right' information (Howarth, 1988). Some of the generic reasons to explain this have already been given, but there may also be local reasons, relating to practical and economic considerations, determining a particular use of a specific technique (see, Noyes *et al.* 1996, for further information on this). In order to combat these difficulties, it is recommended that elicitors:

1. Use a variety of knowledge elicitation techniques;
2. Support the expert's view with other material (e.g. user manuals, relevant documentation, reports, etc.);
3. Become familiar with the expert's domain and terminology, in order to maintain credibility;
4. Engender positive social skills when working with end-users, since the flow of information tends to be one-way, i.e. they are helping the elicitors to achieve their goals, and usually have little to gain from participation in your exercise/research.

2.6 EXERCISES 2 AND 3

Exercise 2 Working With Experts
This exercise requires two people.

First Person:
Think of a task at which you are an expert, e.g. driving a car through the London rush-hour, playing a musical instrument, etc.

Second Person:

You want to find out about the interaction between the person and the task at which they are expert, in order to develop something better.
How are you going to do it?

Outcome:

In this exercise you should experience the difficulties of finding out about knowledge held by the expert.
Further, imagine you had to take the information elicited and use this in the design of a system. How easy would that be?

Exercise 3 Knowledge Elicitation

Task 1:

What makes you learn well?
(Write down the answer to this question.)

Task 2:

1. Think of a time in your life when you have learned to do something very easily. Describe it.
2. Think of a time in your life, when it was difficult for you to learn to do something very easily. Describe it.
3. Give reasons to explain why it was not easy to learn in the first situation, and difficult in the second situation.

Outcome:

The outcome from these two exercises should be the same; it was just that the second task, with more focused questions, should have provided an easier means of eliciting the required knowledge.

2.7 SELECTED REFERENCES

Dan Diaper (ed.), *Knowledge Elicitation*, Ellis Horwood, Chichester, 1989.
A discussion of elicitation techniques, including the detailed chapter by Cordingley mentioned below, and a chapter by Geoffrey Trimble on 'Knowledge Elicitation – Some Practical Issues'.

Nigel Shadbolt and Mike Burton, 'Knowledge Elicitation', in John Wilson and Nigel Corlett (eds.) (rev. edn.), *Evaluation of Human Work: A Practical Ergonomics Methodology*, Taylor and Francis, London, 1995.

A number of techniques are covered (e.g. structured interviews, protocols, concept sorting, laddered grids, the limited information task, automatic elicitation), in conjunction with discussion of their various benefits and shortcomings.

Hoffman, Shadbolt, Burton and Klein, 'Eliciting Knowledge from experts: a methodological analysis', in *Organisational Behavior and Human Decision Processes* 62, 129–158, 1995.

This paper places knowledge elicitation into three categories: analysis of experts' tasks, various type of interview, and contrived tasks. Recommendations on how to conduct knowledge elicitation studies are also covered.

For further information on:

Scenario analysis – see John Carroll (ed.), *Scenario-based Design: Envisioning Work and Technology in System Development*, Wiley, New York, 1995.

Carroll's book is concerned with the application of scenario-based design, i.e. how the use of scenarios provides a means of representing, analysing and planning how a system or product might impact upon users' activities and experiences.

Card sort – Betsy Cordingley 'Knowledge elicitation techniques for knowledge-based systems', in Dan Diaper (ed.), *Knowledge Elicitation*, Ellis Horwood, Chichester, 1989.

This chapter summarises a number of techniques (including card sort) used to elicit knowledge from individuals.

Verbal protocol – the elicitation and subsequent analyses of protocols are discussed at length in Cordingley's chapter.

3 What Will the System Be Used For?

OBJECTIVES OF CHAPTER:

- To consider information exchange across system interfaces
- To examine information presentation and user performance
- To provide some psychological principles to inform the presentation of information in different modalities

HAVING READ THIS CHAPTER, THE READER WILL BE ABLE:

- To relate information types to user requirements
- To choose appropriate information presentation types
- To understand more about best practice in the presentation and management of visual and auditory information

---

3.1 COMMUNICATION OF INFORMATION

An important distinction was drawn by Zuboff (1988) between technology which automates (i.e. provides a means of performing physical tasks), and technology which 'infomates' (i.e. provides a means of performing information-processing tasks). It is particularly relevant in this book, where we take a number of different perspectives on design. However, our concern here is primarily with technology which infomates. Humans use information in their interaction with technology and the nature and quality of the information that passes between the human and the systems, and between the humans operating the technology, is critical to system design. In some respects, human factors could be viewed as the science of effective information communication (Oborne, 1995). In the description of systems in Chapter 1, information is exchanged between components in the system during operation. In order to maximise system efficiency, it is important to ensure that the appropriate information is passed to the appropriate components at the right time. Taking the system description used in this book (physical, operational, environmental and social), we can ask what information will be used at these levels of description, and how to ensure appropriate communication.

Much of the information used at the physical level will relate to the behaviour of the hardware, e.g. the switching of various components, the variations in voltage through the circuit, etc. Information use at the operational level will concern changes in the software, e.g. in response to changes in data, and also changes in the human information processor, e.g. in response to new goals or feedback from the computer. At the environmental and social levels, information use will concern the global changes in the domain of operation. At the environmental level, information use could relate to the management of the physical components of a system, e.g. traffic lights on a road layout, while at the social level, information use could relate to management of operational components, e.g. setting productivity targets for a workforce.

While information is used in each of the levels (and the manner in which it is used concerns the various specialists involved in designing systems), we argue that information exchange is the key issue. Information exchange occurs across the interface between the system components and between levels of the system. Typically, human–computer interaction concentrates on the interface between components at the operational level, i.e. where people interact with software, and between operational and physical level components, i.e. where people interact with interaction and display devices, and where software modifies displayed output, and is modified by input. The manner in which the human works at an operational level will form the basis for much of this chapter. However, it should be noted that in recent years, there has been increased interest in the interface between social and operational components, particularly with respect to computer-supported co-operative work (CSCW).

Inference

Information always conveys a message. This implies isolation, i.e. without reference to the source, medium or receiver, there is no information. In other words, if the component to which the 'information' is passed is unable to process or handle it, there can be no message. Information relies on both parties 'knowing' the appropriate information to use, and on the receiver 'expecting' a particular type of information. We have placed the words 'knowing' and 'expecting' in inverted commas, because when referring to a computer the knowledge and expectation will be typically provided by the software. In contemporary human–computer interaction, it is still important for the person to behave in the manner that the computer 'expects'. Studies of perceptual organisation have led to the development of the Gestalt principles of perception, which can be applied in the design of displays. The German Gestalt school of psychology suggested that we group individual stimuli together during perception to make wholes (or Gestalts), and that it is the whole that conveys the meaning of the object. For example, we know that humans are very good at pattern-matching (de Keyser, 1986, described people as 'furious pattern-matchers'), and users should find systems which capitalise on this feature easier to use. British Rail, when designing train door handles, made use of this human characteristic; e.g. if the doors are all safely closed, the train guard can see this at a glance by looking along the side of the train, as an insecurely shut (or open) door will break the horizontal pattern.

When considering problem-solving behaviour, it has been shown that one of the main weaknesses of human problem-solvers is their 'preference for confirmatory evidence over evidence which will refute their ideas' (Wason and Johnson-Laird, 1972). Since it is likely that this confirmatory evidence will be based on previous experience, it may 'handicap' solving the problem. For example, in 1989, one of the many causes leading to the so-called Kegworth air disaster was thought to be that the crew shut down the wrong engine. The decision to close down that particular engine was based partly on information from a previous flying experience with that particular aircraft when the engine they shut down had been problematic. One solution to help humans in a situation like this is to train them to look for evidence to refute those intended actions which make up their initial response to solving the problem.

3.2 PRESENTING INFORMATION TO THE HUMAN

It is not only the information *per se* that influences human–computer interaction, but also the means of information transmission. Subsequently, it is possible to have a high-quality information path that is ineffectively transmitted. For example, a conversation between two humans may result in perfect understanding and subsequent desired actions, whereas the same dialogue between a human and an automatic speech recogniser may result in poor recognition performance on the part of the technology, and no end-result. In this case, the problem arises because of inadequate reception on the part of receiver, as the information, the verbal message, would have been identical in both situations. Taken a step further, it is not only the reception which needs to be acceptable, but also the interpretation (and understanding), although in many instances, it will not be possible to separate these two aspects. Effective communication therefore depends upon the information being correctly interpreted by the receiver in the way that the transmitter intended. This applies when information is being exchanged at an operational level, i.e. between humans, between humans and technology, or between technology and humans.

In summary, the issue when designing systems centres on the optimal means of exchanging information between operational components of a system, i.e. humans and technology. This involves consideration of both the type and nature of the transmitters and receptors, as well as the characteristics of the information being communicated. The issue concerns how and when the different modes of communication should be used to present information to the human recipient. There are two questions here: first, how should information be presented visually, verbally, etc. in order for the human to gain maximum benefit, and second, when should the different communication modes be used? The latter implies that some form of comparative exercise is needed to determine the characteristics of situations where auditory, visual or combinations of these, should be used.

Words

Oborne (1995) stated that one of the most important aspects to be considered in the presentation of visual information is the position of the target information in the material that the human is searching. This is due to the differences in the sensitivity of various parts of the retina upon which the image is falling, and the subsequent search strategy that will ensue. Research evidence has shown that the further an item is placed from the gaze fixation, the less the likelihood that it will be identified correctly, and the longer this process will take (Schiepers, 1980). Although in this situation, it is not possible to know in advance the position of the gaze fixation, there are features of the visual material, e.g. the use of spaces, which can be used to enhance the presentation of visual information, and hence the human interpretation of it.

It is convenient to consider text in the context of reading information, since this is likely to be the *modus operandi*, although it could be argued that some visual information merely requires an acknowledgement response on the part of the human viewer. The extent to which this is reading then becomes a philosophical consideration about the limits of what constitutes reading. For our purposes, reading can be considered as essentially a four-stage process (see Table 3.1).

In terms of reading visual information, the two primary aspects of comprehension are legibility and readability. Legibility is the ability to detect and discriminate between individual characters, while readability is the transformation of the information into meaningful units. The former is often measured in terms of confusion (or 'lack of confusion'), and is an important consideration in the design of visually presented information. We know that legibility is influenced by character size and resolution. Although it can be generally assumed that legibility increases with character size, there are obvious limits. In terms of screen design, it has been shown that once characters reach a height of 5 mm, recognition performance begins to decrease (Cakir *et al.*, 1979); a lower limit of 3 mm was suggested by Dul and Weerdmeester (1993). In terms of resolution, contrast between the characters and their surround can influence legibility, and colour also plays a role here. Most of the material that we read comprises dark characters on a lighter background. Hence, in terms of design, it is generally recommended that this format is retained, i.e. dark characters on a lighter surround with colour being used sparingly. Although humans tend to like colour, it often adds little to increasing legibility, other than being pleasant. There are, of course, exceptions to all these points, and there may be an occasion that demands the use of reverse-video presentation of text and a large number of colours.

In contrast to legibility, there are a number of ways of measuring readability; these often involve formulae that include counts of the number of letters in words and the number of words, and these can be related to population norms, i.e. a reading age of '8 years' is required. Readability can be affected by the grouping and spacing of items. For example, the presentation of text in all capital letters tends to make it more difficult to read, especially in large quantitities. It has been shown that when reading continuous text, we recognise the characteristic outline of the word initially as a meaningful unit. Using all capital letters loses the outline shape of the word that would be present in mixed text, with ascender (e.g. 'h' and 'l') and descender (e.g. 'g' and 'y') characters. A variation on this is to present text in lower case, but without the top of the ascenders and the bottom of the descenders appearing above and below the rest of the text. In the 1980s, some of the early computer printers produced text in this manner, and it is still the case with some mobile phone displays, presumably on the grounds of space and cost restrictions. Just as presentation of text in all capitals loses some of the cues that help increase readability, likewise right hand justification of text has the same effect. Proportional spacing, which presents characters in accordance with their size (e.g. 'w' is given more space because it is a 'wider' character), also enhances readability. Spacing in a vertical plane is also important, and will differ when text is presented in short columns, as in some newspapers and magazines (see Hartley, 1998, for examples). Finally, the actual design of the characters themselves can affect readability. For example, serif fonts are generally thought to be easier to read, because they have tiny strokes that help lead the reader through the text. In contrast, sans-serif fonts are usually more appropriate for

Table 3.1 Stages of reading (adapted from Cakir *et al.*, 1979 and reprinted with permission from IFRA, Darmstadt, Germany)

Stage 1:   Detection
Stage 2:   and Discrimination
Marker = characters and signs
Mechanism = eyesight
Basic concept = legibility
Stage 3:   Transformation into meaningful units
Marker = spacing of words
Mechanism = eye movements
Basic concept = readability
Stage 4:   Integrating and understanding the message
Marker = text, graphs, tables, layout
Mechanism = mental processing
Basic concept = understandability

special effects, for example, a serif font has been used in this book for the text, and a sans-serif font for the headings and sub-headings.

It is evident that the design of information for presentation on computer screens has been extensively researched, and that a large number of recommendations and guidelines exist. Cakir *et al.* (1979) quoted one author who stated that 'work on the design of (screen) alpha-numerics has become almost an industry in itself'. For example, Smith and Mosier (1986) presented 944 guidelines on display design: at the time of writing, these are available on the World Wide Web. It should also be noted that an International Standard (ISO 9241) is being prepared that considers many design aspects of information presentation on computer screens. It is not the intention of this chapter to provide an extensive overview of design guidelines for computer-based systems – this has been covered in detail elsewhere (see references at the end of the chapter) – but rather to focus on some of the psychological principles that can guide and inform the design of the system.

How to Present Information Visually?

Studies of perceptual organisation have led to the development of the Gestalt principles of perception that can be applied in the design of displays. The German Gestalt school of psychology suggested that we group individual stimuli together during perception to make wholes (or Gestalts), and that it is the whole that conveys the meaning of the object. It also presents several guidelines which are particularly relevant to the production of well-designed icons. Six examples to demonstrate this are given here.

The first set of principles relates to figure–ground differentiation, which is concerned with ensuring that the icon stands out from its background as a coherent object. However, there will be some situations where it might be sensible not to fill in the object. For example, in a drawing package, the icons used to represent drawing tools for circles and rectangles should be kept open so that users do not interpret these as 'draw a filled shape'.

Principle 1: The object should be filled where possible, in order to make it stand out. (Figure 3.1)

Principle 2: The object should be closed, so that all parts relating to the figure belong to the same 'picture'. (Figure 3.2)

Principle 3: The object should have a readily identifiable contour. (Figure 3.3)

Principle 4: Gestalt psychologists also believe that perception involves the grouping of objects into patterns. Figure 3.4 shows how the proximity of objects in a display can lead to the viewer seeing the

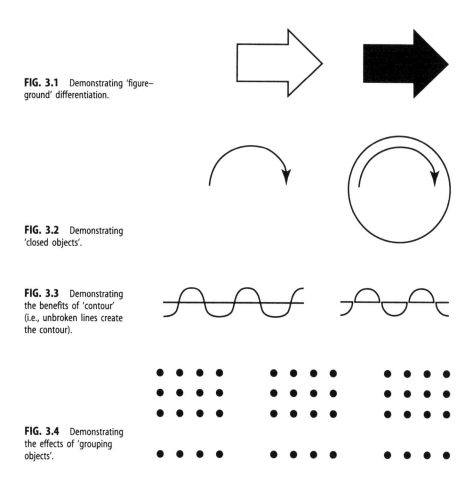

FIG. 3.1 Demonstrating 'figure–ground' differentiation.

FIG. 3.2 Demonstrating 'closed objects'.

FIG. 3.3 Demonstrating the benefits of 'contour' (i.e., unbroken lines create the contour).

FIG. 3.4 Demonstrating the effects of 'grouping objects'.

objects being arranged in groups. If these objects are unrelated, or if the designer intends the viewer to read the display in rows or columns, then this design can lead to misinterpretation. The figure shows how similar objects can be interpreted as belonging together. In this example, the viewer could read the display according to the groups of information.

Principle 5: Humans will also attempt to apply principles of symmetry when reading displays. Thus, in Figure 3.5, if the two sides of this display do not operate symmetrically, the viewer may misinterpret one side, e.g. if the needles rise on both sides of two displays, does this signify rising values on each display?

In Figure 3.6, the viewer may interpret the components in the display as belonging to the same dimension, which might not be true.

The final points to bear in mind when designing icons concern the intended audience of the icons. The International Standard (ISO/IEC CD 11581-1.2, 1993 Draft Standard) suggested that provided that two-thirds of a population can interpret a symbol or icon, then it can be used justifiably. The fact that two-thirds is acceptable (rather than 100% of the population) indicates the problems in gaining consensus as to what the icon means. These problems can be made worse when the target population features people from different cultures. One oft-repeated anecdote concerns the use of a picture of a snowflake to indicate that a food product was suitable for freezing, where prospective users in a tropical country (with no experience of snow) had to learn what a snowflake looked like in order to understand the icon. Similar tales have been told of a penguin icon to indicate frozen food. Thus, while these icons may appear intuitive, their interpretation relies on appropriate

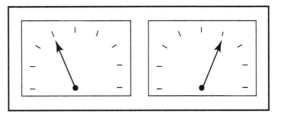

FIG. 3.5 Demonstrating 'symmetry'.

FIG. 3.6 Demonstrating 'common fate'.
(Copyright John Wiley & Sons, Ltd. Reprinted with permission.)

experiences. Furthermore, some icons are used to indicate actions or objects specific to one machine, and require knowledge of the machine to interpret them. This is particularly true of the icons used on car dashboards, where people may have difficulty in interpreting the icon. For example, Baber and Wankling (1992) found that the icon for 'catalytic converter' was correctly interpreted by few of the people in their study (this may have changed in recent years, as more people become familiar with catalytic converters). More importantly, Baber and Wankling found that, even when people correctly interpreted the icon, they did not always identify the appropriate meaning of the icon. For example, while most of the participants correctly identified a picture of a battery to indicate the battery, less than half of them were able to say what the icon meant. The most common suggestion was that there was a problem with the battery, whereas the icon is intended to mean a problem with the charging of the battery. The solution to the problem was to provide text indicating the name of the icon and the correct action to perform.

Although icons often provide a short-cut way of communicating information, they often have to be accompanied by text. There are a number of ways of categorising them (see, Macaulay, 1995). The most common approach is to consider icons as either 'concrete' (where the icon uses an object to represent an object or action using that object, e.g. using scissors to indicate 'cut'), or 'abstract' (where the icon represents a function, e.g. two overlaid pieces of paper to represent 'copy') (Rogers, 1989). Stammers (personal communication) has shown that 'concrete' icons are easier to interpret than 'abstract' icons. His measures included the number of people correctly identifying the meaning of the icons. Consequently, it is suggested that the 'abstract' icons retain some ambiguity that is not so apparent in the 'concrete' icons. However, even 'concrete' icons can be difficult to interpret correctly. For example, that used to indicate 'save' on the Microsoft word processing package represents a computer disc. While this can be interpreted as save to disc drive, it also means save to hard disc. Faced with this icon, the user might decide to look for another icon to signify save to hard disc. Microsoft does provide text labels for their icons, which reduces the potential for ambiguity, and once the icon has been encountered it is easy to recall its meaning. This example illustrates the difficulty of designing icons which can be used with no training or additional support (in this instance, the 'training' arises from reading the manual or 'help', or from testing the icon to see what it does, and the support comes from the text label). Thus, while system designers may be tempted to use icons in preference to words, assuming that icons are easy to interpret and have universal application, this is unlikely to be true, and the design of good, clear, usable icons is very difficult.

Consider the design of road signs; these are intended to be perceived whilst driving, often at speed and in low levels of illumination. Perception of symbols is faster than perception of words in such conditions (Ellis and Dewer, 1979). Presumably this is due to the fact the symbols contain fewer bits of information than words. However, if the signs used short words, then time to perceive words was no different to that to perceive symbols (Steiner and Camacho, 1989). Furthermore, as the Baber and Wankling study (1992) suggests, simply perceiving a symbol may not be sufficient to interpret it. Christ (1978) demonstrated that, with sufficient practice, people could comfortably use any symbol set. This could be taken to support the (familiar) assertion that people can be forced to adapt to any system, given sufficient time and training. Unfortunately, this proposition collapses in the face of two counter-arguments: first that users of computer systems are not always appropriately trained in their use, and second that when people encounter stressful situations, their performance often reverts to pre-training behaviours.

How to Present Auditory Information?

There are two main aspects to the role of auditory information in human interaction with technology. First, understanding how humans hear and perceive sounds has implications for systems design, e.g. when designing alarms for a process control application, the information conveyed by different types of sounds has implications for the design of auditory warnings. Second, given that most human work depends on verbal communication and concentration, the ability of humans to handle information and communicate in environments where noise is a characteristic has to be considered in the design of systems.

Auditory displays tend to be used in one or more of the following conditions:

1. When the message is simple and short.
2. When the message is to be presented to a number of people.
3. When the user's vision will be occupied with other tasks.
4. When vision is not possible (perhaps due to poor illumination).
5. When the user is not at a fixed location.

Stanton (1994) has shown than a minority of auditory signals can be classed as warnings, and many are used as advisory. There is a tendency to put auditory alarms on to all manner of equipment. Edworthy (1994) showed how this can create real problems, by examining the auditory alarms used in an intensive care ward of a hospital, with different pieces of equipment either having similar sounds for different events or different sounds for the same event.

Auditory information can be presented as a simple signal, e.g. on or off, safe or critical, and is designed to elicit an action on the part of the operator (Stanton and Baber, 1995). More sophisticated warnings not only convey the state of the system, but also provide additional information, e.g. the use of earcons (Gaver, 1989). The third and final group includes auditory information utilising human speech; this could take the form of (i) guidance warnings; (ii) giving instructions; (iii) 'speaking' written text; or (iv) providing feedback. It should be noted that speech generation (from simply reproducing recorded human speech, through to the complete synthesis of human speech) has been employed to carry out all these activities (Noyes, 1993). Examples of systems which include (i) guidance warnings are often those associated with transportation, e.g. on the London underground trains, passengers are reminded to 'mind the gap', also seatbelt reminders in cars. It is not easy to delimit warnings that merely offer guidance or provide instructions, as the same auditory information in a different context may move from providing guidance to acting as a warning. In terms of (ii) giving instructions, there are many examples where natural or synthesised speech has been used: e.g. programming video recorders, and setting up computer spreadsheets by following verbal prompts. Both guidance warnings and instructions are likely to include short messages; this is in contrast to the conveyance of what is the equivalent of continuous 'written' text presented via the auditory channel. This is a well-researched area and includes commercial systems such as the 'talking typewriter', the 'language master' and the 'talking text writer'. Again, it could be argued that there is a degree of overlap between (ii) and (iii) 'speaking' written text, since educational systems which use synthesised speech instructions also provide speech output of written text (Davidson *et al.*, 1991). The fourth category is the use of auditory information to provide specific feedback. For example, in some applications using speech synthesis, it is seen as a natural progression for speech feedback to follow speech instructions given by the system, or speech recognition commands given to the recogniser. However, it should be noted that all auditory information could be viewed as 'feedback' in one context or another, also that there are other classifications of auditory displays. For example, Simpson *et al.* (1985) classified auditory displays in terms of five basic types:

1. Warnings – which indicate safety critical failures or problems.
2. Advisories – which indicate potential problems.
3. Commands or prompts – which are designed to provoke operator response.
4. Responses – typically to operator requests for information.
5. Feedback to control input – for example, making a touchscreen 'beep' when touched.

In terms of designing auditory displays, there are a number of principles that can be applied:

1. Making sure the auditory message stands out – the sound should be clearly discernable from background noise. Baber (1991) argued that one problem with using speech in a control room related to the problem of making a speech message distinct from other spoken exchanges; the obvious solution is to use synthesised speech, but this introduces problems of interpretation and is not appropriate for all types of task (Baber *et al.*, 1992). This is discussed in more detail in Chapter 4.

2. Providing no more information than is necessary for the intended interpretation. Fire alarms provide a good example here. A ringing fire bell is the auditory signal to indicate that there is a fire in a building. It is universally recognised, and usually sufficient to result in the evacuation of a building. At an operational level, this signal is usually enough to ensure that people leave the building. However, when considering this alarm as part of a system, the social level of description suggests other meanings to the bell. People may interpret the alarm as a practice fire drill, or as the result of an equipment malfunction. The result will not be the required response, as some may not leave the building and others may do so, but with no great haste.

3. Matching with user expectations – the sound used (or speech message used) should fit the expectations of the listeners. For instance, naturally occurring sounds could be used in much the same way as icons, e.g. a knock on a door to signal the arrival of a message on an electronic mail system (Gaver, 1986). Edworthy and Adams (1996) suggested that the characteristics of sounds, such as intensity and frequency, could be used to assign urgency to a warning signal.

3.3 STIMULUS-CENTRAL PROCESSING-RESPONSE COMPATIBILITY

In an influential account of how people process information, Wickens (1984) proposed that there is a relationship between information received by a person and the action to be performed. If the relationship is optimised, performance will be efficient, i.e. fast and error-free. This relationship is described by Figure 3.7.

From Figure 3.7, it is possible to see that information (stimulus) could be presented in either visual or auditory form. Clearly, this means that the perception of the information will follow a route from the eyes or the ears to the brain, and that the processing will be affected by the route followed. Furthermore, the response made could be either vocal or manual, and this also influences information processing (in terms of planning actions). Thus, a 'direct' route ought to link stimulus to response via the appropriate information-processing route, with any switching interfering with performance. This suggests that an auditory signal will be best responded to vocally, and a visual signal will be best responded to manually.

Building on his earlier work (1992), Wicken's multiple resource model has been considered a useful framework upon which to base interface design. Multiple resource theory specifies that there are several separate information-processing capacities, categorised by the dimensions of stages (either perception/early or output/late processing), modalities (either auditory or visual), and processing codes (either spatial or verbal). Wickens (1991) argued that there is better timesharing between two tasks that use separate, rather than common resources. Changes in the difficulty of one task will be less likely to influence performance of the other task when they use separate resources. Conversely, tasks that use the same resources will degrade performance. However, there are some qualifications that restrict this initial simplicity. Wickens listed these as 'switching', 'co-operation' and 'confusion'. Switching between tasks rather than time-sharing between tasks could account for poorer task-sharing performance of similar tasks, rather than resource consumption *per se*. Co-operation can have the opposite effect on dual task performance. Two difficult tracking tasks timeshared have been found to degrade task performance less, compared with performance on a single easy or hard task (Fracker and Wickens, 1991). It would appear that timesharing similar tasks can facilitate task co-operation and enhance performance. Confusion, on the other hand, can cause dual task degradation that is not attributable to resource interference. These

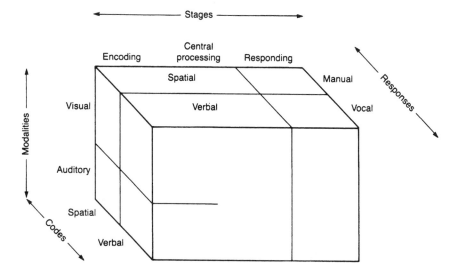

FIG. 3.7 Stimulus–response–compatability box diagram. (From Wickens, 1992.) (Reprinted with permission of Academic Press.)

mechanisms of confusion, co-operation and switching go beyond the simple resource construct, and can partly account for some aspects of dual task performance, although they do not eliminate the need for resource constructs.

Some have commented that multiple resource theory suffers from a lack of parsimony, i.e. the theory has a surfeit of mechanisms which are not required to explain the outcomes (Kantowitz, 1987). However, the theory's parsimony may partly explain why it is so attractive for system design. It provides a holistic model of human performance that considers many structural aspects of tasks, and enables researchers to predict both workload and performance before designing tasks (Sarno and Wickens, 1995). Hence, it should be possible to design interfaces which require dual task performance to use separate resources, and thus maximise the amount of attention directed towards the complete task. Such a premise has been used to justify the integration of novel input mediums, e.g. automatic speech recognition in high stress environments (Enterkin, 1991; Baber and Noyes, 1996).

3.4   CONCLUSIONS

The focus of this chapter has been on how we can design systems in order to optimise the communication and management of information. This is a particularly pertinent (and timely) question, given the increase in expert systems, which are often information-rich. Thus, in these so-called 'intelligent systems' the capability exists to present a large array of possibly divergent information to the human operator. Further, the last couple of decades has witnessed an interesting use of PCs - a situation that has gathered momentum in recent times with the development of the internet and the World Wide Web. 'Information overload' is an increasingly-used term, as the paperless office concept of the 1980s fails to be realised, and we become subject to more and more paperwork, bombarding us with information generated by technology.

The problem for the human factors specialist and system designer is how best to present relevant information, and how to employ the technology to maximum effect. For example, the question we addressed in our civil flight deck design work was whether information should be displayed temporally as problems arise, or whether it should be prioritised according to level of urgency. Intuitively, there are no obvious answers to this. If established guidelines do not exist, one approach to locating the answer to this type of question might be to carry out some summative evaluation work, as described in Chapter 9.

In conclusion, it becomes evident that a tremendous number of guidelines and recommendations already exist for the design of the management of information at the interface.

3.5 EXERCISE 4

Exercise 4: Redesigning Instructions

These are actual instructions taken from a child's video game.
Can you list some suggestions for making improvements?
* TO START PLAY
1. Turn your television on to Channel 3.
Note: If Channel 3 is broadcasting in your area and interfering with the game, set the switch on the back of the control deck to Channel 4.
2. If your TV has an automatic fine tuning control (AFC), turn it off. (Use the manual fine tune dial to adjust the picture after inserting the game pak, as described below.)
Note: If you have a color TV that turns black and white when the AFC is turned off, leave the AFC on.
3. Make sure that the power switch on the control deck is off.
CAUTION!! ALWAYS MAKE SURE THAT THE POWER SWITCH ON THE CONTROL DECK IS OFF BEFORE INSERTING OR REMOVING A GAME PAK !!
4. Open the chamber lid on the control deck.
Insert a game pak into the chamber (label facing up) and push it all the way in. Press down on the game pak until it locks into place and close the chamber lid.

Some suggestions:

1. Consider the user group – is text the right medium for providing these instructions?
2. Consider the terminology – is it an appropriate level of readability for the intended user population?
3. Consider safety – what are the implications of *not* following the instructions?
4. Consider reversion – what is the back-up if the user cannot make sense of the instructions?
5. The text implies that the reader has knowledge of the technology – is this justifiable?
6. Do the instructions take account of local differences in transmission, e.g. individuals who have cable/Sky TV and a large number of channels? How could this be addressed?
7. Could the layout of the instructions be redesigned to help the reader?

3.6 SELECTED REFERENCES

A. Cakir, D.J. Hart and T.F.M. Stewart, *The VDT Manual*, Wiley, Chichester, 1980 (also published by IFRA, 1979).
Now a somewhat ageing text on the design of visual display terminals, but still providing a comprehensive and thorough coverage of display design.

L.N. Smith and J.N. Mosier, *Design Guidelines for User-System Interface Software. Report MTR-9420*, Mitre Corporation, Bedford, MA, 1996. (Also available on the Web.)
This text is remarkable in that it provides 944 guidelines for screen design.

C. Marlin 'Lin' Brown, *Human–Computer Interface Design Guidelines*, Ablex, Norwood, NJ, 1988.
This text presents the guidelines in a succinct and practical way often giving examples to support a guideline in a 'USE' table, followed by the converse in a 'DON'T USE' table. Sometimes there is page after page of this type of table.

David Travis, *Effective Color Displays: Theory and Practice*, Academic Press, London, 1991
Published as part of their 'Computers and People' series, this is one of the few texts totally devoted to the use of colour in electronic displays. As the title suggests, it covers both the theoretical background and the practical applications necessary for using colour in displays, by considering the human visual system in detail, and the technical aspects of producing colour electronically. The book also considers aspects of the workplace, and an environmental ergonomics checklist is included in the appendices.

Christopher Wickens, *Engineering Psychology and Human Performance*, Harper Collins, London, 1992.
An authoritative text, that is intended to bridge the gap between the problems of system design and the research findings from cognitive experimental psychology and human performance, and includes extensive coverage of Wickens' stimulus-response compatibility model, as well as many other applications relating to human information processing.

Kevin Cox and David Walker, *User Interface Design*, Prentice Hall, Singapore, 1993.
This is a text on the design of interfaces for computer systems which draws on theory, but is primarily meant for practitioners in the field. Hence, there are lots of practical examples and tips to help usable systems to be developed.

Linda Macaulay, *Human–Computer Interaction for Software Designers*, International Thomson Computer Press, London, 1995.
Published as part of the Thomson Tutorial Guides in Computing and Information Systems series, this a practical book for students studying courses in HCI, software design and systems design.

Alan Dix, Janet Finlay, Gregory Abowd and Russell Beales, *Human–Computer Interaction*, Prentice Hall, Hemel Hempstead, 1998.

This book, currently in its second edition, provides a comprehensive coverage of HCI, from some of the basic concepts through to leading-edge technologies, such as virtual reality. It has a design focus, and includes numerous practical examples and tips, including extensive web-based support materials.

4

What Are the Main Components of the System?

OBJECTIVES OF CHAPTER:

- To introduce the main components of the human–computer interface
- To consider the design and use of common input and output devices and technologies
- To focus on the human factors issues associated with the use of these technologies

HAVING READ THIS CHAPTER, THE READER WILL BE ABLE:

- To select appropriate forms of input and output devices and technologies
- Be aware of the human factors issues associated with the use of the main components of human–computer interaction

4.1 OPERATIONAL LEVEL INTERFACES

The communication link between the human and the technology is a key operational level interface; it is at this level that the human is able to exert control over the machine, or to enter data or receive information from the machine. This means that the devices that support the interaction across this interface will fall into two classes: input and output, synomonous with control and display (at least as far as the human is concerned). If we make the simple assumption that control can be discrete or continuous, then we can begin to determine the sort of information a person might require to perform such control, and the type of device which would support the control actions.

Discrete control actions would be made on an intermittent basis, usually in the form of a single action. This suggests that some form of two-state device, such as a switch, button or lever would suffice. The person would need to know (i) how the device operated, and (ii) that the operation had been successful, i.e. that the desired outcome had been achieved. For simple devices, such as switches and levers, there is a minimal range of information that can be provided to the user on how to operate the device. However, there are many instances where poor design encourages the wrong action.

Buttons or Labels?

An ATM, designed to respond to button presses, has buttons mounted around the screen. The buttons' 'labels' are positioned on the screen, as they have been designed to look like buttons, and a user presses the screen rather than a button. As far as the user is concerned, 'information' has been communicated, in that the request for the machine to perform an action has been signalled by a button press. However, the machine, of course, will not respond. In this example, the labels are interpreted as controls, leading to user error. In an alternative example, the alignment between buttons and labels was not true and the user pressed a button that did not correspond to the desired request.

Discrete controls provide users with two forms of feedback: (i) primary feedback arises from the action of the control itself, i.e. whether it moves or not, whether it makes a noise etc., which confirms that control has been operated effectively; (ii) outcome feedback arises from the performance of the machine, i.e. whether it has responded in the anticipated fashion. The opportunities to correct or otherwise modify the consequences of a control action are thus limited.

Continuous control devices, on the other hand, allow a great deal of scope for effecting small changes in the control actions, e.g. when using a steering wheel to manoeuvre an automobile, or when using a mouse to move a cursor across a screen. In this instance, the primary feedback will be obtained from the performance of the machine, with feedback arising, for example, from the movement of an object being controlled. In this instance, the movement or feel of the control might be less obviously relevant to the performance of the user, and the notion of outcome feedback becomes difficult to define, in the sense that there need not be any obvious termination of the action.

From this short discussion, we can see that not only do the two types of control differ in the superficial aspect of how they are performed, but also in terms of how the control devices are used, and the type of feedback useful to the person performing the task.

4.2 INPUT TECHNOLOGIES

A control (input) device might be defined as any instrument, apparatus or mechanism that is used to influence the state of a system, whereas a display device is used to present information to the user. When considering the design of control/display technologies from a user perspective, the aim is to create devices that maximise the advantages of human physical and cognitive characteristics, and so promote efficiency and reliability. This is to ensure that learning times will be expedient, and the risk of accidents minimised, especially when the user has less reserve capacity, due to stress or overload. The type and function of the majority of control/display devices reflect this intrinsic link with computing, and the technologies covered here will reflect this.

The importance of control design is evident from the frequently used term 'knobs and dials ergonomics', where the first part of the expression refer exclusively to the design of push-buttons, switches, knobs, cranks and wheels. In the avionics and process control applications of the 1940s and '50s, the design of controls was particularly relevant, and much of this work pre-dates the growth and advances in computer technology. For example, in 1947 Fitts and Jones carried out a survey of aircraft controls' design (published 1961), and concluded that poorly designed controls were leading to inefficiency in human performance.

Although the generic term 'input technologies' is being used here to cover control technologies, control devices are generally thought of as a category of input devices. Hence, the term 'control' is being used to indicate both a class and a type of input device. Input devices are generally categorised into three broad types: 'controls', 'pointing' and 'non-pointing' devices.

Controls

Continuing the theme of classifying according to whether actions are discrete or continuous, Oborne (1995) provided a comprehensive review of control design. He classified the various controls into two types: those that make discrete changes in the state of the system, and those used for making continuous settings. For example, a discrete control would be a toggle switch which is either off or on, while a continuous control would be a volume control on a radio.

When considering the design of controls, decisions have to be made relating to choice, location and spacing. The choice of controls can be determined by:

1. applying information relating to knowledge of human anatomy and physiology, e.g. the fingers and hands are more suited to quick,

precise movements, while the arms and feet are best used for controls which require force to be applied;

2. the physical characteristics of the controls, e.g. size (finger controls should be spaced not less than 15 mm apart), shape, colour, texture, resistance, labelling, allowance for clothing;

3. the need to avoid ambiguity, i.e. the operation of the controls should be immediately obvious (whether to push/pull/turn, etc.);

4. the nature of the controls, e.g. whether emergency controls or important controls need to be recessed. In terms of location, as a general rule, emergency controls should be separately located.

Table 4.1 Types of controls and their functions (from Oborne, 1995). (Copyright John Wiley and Sons, Limited. Reproduced with permission.)

Control type	Activation	Discrete setting	Data	Quantitative setting	Continuous control
Hand push-button	Excellent	Can be used, will need as many buttons as settings – not recommended	Good	Not applicable	Not applicable
Foot push-button	Good	Not recommended	N/A	N/A	N/A
Toggle	Good, but prone to accidental activation	Fair, but poor if more than three possible settings to be made	N/A	N/A	N/A
Rotary selector switch	Can be used but on/off position may be confused with other positions	Excellent, provided settings are well marked	N/A	N/A	N/A
Knob	N/A	Poor	N/A	Good	Fair
Crank	Only applicable if large forces are needed to activate, e.g. open/close hatch	N/A	N/A	Fair	Good
Handwheel	N/A	N/A	N/A	Good	Excellent
Level	Good	Good, provided there are not too many settings	N/A	Good	Good
Pedal	Fair	N/A	N/A	Good	Fair

When designing controls, there are a number of issues that need consideration, including clarity, visibility, and colour. A further consideration is the need for standardisation. For example, car manufacturers position windscreen wiper and indicator sticks in different locations, thus making the change from driving one car to another problematic. There is also a need to consider maintenance requirements in the design of controls and control panels.

Pointing Devices

It is implicit in the notion that those input devices that have a pointing component also require a medium upon which to point. Consequently, most pointing input devices are used in conjunction with a screen. Pointing devices fall into two groups: those with direct control on the screen's surface, e.g. lightpens (including pen-based computing in character recognition systems), touchscreen technologies, and those which have indirect control away from the screen, e.g. mouse, tracker balls, cursor keys, joysticks, graphics tablets with stylus.

Lightpens

This is a misleading description, in that it implies that the device is like a pen (or a gun in the term 'lightgun') and emits light; in fact it detects it, signalling to the computer when (not where) there is light. Light enters the pen from the screen, reaching a high-speed light detector that generates an electrical pulse. Usually, the detector is a phototransistor or a photodiode inside the pen, but it can be a photomultiplier tube outside of the unit. The impulse is amplified, filtered (to remove ambient light from the room), and the voltage adjusted to remove interference. A digital pulse generator picks up the electrical impulse and sends a 1-bit digital code, indicating where the light pen is active, to the main computer. Typical response time is in the region of 10^{-6} seconds, although the photomultiplier is faster.

The lightpen is generally used in conjunction with a display for pointing, selection and drawing activities. It is the only device that is primarily suited for pointing at graphics objects, and like the touchcreen, is an input medium, where the user physically touches the screen. Advantages include the fact that this device has a similar feel and action to a pen or pencil, and the term 'natural' is often used, although some would dispute this. Feedback is immediate, and learning time should be minimal.

There are a number of difficulties yet to be resolved concerning the ease of use of this device. It can be triggered by stray light, and can be moved only at a moderate rate, as there is a need to attain a virtually constant speed to maintain contact with the cross-hair image, which may prove frustrating for some users. Furthermore, precision is not high, due to the pen's aperture and the problems of parallax, and fatigue may arise, as operation requires the user to hold the device perpendicular to vertical surfaces. Many lightpens have trailing leads, which can prove cumbersome and awkward to manage. A final point concerns costs. As lightpens cannot be used in isolation, they require the use of some form of display surface.

Touchscreens

With touchscreens, the screen reacts to light finger pressure, which is transmitted in the form of 'finger co-ordinates' to the host computer.

The advantages emanate from the flexibility of this device, as it can be operated by direct finger pressure. Learning time is generally minimal, since operation of touchscreens is relatively self-evident and straightforward, and possibly more accurate than typing. It is potentially inexpensive, since input is via the screen and touch matrix (i.e. no keyboard is necessary). This also results in saving space, e.g. touchscreens have been considered as appropriate in aircraft cockpits where space is at a premium. Furthermore, operation can be relatively silent, which may be beneficial in shared workplaces, and reliability is enhanced by the fact that there are no mechanical parts. Unlike the lightpen, there are no trailing wires to act as a hazard.

Disadvantages stem from the fatigue encountered using touchscreen technologies for any length of time. Sometimes the fingers will obscure the target, and the remedy of moving above the target can also be equally confusing. This difficulty manifests itself in a lack of feedback for the users. From our own experience, parallax can be a problem (despite repeated recalibrations for individual users), as well as a screen that very quickly becomes covered in greasy fingerprints.

Joysticks

These devices control the screen cursor rather than setting its position by absolute co-ordinates, as a digitiser does. A joystick (like a trackerball) provides a different means for controlling a sensor that passes an analogue signal or incremental count to the control unit which, in turn, converts this into a digital format.

There are a number of different types of joystick available, with varying means of operation. The displacement joystick allows tilting of the handle up to 30°, and the speed of the cursor is a magnitude of angles. The sensor is a potentiometer generating four analogue signals (forwards, backwards, right, left), or six if the joystick is three-dimensional (optional rotating knob on top). The force-operated or isometric joystick responds to the pressure from the operator's fingers. Precise pointing is possible as one 'bump' can move the cursor one unit of resolution. Normal cursor speed and force are applied. The sensor generates two analogue voltages, corresponding to the amount of force applied in the x, y directions. The switch-activated joystick activates eight switches, corresponding to the eight points of a compass. This particular type is not used much in graphics applications.

In human–computer interactions, the joystick is most frequently found in the context of playing games. Benefits include relative cheapness, robustness and increased functionality in terms of degrees of freedom when compared to other pointing devices. However, prolonged joystick use may be tiring, since they are not specifically designed to allow the wrist to be rested whilst in use.

Mouse and Trackerballs

The mouse and trackerball have been designed specifically for use with interactive graphics systems (with the mouse simply an upsidedown trackerball). The mouse usually has a small ball in the region of 1–2 cm diameter, while trackerballs are 7–8 cm in diameter, mounted on rollers; both devices need to be used on a flat surface, and can be operated by using the palm of the hand, moving in all directions. Sensors can be either a potentiometer, or four optical encoders (as in incremental digitisers). These count the increments of ball rotation in each of the four component directions, and the four (data carrying) pulses are converted into digital data. Distance moved by the cursor, number of resolutions of the ball, and direction of the cursor corresponds to direction of rotation. Three revolutions can move the cursor across the screen, or 300 revolutions for finer control, which is more accurate than a joystick.

Advantages include the ubiquity of the mouse, whilst most people have the ability to operate the mouse for long periods of time without fatigue. However, it is postulated that in years to come, we will witness mouse-related RSI (repetitive strain injuries), in the same way as has been experienced with keyboards (see work by Karlqvist et al., 1994; Harvey and Peper, 1997). In terms of disadvantages, some would cite the learning time needed to use the mouse and trackerball successfully.

Graphics Tablets with Stylus

The graphics tablet is a square or rectangular device embedded in epoxy, with a grid of co-ordinating wires just below the surface. Drawing on this surface results in the appearance of the trace on another surface, providing a fast mode of interaction; many of the fatigue problems which arise from operation in a vertical plane are alleviated, because the device is used whilst horizontally mounted. Although there are problems with parallax, ambient light does not create any difficulty. Graphics tablets are somewhat dated now, having first been developed in the 1950s, and replaced in recent times by the increased functionality offered by GUIs (graphical user interfaces) and advances in digitising tablets and flat panel display technology.

Character Recognition

Despite the recent interest in pen-based personal communicators, the concept of pen-based computing is not new. The pen as an input device for computer systems was considered back in the 1950s, with one of the earliest devices being the Stylator (Dimond, 1957), followed by the RAND tablet in 1963 (Davis and Ellis, 1964). These early digitising tablets employed a variety of electromagnetic techniques to detect the position of a pen point on a writing surface, and although resolution was fairly poor, attempts to program character recognition were carried out with some success. Since then, other techniques have been used for detecting pen input, including utilisation of electrostatic properties, pen pressure, and ultrasonics (see, Leedham, 1994). However, it is only in the 1980s that we witnessed real advances in character recognition, with major developments in display technology.

Character recognisers can be divided into two types according to whether they operate on- or off-line. On-line recognition results in the processing of the handwriting taking place at the same time as the person is writing, so that feedback is nearly immediate. Hence, the system has to operate in real time, handling writing speeds of around 20–30 words/ minute. In contrast, off-line systems deal with the processing at a later date, and thus lose any of the dynamic information associated with the input. Speed of operation will be dictated by the system; Leedham quotes the example of the automatic processing of postal addresses at a speed of 80 words/second. This is 160–240 times the speed of on-line systems.

It should be noted that with on-line systems, the pen can be used for pointing and selection, as well as the creation of ink traces – the so-called 'digital ink'. Here, data about stroke number, order, direction, relative scale and position, and the temporal sequencing of strokes can be collected (Bricklin, 1993). Ink traces might take the form of conventional alpha-numerics and punctuation, as well as 'gestures' used as commands and edits. These gestures are allegedly based on proofreader symbols (Mezick, 1993). As with other recognition systems, one of the difficulties concerns the end-point detection of words. These segmentation problems make the recognition of cursive script particularly difficult, and not surprisingly, the highest recognition rates are attained with single character input.

There are a number of human factors issues associated with the use of character recognition systems. (For further information on the human factors issues of pen-based computing, see Noyes *et al.*, 1995). One of the main considerations determining the success of character recognition as an input technology concerns the task. Studies by Rhyne and Wolf (1991, 1992) and Frankish and colleagues (see, Frankish *et al.*, 1994, 1995; Frankish, 1999) have looked at task design, and concluded that applications where handwriting is not a major component can achieve satisfactory results. This may appear counter-intuitive, given that the system is concerned with character recognition, but the use of the pen for pointing and selection rather than the generation of digital ink has many advantages. For example, the tip of the 'pen' allows objects to be selected with a high degree of accuracy, and with immediate feedback given to the user. Using a pen for the generation of non-standard text, e.g. musical notations, Greek letters, etc. might be advantageous (Wolf *et al.*, 1989). This is in contrast to cursive writing, where a number of factors make character recognition difficult. These include:

1. the endpoint detection of letters (as already mentioned);
2. inter- and intra-individual differences and inconsistencies;
3. the mismatch between how users expect the system to recognise handwriting based on their own knowledge and experiences of reading handwritten text, and how the technology actually works.

The difficulties of individual variations and inconsistencies in handwriting are exemplified when considering signature verification. This is an application that has attracted a lot of interest (Smithies, 1994), given that an increasing number of transactions in the financial, legal and retail businesses are now being conducted electronically. An electronic means of verifying signatures would mean that the whole process could take place at the computer interface, without the need for paper. If the technology could become sufficiently sensitive and accurate at signature verification, this could also act as a security check in the system. However, this scenario is still some way from being realised.

In summary, uses for character recognition are numerous, spanning a number of applications from the optical character recognition of printed text to 'free writing', as in the case of note-taking on a PDA (personal digital assistant), or scribbling in a brain-storming session. There are also a number of exciting, potential applications, such as signature verification. Current applications achieve varying degrees of successful recognition according to the extent that the pen is used as a pointing device, and handwriting is constrained. In principle, there is no reason why all tasks that we currently carry out with a pen and paper could not eventually be reproduced using a pen-based system. This would have a number of benefits, allowing users who are not computer-literate to have access to computer-based facilities. For example, Buell and Brandt (1990) reported that a group of USA rail workers was using pen-based computers in place of pen and paper to record information. However, caution is warranted here. The perceived naturalness of the interface is based primarily on the assumption that users' experience and knowledge of using pens and pencils will be to their advantage when they come to use a pen-based computer system. This may not be the case; indeed, it may even work to their disadvantage, since they bring unreal, but well-established perceptions of using a pen to the interface. These, coupled with high expectations of how easy pen-based systems will be to use, are unlikely to be met when users actually encounter the technology. It could almost be concluded that users would be better off if they had never used pen and paper; then they would be unable to expect the character recognition system to react in the same way as a human reading the writing. This is particularly noticeable when individuals attempt to 'help' the system recognise their script. They use techniques such as pressing harder, going over the letters already written (to make them bolder and more prominent), writing slower, writing in capitals, etc. Although all these would be appropriate and acceptable in human to human communication, they do not relate to the way that the computer algorithms recognise handwriting, and are unlikely to prove successful.

Non-pointing Devices

This group of input devices includes the keyboards, which are probably the most frequently used and most familiar of all the input technologies, and speech recognition (commonly called ASR – automatic speech recognition).

Keyboards

Keyboards can be either sequential, e.g. the ubiquitous QWERTY keyboard, where a single character has a dedicated single key press, chord, which involves patterned pressing of keys, or a combination of both operations, e.g. the so-called hybrid keyboards, such as ANTEL. All these keyboards may or may not have a numeric keyboard option attached.

Most alpha-numeric keyboards used in human–computer interactions adopt the QWERTY layout (so-called because of the first six letters on the top row). This may seem somewhat surprising, given that this keyboard layout was devised over a century ago, with the invention of the typewriter. There has only been one change (moving the letter 'M' from the middle to bottom row) since it was patented by Sholes *et al.* 1868 (US Patent Office, No. 79,868). Furthermore, it has survived many challenges from other keyboards, some of which will be briefly reviewed here. The standard QWERTY keyboard (as shown in Figure 4.1) became an international standard in 1966, and has subsequently become documented

FIG. 4.1 Standard QWERTY layout (referred to as the universal keyboard since 1905).

in many other standards (ISO 4169, 1979; BS 5959, 1980; ISO 9241, in draft).

Despite the extensive use of this keyboard throughout the Western world, there is no substantiated factual information relating to the rationale for the arrangement of letters in the QWERTY layout. Suggestions range from a variation on the alphabet, to trying to avoid the mechanical problems of returning type bars clashing, through to relating the layout to the inventors' occupations as printers and salesmen. Further explanations concerning these are given in Noyes (1983a).

During the last 130 years, the QWERTY keyboard has been the subject of much criticism, and has been 'challenged' by many other keyboard designs and layouts. Noyes (1998) gave the following examples of poor design.

1. When typing English text, QWERTY overloads the left hand – this is the non-preferred hand for the majority of the population.
2. It also overloads certain fingers, especially the little fingers.
3. Too little typing is carried out on the home (middle) row of keys – the distribution of typing loads across the three rows is uneven, with 52% being carried out on the top row, 32% on the middle, and 16% on the bottom row.
4. Excessive row hopping is required, often from the top to the bottom row and back again – this occurs in such high frequency letter sequences as 'br, un, in', etc.
5. Many common words are typed by the left hand alone, e.g. taking a sample of 3000 words, it was found that for every 10 typed by the right hand alone, 90 words are typed by the left hand.
6. Forty-eight per cent of all movements to reposition the fingers laterally between consecutive strokes are one-handed, rather than the easier two-handed motions.
7. QWERTY requires reaches from the home row for 68% of all typing – on a well-designed keyboard, these reaches can be reduced to 29%.
8. The easiest keying movements are two-handed, without reaches from the home row – only 4% of words fall into this category on the

QWERTY keyboard, whereas it has been suggested that on a well-designed keyboard, this could increase to 34%.

9. The QWERTY layout slopes diagonally from the top left to the bottom right – this results in the little fingers having to stretch up to the top row.

10. The division of keys into diagonal 'strips' for the different fingers is made by oblique parallel lines, resulting in the strips for the fingers of the left and right hands being identical, regardless of the fact that the hands are not congruent, but inverse images of each other.

Despite these criticisms, challenges to the QWERTY keyboard have met with little success. A large number of keyboards has been produced over the years; these are listed in Noyes (1998). It would seem plausible to consider an alphabetical layout, and indeed some children's toys and a few systems (e.g. an airline reservation system used in the 1970s) have this arrangement of keys. However, the alphabetical layout has not been successful, partly because it has been shown experimentally that the novice user takes longer to use this keyboard, because he or she first carries out a mental search, followed by a visual search of the keyboard. This takes longer than the purely visual search that is demanded by QWERTY (and its apparent 'random' arrangement of keys). In terms of serious and sustained contenders to the universal keyboard, it is probably worth mentioning one – the Dvorak Simplified Keyboard. In the 1930s, Dvorak and his colleague, Dealey, experimented extensively with developing a new keyboard. They based their design on data relating to the frequency of use of different letters, digrams, trigrams, four- and five-letter sequences, in order to address the deficits in the QWERTY keyboard. The end-result was the DSK (Dvorak Simplified Keyboard), patented in 1936 (US Patent No. 2,040,248) and shown in Figure 4.2.

Although there has been some support for the DSK over the years (e.g. the world record typing speed of 128 words per minute was set with this keyboard, and some organisations have claimed to be converting to the DSK), QWERTY has become the *de facto* standard. Looking to the future, it is unlikely that this position will change. Reasons for this include:

1. It has been argued that QWERTY can be operated at near-optimal speeds for a typewriter keyboard – an imaginary 'ideal' keyboard would only attain speeds 8% faster. (We could also question whether

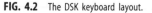

FIG. 4.2 The DSK keyboard layout.

'speed' is important, since on very few occasions do individuals type for long periods of time at high speed.)

2. One of the benefits of QWERTY is that many common sequences of letters are typed by alternate hands – it is thought that this benefits the user, by providing greater kinaesthetic feedback.

3. Movement from the mechanical and electric keyboards of the 1950s and 1960s to the electronic keyboards that came in with PCs would have provided an opportunity to move away from QWERTY.

4. QWERTY is well established in terms of the user population – one estimate in 1990 was that there were 40 million computer keyboards in the USA alone. Hence, the upheaval and costs associated with changing the keyboard would be considerable.

5. The number of tasks undertaken via the keyboard is increasing. No longer do we use the computer keyboard solely for the generation of text, but also for access to the Internet, intranets and various databases, the sending and receiving of electronic mail, as well as word processing and related activities.

Many of the criticisms aimed at QWERTY have been concerned with the layout of its alpha-numerics. However, its design where the keyboard slopes from the top left to the bottom right has also been the subject of criticism. It has been suggested that a better design would be a keyboard in keeping with the shape of our hands, i.e. in two divisions, with arcs of keys emulating our hand shapes with higher keys for the shorter fingers. This 'split keyboard' concept is not new, and was suggested as early as 1926 (Klockenberg, 1926). It has also been more recently adopted in the Maltron keyboard (Malt, 1977; Hobday, 1996), the kinesis ergonomic keyboard (Gerard et al., 1994) and the STINGRAY (White and Hutchinson, 1996). Although there has only been a small number of evaluative studies comparing the split keyboard design with the standard QWERTY design, it has been suggested that the more natural position of keys on the former results in reducing musculo-skeletal loading during operation (see studies by Hedge and Powers, 1995; Mechan and Porter, 1997).

Since the Second World War, there has been a move away from the traditional sequential keyboards, with the development of chord keyboards. Chord keyboards, as the name suggests, are operated primarily by pressing groups of keys simultaneously (or within a short space of time), the main advantage being that the number of keys can be dramatically reduced, e.g. five keys for the five digits allow 31 chords to be made (i.e. 2^5-1, where '1' is the invisible 'no keys pressed' chord), while only ten keys allow 1023 patterns to be made available. An alternative approach is to give more keys to one digit, so that five keys plus the inclusion of a second thumb key increase the number of possible chords to 47, a third key to 63, and so on. Alternatively, a key could be introduced to act as a shift key; hence, four finger keys plus two thumb keys used in this way could generate 62 characters. One of the advantages of chord key pressing is that it allows a relatively small number of keys to generate a large number of options. The disadvantages are that the learning time to achieve successful chord key presses can be considerable (Noyes, 1983b; Greenstein and Muto, 1988). This is partly because there is a memory element involved in retaining the various combinations. Further, some of the chords are difficult to form, e.g. the chord involving all digits except the ring finger. As a result, there have been few chord keyboards marketed for general word processing activities, as the majority have been developed for specialist applications, e.g. mail sorting, word processing by disabled users.

A hybrid keyboard exhibiting features of both a sequential and a chord keyboard exists in the form of the ANTEL keypad. It was patented by Stewart and Miles in 1977, and is shown in Figure 4.3. This pocket-sized device has a number of keys operated by single key presses, e.g. 'A', 'C', 'E', some that require two key presses simultaneously, e.g. 'B', 'D', and some that need four keys to be pressed at the same time, e.g. '?'. Due to the close proximity of the keys, it is sufficient for a single finger to make contact with all four keys. Unlike 'true' chord keyboards, such as the Microwriter and the Writehander (Noyes, 1983b), the ANTEL keyboard resolves the difficulty associated with remembering the various chords.

As well as the chord keyboards, there have also been a number of specifically designed ones, e.g. numeric and function keyboards. An interesting situation exists with numeric keyboards, in that there are two recognised layouts, as ISO 9241 permits both arrangements. These include the 'telephone layout' given in Figure 4.4, and the 'calculator layout' in Figure 4.5. The telephone layout arranges the numbers in a form we would expect when reading from left to right, and has been shown to be slightly superior in terms of user performance (Lutz and Chapanis, 1955; Conrad and Hull, 1968; Chapanis, 1988; Straub and Granaas, 1993). In contrast, the numeric keypad shown in Figure 4.5 arranges the keys in a somewhat bizarre arrangement beginning '7', '8', '9' on the top row. This layout, found on calculators and PCs, probably emanates from that found on adding machines, where the higher numbers are positioned towards the top of the device. The origins of this arrangement presumably relate to the internal mechanics of this device necessary for successful operation. The layout became a British Standard in 1963. Although both arrangements are in frequent use (in fact, some users are unaware of the difference until it is brought to their attention), difficulties are likely to arise when transferring from one keypad to the other. Take keying in a PIN when using an ATM. Frequent practice at this activity results in a motor action that is carried out effortlessly, usually

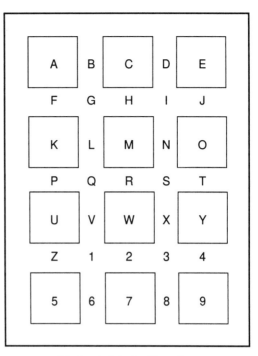

35 clearly labelled functions

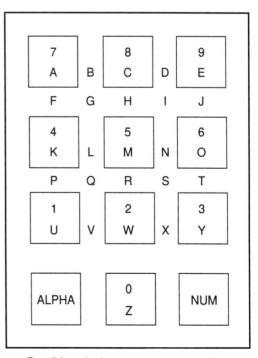

FIG. 4.3 The ANTEL keyboard.

Possible calculator or computer version.

1	2	3
4	5	6
7	8	9
	0	

FIG. 4.4 Telephone layout for numeric keypad.

7	8	9
4	5	6
1	2	3
	0	

FIG. 4.5 Calculator layout for numeric keypad.

with greater accuracy than would be immediately attainable using the 'alternative' keypad arrangement.

Function keyboards, as the name suggests, are keyboards with keys labelled with specific functions. In this sense, they are application-specific, although standard QWERTY keyboards usually have a row of function keys positioned at the top of the keyboard. These function keys are often used as 'short-cuts', allowing the user to 'undo' a command or select help by a single key press. There is still little standardisation amongst function keys; this is possibly because they are little used in word processing tasks, and there is often a facility to set them up according to your own needs (although anecdotal evidence suggests that most people probably do not bother to do this). Function keyboards, on the other hand, are tailored to meet an application, such as air traffic control (ATC) tasks (Lam and Greenstein, 1984). Due to the diversity of special function keyboards, it is not easy to draw any generic conclusions concerning their use. Lam and Greenstein found that for the ATC environment, function keyboards resulted in faster key times with fewer errors, when compared with QWERTY. However, this is hardly surprising, given that the function keyboard had been designed to meet the task requirements.

Speech Recognition

There is an increasing number of products and devices being developed to allow automatic speech recognition (ASR), whereby humans can input information to a computer using speech. The word 'speech' is not entirely accurate, since most recognisers are not programmed to differentiate intelligible speech from mere vocal utterances or other sounds. However, within the context of human–computer interaction, the quest to find a reliable means of allowing humans to communicate with their machines continues to attract much commercial and research interest.

The history of ASR mirrors that of pen-based systems, with the earliest recognisers being developed in the post-war period. In 1952, a recogniser was demonstrated that could recognise 10 digits with near-perfect accuracy when they were spoken singly into the device (Lea, 1980). It took another 20 years for ASR to move from the experimental laboratory into operational use, and it is thought that the first applied use of speech recognition was during a manufacturing task at the Owens-Illinois Corporation in the USA (Martin, 1976). In 1973, they introduced voice input into the quality control and inspection of face-place components during the manufacture of televisions. The 1980s were a time of growing interest in ASR. This is largely explained by the expansion in computer processing capabilities around this time, and research developments in the pattern-matching algorithms for recognition. Today, we have a situation where ASR is being used very successfully in a number of dedicated applications, but the goal of communicating with machines using natural language is still to be achieved. There are a number of reasons for this.

Users – most of us acquire and use human speech with relative ease. The 'naturalness' aspect of communicating with machines using speech is often cited as one of the advantages of this mode of input. However, although human to human communication is frequently executed using speech, it is questionable whether this naturalness extends to human to machine interaction. One of the outcomes of this familiarity that we have with talking to each other is that users can have unreal expectations when they attempt to use ASR. They anticipate that using speech input will be similar to speaking to a fellow human. When misrecognitions occur, it is likely that they will adopt well-rehearsed strategies to make themselves understood, e.g. talking louder, slower, emphasising and stressing various syllables, repeating words and phrases. However, these strategies do not relate to the characteristics of the pattern-matching algorithms that the recogniser is using. Hence, the user's approach to enhancing recognition performance is unlikely to be successful.

The key to achieving successful recognition is consistency. Since most recognisers work according to pattern-matching incoming utterances to pre-stored templates, it is important that users generate consistent vocal utterances. At this point, it is useful to consider the notion of intelligibility. Human utterances can be unintelligible but consistently produced, as is the case with some disabled users (Noyes et al., 1989). Likewise, some human speech can be extremely intelligible, but inconsistent, and inappropriate for successful ASR use.

Products – the differences in the technology have already been alluded to: there are essentially two types of recogniser, allowing speaker dependent and speaker independent recognition (Baber, 1991). The former requires knowledge of the vocal utterances of the user, usually facilitated by setting up templates of speech items in a process known as enrollment. Once the user has trained the system, incoming utterances are then matched to the pre-stored templates, and a selection made, based upon the best match. Hence, the need for consistency. Also, this type of recognition does not require words only to be input, since it is of no interest whether the utterances are intelligible to other humans or not. Speaker-independent systems, on the other hand, do not require this formal training period, and in theory could be used immediately by any user. Consequently, successful recognition performance is more likely with speaker-dependent than speaker-independent systems.

Applications – one of the major problems for ASR is the end-point detection of utterances. In human to human communication, the use of other cues, e.g. gestures, posture, facial expressions, plus the context in which the dialogue is taking place, and the built-in redundancy of human speech, allows us to understand the other speaker. Recognition technology currently does not have access to this other information, and unless there are distinct pauses after each incoming utterance, there will be segmentation difficulties. In summary, ASR is more successful when handling isolated items, rather than continuous (or connected) speech. A better recognition performance is also attained when smaller vocabulary sets are used. It could therefore be concluded that those applications that have a dedicated user group, a small vocabulary (say, up to 100 items), and 'isolated' input mode, are currently more appropriate for ASR. Examples include the previously mentioned quality control and inspection task, environmental control units (ECUs), primarily for use by disabled individuals, and the use of speech in information overload situations, where other channels are exhausted. An example of the latter is the use of ASR by cartographers and hydrographers, who have integrated speech input into a CAD (computer-aided-design) task where their eyes, hands and feet are already operating controls (see Noyes, 1993). Here, utilising speech comprised one of their few remaining options for entering information. Hence, it can be seen that the use of speech recognition for natural language applications with vocabularies of 20 000+ items is still some time off.

Multi-modal Aspects

When interacting with computers and advanced technologies, the keyboard is often used in conjunction with some other input device. In PCs, for example, this is usually a mouse or a trackball. Table 4.1 provides a summary of input devices and their application, while Figure

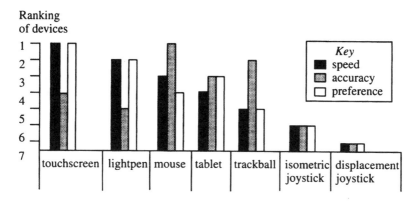

FIG. 4.6 Summary comparing seven input devices. (Note: the scale on the y-axis is intended to denote the ranking, with '1' being the best and '7' the worst.) (Reprinted with the permission of Academic Press.)

4.6 compares seven input devices, according to the parameters of speed, accuracy and user preference. The issue concerns the extent to which these other modes complement or disrupt the primary task of keying. There is a certain irony in the fact that all the ancillary devices in Table 4.2 require hand operation; thus inevitably interrupting use of the keyboard. The conclusion reached is that speed of typing is not important. This viewpoint is not new, and various statistics quoted by Noyes (1983a) demonstrated that even skilled typists spent surprisingly little time actually touch-typing. Fifteen years later, it is likely that keyboard users are spending even less time typing, because of the increased range of functions offered by computer technologies. Hence, the need for parallel use of the keyboard and an ancillary device (if indeed it was possible) to maintain typing speed is not necessary. There may also be other benefits of sequential operation of two modes, e.g. reducing the repetitive physical movements demanded by sole keyboard use. It might also be hypothesised that keyboard layout and design become less important in multi-modal operation.

4.3   OUTPUT TECHNOLOGIES

There are three main types of output devices: printers, displays and speech. As a technology, printers have attracted little attention, other than in the early days of HCI, when the noise they generated was often considered a disruptive influence in the workplace. Various actions were taken to overcome this problem, such as using shields to dampen down the noise, and placing printers in their own rooms, away from the centres of activity. Since the computer display is often used in order to see what you will eventually print (i.e. a hard copy display), it is this that has

Table 4.2 Summary of input device function, disadvantages and recommended use

Device	Functions	Disadvantages	Recommended for:	Not recommended
Light pen	Move cursor, select, draw	Parallax, tires arm	Infrequent use, tasks with little keyboard use	Frequent pen-keyboard changes, continuous use
Touch screen	Select	Accidental activation, tires arms	Infrequent use, coarse pointing	Continuous use, precise pointing
Mouse	Point, select, draw, drag, move cursor	Requires desk space	Tasks requiring little keyboard use	Frequent mouse to keyboard changes
Cursor keys	Discrete cursor movement	Slow for moving cursor 'long' distances	Tasks requiring short cursor movements	Extensive or fine cursor movements
Tracker ball	Track, select, move cursor	Mouse may be faster for selecting text	Integrating graphics with keyboard entries	Frequent change to and from keyboard
Joystick	Track, select, move cursor	Mouse may be faster for selecting text	Tasks with intensive cursor positioning	Frequent change to and from keyboard
Graphics tablets with stylus	Move cursor, select, point, draw	Parallax		

attracted the human factors interest. In this sense, we have already covered a number of display design issues in Chapter 3. The following section will focus on speech output.

Speech Output

The generation of human speech can take many forms, from copying fixed messages using a tape recorder to complete synthesis using artificial means. When considering the development of technology for speech input and output, the 'tube of toothpaste' analogy has been applied, whereby the latter is like squeezing the toothpaste out, while the former is akin to pushing it back in. Hence, it is not surprising to find that attempts to reproduce human speech precede developments in ASR. As long ago as the eighteenth century, a talking machine was invented (Sclater, 1982), although it was not until the 1930s that the first electrical voice synthesiser was produced (Bristow, 1986). A further milestone was reached in 1978, with the development of the first single chip synthesiser (Schalk et al., 1982).

There are two main approaches to generating synthesised speech: synthesis-by-analysis and synthesis-by-rule. Synthesis-by-analysis takes human speech and analyses the pitch, voice quality and formant characteristics, in order to produce digitised speech that sounds very similar to human speech. Synthesis-by-rule, on the other hand, generates human speech totally by rules derived from linguistic and acoustic parameters, i.e. with no reference to an original recording of human speech. Although this allows greater flexibility, in that messages can be constructed in response to local demands, synthesis-by-rule generated speech does not always sound natural. The result is often a monotonic, robot voice that some individuals find unacceptable. One of the reasons for this is that listeners have to make a greater effort to comprehend this type of synthesised speech. This has been extensively documented in the human factors literature (see Luce et al., 1983; Waterworth and Thomas, 1985). However, unnatural-sounding speech is not necessarily unintelligible, and often the so-called computer accent is easy to understand. The converse is also true where speech that sounds natural is, in fact, unintelligible. Together, naturalness and intelligibility determine the quality of speech output, which is dependent on the individual preferences of the listener to a great extent (Lienard, 1980).

Speech output has been used in a wide and diverse range of applications, although Spiegel and Streeter (1997) argued that its enormous potential has yet to be realised. Often in human–computer interaction, speech output is an add-on, as opposed to an integral part of the system. In this sense, its use will be intermittent, e.g. automated public address systems giving information about evacuation procedures in the event of a fire. One of the benefits of using speech output is that it grabs the attention, and can alert/direct the listener. A disadvantage is its ephemeral nature, making it inappropriate for tasks where a lot of information has to be 'digested' by the user. In the past, speech output has received adverse publicity, because its repetitive nature can eventually lead to irritation on the part of the user. Spoken seat belt reminders in cars were an example of this, with many individuals eventually disabling their systems. One area where speech output has an obvious application is with the disabled user group (Edwards, 1991). Individuals who lack the physical ability to generate their own speech, and those with visual impairment who cannot access information in written form, will benefit from a technology that communicates human speech (and doubles up as both an artificial mouth and an artificial eye). Unlike ASR, speech output technology does not have to meet the high performance requirements of speech input. It plays a more passive role in human–computer interaction, usually as a provider of information rather than an interactive communications device. Consequently, the human factors issues are not so critical to successful operation of this technology.

4.4 CONTROL–DISPLAY RELATIONSHIPS

In Chapter 3, stimulus-response relationships were discussed within the context of Wicken's model. Although this chapter has focused primarily on input/output technologies, it is important to draw attention to the fact that the design of one (the stimulus) may affect the operation of the other (the response). A classic experimental study that demonstrated the importance of control/display relationships was concerned with the design of oven controls (Chapanis and Lindenbaum, 1959). Individuals were presented with a four-burner hob and asked to state which control lit which burner. Where there was a direct spatial correspondence between the positioning of the control and the display, participants were extremely accurate. But, as can be seen from Figure 4.7, this was not so when this compatibility was lost.

This study has been replicated, with slight variation, by a number of researchers, and each time the importance of display/control compatibility was highlighted. This feature of compatibility, and our expectation that it will be present in control design also applies to its mode of operation, i.e. we expect movement compatibility. If a control is turned clockwise, we would expect an associated display to show an increase. This is known as a population stereotype (Oborne, 1995). With respect to this particular example, there are a number of violations of the population stereotype, such as materials that are stored under pressure

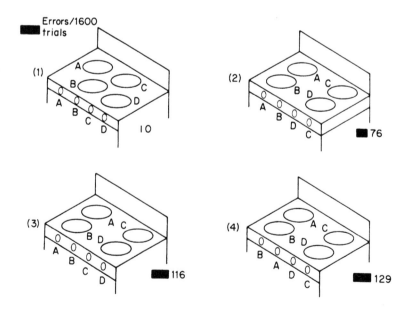

FIG. 4.7 Control–display arrangements used by Chapanis and Lindenbaum in their study (Chapanis A., and Lindenbaum L.E. *A Reaction Time Study of Four Control–Display Linkages, Human Factors*, Vol. 1, No. 4, 1–7, 1959).

(water, gas), which do not obey the clockwise/increase phenomenon (Petropoulos and Brebner, 1981).

A third type of compatibility is 'cognitive' compatibility. Whereas spatial and movement compatibility refer to physical aspects of the control–display relationship, it is also important that the cognitive requirements of the human are met in the design. When considering the design of computer systems, the memory load placed on the user must be compatible with the memory capabilities of the individual. For example, delivering a long message via speech output will be inappropriate if the user cannot remember all of it when they attempt to complete a task that demands they do.

4.5 CONCLUSIONS

This chapter has focused on commonly-used control and display technologies in HCI. In this sense, it has not dealt with some of the more specialised input/output devices, such as head-up displays (HUDs), and data gloves. Neither has it covered what must be the ultimate control technology – the use of thought. Although this topic has attracted researchers for a number of decades, little progress has been made in terms of relating our brain waves (via EEGs – electroencephalograms) to various words or thoughts. For the time being, this is likely to remain a future development.

In terms of HCI, the QWERTY keyboard currently dominates the control devices. It has survived the move from character user interfaces (CUIs) to graphical user interfaces (GUIs), as well as miniaturisation in the form of PDAs and handheld devices. The next 'challenge' for QWERTY could be wearable computers, but its establishment on PCs, coupled with the growth in internet use, means that its demise is unlikely.

Comparison of input technologies is not easy. Common performance measures include speed, accuracy, and user preferences (as demonstrated in Figure 4.5). But, as Baber (1997) pointed out, the fact that empirical evidence suggests one device is faster than another, does not always mean that this will be so. Little more can be concluded other than that the device was faster (or slower) in that particular experimental setting. One of the main determinants of performance appears to be the type of task, and it is evident from considering the characteristics of ASR and pen-based input that judicious and careful selection of task can result in high recognition rates and successful performance. It could therefore be suggested that, in the context of HCI, interface design should be viewed primarily in terms of task design.

Likewise, despite the plethora of output technologies, the display screen dominates. This includes both general PC-based and specific applications. It is evident from the previous chapter that a great deal of research has gone into the design of displays, and our understanding of the human factors issues is considerable.

4.6 EXERCISE 5

Exercise 5: Designing a Control Panel
You have been employed by a manufacturing company to design their new product. The company is considering combining the following into one item:

AF-FM radio
Cassette player
CD player
Telephone plus answering machine
Alarm clock
Desk or bed lamp

The company is trying to decide whether to include a small (10 cm. screen) TV set, and a switched electric outlet that can turn on a coffee maker or toaster.

Your tasks are:
1. To design the control panel,
2. To certify that it is actually what customers want, as well as being easy to use.

Outcome:
Draw a rough sketch of a control panel for the items in the list.
Indicate how you would incorporate the needs of the user population.

4.7 SELECTED REFERENCES

Wilbert O Galitz, *It's Time To Clean Your Windows: Designing GUIs That Work*, Wiley, New York, 1994.
This continues the theme of Galitz's previous book on office automation and user interface screen design, by focusing on display screen design. He does this within the context of graphical user interfaces, covering direct manipulation, windows, menus, icons, etc., as well as user considerations.

David Oborne, *Ergonomics at Work: Human Factors in Design and Development*, Wiley, Chichester, 1995.

This text, first published in the 1980s, and now in its third edition, provides an excellent introduction to the topic of ergonomics, covering interface, workplace and environmental design issues. The approach taken tends to be from the physiological perspective: for example, two of the early chapters cover the structure of the body in terms of the sensory nervous system, body size and movement. However, the level of detail is generally impressive.

Chris Baber, *Beyond the Desktop: Designing and Using Interaction Devices* (Computers and People Series), Academic Press, London, 1997.

This text considers how interaction devices in human–computer interaction have developed and how they are used, as well as discussing implications for future design and development. It considers the ergonomics of keyboards, pointing devices and speech input, and covers devices for use in 'restricted environments' and multi-modal interactions.

Jeffrey Anshel, *Visual Ergonomics in the Workplace*, Taylor and Francis, London, 1998.

To quote the backcover, this text is an easy-to-read introduction to the role of the visual system in the workplace. It covers how the visual system works, including an historical perspective of how it has evolved, and issues relating to computer use, and includes many practical exercises and tips. The appendices provide an incredible amount of information relating to resources for visually impaired individuals.

Part 2
Developing Systems

5 How Will the System Be Designed?

OBJECTIVES OF CHAPTER:

- To consider system life cycles, in particular, user involvement
- To overview different approaches to system design
- To look at the human factors activities associated with general development life cycles

HAVING READ THIS CHAPTER, THE READER WILL BE ABLE:

- To specify the main stages and attributes in system development
- To describe the role of human factors in life cycles
- To recognise the various benefits and shortcomings of different methodological approaches to design and analysis

---

5.1 LIFE CYCLES

The actual design and development process of a system (or product) will vary according to the nature, type and size of the proposed system, its application, approved standards, and project management, but in general it will be an iterative process, involving a number of stages. Many life cycles representing the design process are to be found in the literature; some of the more frequently cited will be presented in this chapter. It is worth pointing out that few systems or products are actually designed from start to finish, as demonstrated by these development life cycles. For example, some products will arise as a result of systems integration of a number of components, e.g. lawn mowers or computer workstations, or will involve the redesigning and modification of an existing product, e.g. Pyrex measuring cups (Younge, 1985), and 'Reach' toothbrushes

(Kreifeldt and Hill, 1976). However, even if a system is developed from the conceptual stage through to operation, it is unlikely that its development will follow the neat packaging portrayed by the system life cycles that abound in the literature, primarily because they are an abstraction representing an ideal process, and the reality is likely to be very different, where economic, time and resource considerations have to be taken into account. In this sense, life cycles do not indicate the dynamic and iterative processes of system development as they unfold; they are inaccurate and simplistic, and merely represent a starting point. System building in the real world is subject to 'constraints, interruptions, distractions, emotions, personalities and politics' (Rubinstein and Hersh, 1984), and actual projects are not likely to be sequential or orderly, or linear processes in the rigid way that the life cycles suggest. When looking at the more commonly cited life cycles, the actual development and design of systems has to be considered within the conditions and influences already mentioned.

Many documented life cycles relate to the development of software, and have arisen from the interest in human–computer interaction emanating from the growth in computer technologies in the 1980s and 1990s. Perhaps inevitably, they have many common features, as illustrated by some of the life cycles considered here.

The development of a system is commonly represented as a number of sequential steps, usually beginning with some sort of information gathering of requirements, and ending with final delivery of the product. For example:

1. Pre-design stage, i.e. user and usage needs analysis, in order to determine objectives and performance specifications.
2. Design and specification of the new system, i.e. the application of tools and techniques in order to begin to design the system. This may include analysis of a system (or the system) currently in use.
3. Review stage, i.e. more detailed design assessing the requirements of users, their tasks, and extending to workplace and environmental considerations.
4. Delivery and implementation, i.e. product building followed by validation testing, evaluation and product release.
5. Fine-tuning, then operation and maintenance of the product.

Often the final 'maintenance' stage is omitted from the development process. It could be argued that it should be present in life cycles, given that the majority of systems spend most of their time at this point in the cycle, and systems (software in particular) will continue to be developed and modified after product release and implementation. It may also be necessary at this stage to have the final product certified by an outside body. For example, the CAA (Civil Aviation Authority) in the UK are concerned with the certification of avionics systems on civil aircraft. There are also International Standards, Health and Safety regulations and legislation that may need to be taken into account. For example, ISO 9241 is concerned with the usability of office workstations, and there are various pieces of legislation in the UK relating to consumer safety. Page (1998, p. 133) summarised three such acts:

1. Product Liability and the Consumer Protection Act of 1987

This act states that any person suffering injury or damage because of a defective product can obtain redress (usually from the manufacturer of the product).

2. General Product Safety Regulations, 1994

The purpose of these regulations is to ensure that all consumer products are safe. Safety will be assessed by consideration of the product's characteristics, its packaging, its instructions for assembly and maintenance, use and disposal, any possible effects on other products with which it might be used, labelling and other information provided for the user, and the categories of consumers who may be at serious risk when using the product, e.g. children.

3. Sale and Supply of Goods Act, 1994

This act supersedes the 1979 Sale of Goods Act, and is primarily concerned with the fitness of purpose for which the product/system is intended. This might encompass factors such as appearance, safety, and durability.

Meister (1986) also included a further (sixth) stage in his system design process, which he developed primarily for use in the design of military and space systems. This was 'facilitator design', i.e. the design of supporting documentation, and referred to all the materials which will support human activities and performance, e.g. instruction manuals, performance aids, training devices and programmes. Of all the parts of the design process, this is probably the most neglected; anecdotal experience about the design of software manuals often reports this.

It is also worth noting that life cycles tend to focus on addressing the functional requirements of the system, i.e. those aspects which must be present in the operational domain, rather than non-functional requirements, i.e. those aspects relating to the way in which the requirements are provided, such as safety features of the system. However, there is a standard (IEC 1508) currently at the draft stage that will cover the life cycle of a safety-related product, from initial concept through to decommissioning or disposal.

Classic Life Cycle (or Waterfall Model)

Most of the life cycle models generated relate to software development, and this applies to the classic life cycle, often referred to as the waterfall model. Its graphical representation is similar to a waterfall, and it is intended that each activity will naturally lead (flow) into the next. In the waterfall model presented in Figure 5.1, the initial stage is 'system engineering', encompassing the following activities: task analyses, user and system requirements, and allocation of function between users and system. One of the problems associated with this early stage is that it is often difficult to identify all the product requirements at the beginning of its development, primarily because the purpose of the system may be ill defined at this point, and it would thus be problematic to generate an accurate list of user and system requirements.

This life cycle is claimed to be 'the most widely used model of software design and development, at least among large software projects' (Johnson, 1992, p. 77). It is sometimes shown in a 'V' shape, and referred to as the 'standard V' life cycle. Although, as already stated, it

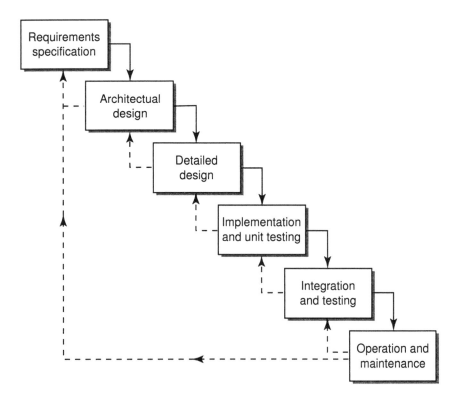

FIG 5.1   The classic life cycle (or waterfall model).

may not be realistic to expect system development to proceed in this comprehensive manner, it does provide a template for the process.

Pressman's Model of System Development

In the last couple of decades, the traditional life cycles have been enhanced by the adoption of new techniques and methods (Skidmore, 1996), involving improvements in communication, e.g. the application of graphical notation rather than text, and the progression through the life cycle. The impetus for these developments relates to the difficulties already described in applying system life cycles: they are often too abstract, difficult to comprehend, and lengthy in execution. Skidmore stated that by the time the system development life cycle has been drawn up, the whole operation has often moved on, and the requirements have changed.

An alternative to the so-called classic life cycle is the prototyping approach, which is appropriate when the requirements are not (or cannot be) well defined. Prototyping is not new; indeed, reference can be found in the literature from the 1970s (Basili and Turner, 1975). Prototyping allows the designer to develop a model of the system under investigation, which may be regarded as an obvious part of the life cycle activities. These 'models' may range from elaborate simulations of part or all of the system, to paper or computer-based projected designs. In terms of the latter, the 'storyboarding' technique may be used, whereby, sketches are used to demonstrate what an interface might look like, and they change as an interaction proceeds, or different inputs are made into it. Dix *et al.* (1993) stated that there are three main approaches to prototyping:

1. 'throw-away' – where the prototype is built, tested and then discarded;
2. 'incremental' – where the prototype is built as separate components one at a time, with the final system being released as a series of products;
3. 'evolutionary' – where the prototype is not discarded, but used as the basis for the next iteration of the design.

Prototyping has many advantages: it allows the interface to be tried and tested before the final system has been constructed, as well as allowing fuller requirements to be elicited from the users (or potential users). However, as pointed out by Johnson (1992), it is essentially a trial and error approach to design, and should be considered in that context. Naumann and Jenkins (1982) defined prototyping as a four-step procedure:

1. Identification of information requirements. Naumann and Jenkins stated two distinct approaches to the gathering of information from

users about their requirements in the design of the system. They called them the 'data abstracting approach', where system design begins with identification of entities, attributes and data structures, and the 'process simulating approach', where the first step is to model the process. It is generally accepted that whatever approach is used, completeness is not important at this stage. A CASE (computer-aided software engineering) tool may be used to capture the requirements. In the past, CASE tools have been cumbersome to use, often expensive, especially for one-off designs, and have had poor graphics (Yourdon, 1986). Alternatives included the use of manually constructed data flow diagrams and dictionaries. Given that the latter holds all the information relating to data in the organisation, these approaches were often unsatisfactory, and 'structured methods' began to receive a 'bad press'. However, the situation has changed, and there are several quality CASE tools now available at low cost.

2. Development of the working prototype. The emphasis here is on the production of a prototype within a very short time; hence the use of the term 'rapid prototyping'.

3. Implementation of the prototype. This allows users to have 'hands on' experience of using the system.

4. Modification of the prototype. Users' comments will enable the prototype to be modified accordingly. Again, the emphasis is on speed of turnaround, and several iterations may be needed until the system is 'complete'.

Table 5.1 Full and mock-up prototyping. (From Lantz, 1984.)

Advantage	Full prototype	Prototype as mock-up
System meets user's needs	X	X
User participates in design	X	X
Early discovery of design problems	X	X
Requirements are developed experimentally, not theoretically	X	X
User participates in development	X	
System interface problems must be solved from start	X	
Work of several phases concurrent with development	X	
Excessive documentation not needed	X	X
Unexpected problems that consume major amounts of time do not occur	X	
Much user training is a by-product of development	X	

In summary, prototyping requires powerful tools to allow the process to proceed rapidly. There are also various advantages associated with producing a full prototype as opposed to a 'throw-away'. Lantz (1984) referred to the latter as a mock-up prototype and summarised the benefits of full and throw-away prototyping in the following table:

Despite the many advantages of prototyping, there are also a number of problems associated with its use, relating mainly to the management of the approach (detailed by Sommerville, 1996). These include:

1. Temporal aspects: building prototypes is a time-consuming activity, especially if they are destined to be discarded. (This partly explains why the term 'rapid prototyping' came into existence, as prototyping needs to be an activity that can be carried out quickly.) The length of time taken may also result in users' enthusiasm and interest waning. Alavi (1984) found that users were often reluctant to spend time modifying a prototype again and again, and were keen to move onto a new project. There may be conflict here between the users' motivation levels and that of the designers, who may view the prototype as being in the early stages of development.

2. Planning: prototyping is a specific technique, thus it may be difficult for individuals to 'cost' it into the design process. However, it has been suggested that the use of prototyping can reduce total systems development by about 25% when compared with a more traditional approach (Gremillion and Pyburn, 1983). This could be partly explained by the fact that the end-product uses fewer computing resources as a direct result of prototyping – users tend to think they want more screens, programs, reports, than they actually need. Prototyping allows them to find this out in the planning stage. Boehm *et al.* (1984) supported this by concluding that prototyping tended to produce a smaller product; prototyped products being about 40% smaller and requiring 45% less effort to produce.

3. Non-functional features: prototyping does not allow examination of some of these features, e.g. safety and reliability. It is also difficult to prototype large information systems, and sometimes it is not obvious how to divide a large system for prototyping.

4. Art versus methodology: some may view prototyping as an art rather than a tried and tested methodology. If this is the case, the organisation may be concerned that prototyping is being executed by particular individuals, and not documented in such a way as to be reproducible (Lantz, 1984).

Pressman's view of system development is essentially an extension of the prototyping approach, by including the use of fourth generation tools (Pressman, 1987). There is no agreed definition on what exactly constitutes a fourth generation language (4GL), other than that it is a further development to the first three generations of computer languages (Skidmore, 1996). It is generally recognised that the first generation comprised machine code, the second generation included the assembler languages, while the third generation languages consisted of the high-level languages, such as Fortran and COBOL. In contrast, the 4GLs allow software to be designed at a high level of abstraction, with the result that the tools then automatically generate the source code from the specification. For example:

1. Requirements' analyses: this would be specified in a form which could be interpreted by a specification tool.
2. Design: this would involve the use of 4GL to address various aspects of the design, e.g. evaluation techniques.
3. Implementation: this involves the designer describing the design in terms of the fourth generation language used by the tool.
4. Fine-tuning: testing and evaluation of final product.

Pressman (1987) argued that the three approaches: namely, the life cycle model, prototyping, and the use of 4GLs, could be combined to provide a single model of system development. This includes the following stages:

1. Requirements' analyses: this is essentially the information-gathering phase;
2. Prototyping: early designs of the interface and system are developed and evaluated;
3. Final product – testing and evaluation.

It should be noted that the use of development tools, such as the 4GLs and CASE does entail more computer resources than prototyping, which takes place without them. Some development teams will not be equipped with the necessary hardware and software, and will lack the appropriate training for their use. It may also be the case that the use of 4GLs and CASE is inappropriate, and the prototype would be better developed using a third generation language.

5.2 GENERIC ACTIVITIES IN SYSTEM DEVELOPMENT

There are a number of different approaches to system development, and two have been discussed in detail here. In summary, they all include common features and several generic activities; Johnson (1992) gave these as definition, development and maintenance.

Definition is involved with defining the scope of the system, the requirements of the users, the tasks and the domain, and finer details relating to the planning of the other activities in the development of the system. This is essentially the starting point of the design process, where the requirements of the eventual product are specified in some way. The form of specification can vary widely, from the more formal, e.g. data flow diagrams, through to informal written or verbal specifications. On some occasions, the next stage, involving the development of the system, may begin before the requirements' analyses are complete. This only becomes a problem if completed before the definition stage!

Development is concerned primarily with the details pertaining to the actual design of the system, particularly the interface design. From a human factors perspective, the design of the interface between the users and the system is of paramount importance, since this is the part of the system with which the user comes into contact. Indeed, interface design has been considered a major element in the successful design of a sophisticated warning system (Palmer *et al.*, 1987). Development of the system is best carried out by design engineers in conjunction with the users. The optimum approach is to involve both parties, and sometimes a third group, if customers/suppliers are included. Although users will have developed their model of the system requirements and operation, this could be far removed from the actual system model; hence it is important to involve the users in system development. However, there are difficulties in relying totally on the user-centred design approach, because users are often too close to the situation to be able to produce a flexible solution that could be modified in the light of changing requirements. Moreover, they do not usually have the technical knowledge and expertise to know of possible alternatives for design solutions.

Maintenance usually occurs after product release, and is concerned with the minor adjustments and modifications necessary to 'maintain' the functions of the product. Documentation previously designed during the development stage will be used here to support system use. It generally describes what the system is supposed to do, how to use various aspects (perhaps in the form of tutorial support), as well as providing help and advice. The generic development life cycle defined in the ROBUST research programme included production, in-service support and decommissioning in this third stage (ROBUST, 1996).

5.3   USER INVOLVEMENT

At the Beginning . . .

Over the last couple of decades, user involvement in system development generally has become more salient. This is recognised as a positive move, since it should lead to better designed products from the perspective of the user. To quote Nielsen (1993, pp. 12–13), 'users are not designers, and designers are not users'. One way of overcoming this is for the designers to work in conjunction with the users, involving the users early in the development process, when their contributions to the eventual design of the product are thought to be greater (Booth, 1989). Monk *et al.* (1993, p. 11) went even further by stating that 'close involvement with users is the only way to get sufficient initial requirements'. Further, in order for user activities to have any impact, they must provide information that is appropriate to particular stages of product development (Gould and Lewis, 1985), and studies involving major conceptual issues are likely to be wasted if they are carried out late in the life cycle. In contrast, the approach carrying the highest risk is the development of a product that has had no input from the users (Weisberg and Lanzetta, 1991). The overall trend towards greater user involvement in product and system development is indicated by most of the larger software developers now consulting users by bringing them into usability laboratories and kiosks, and actively involving them in the design process (Bawa, 1994; Dieli *et al.*, 1994; Nielsen, 1994a).

At the End . . .

It is acknowledged that in some applications, user involvement with the finished product could be only worthwhile if changes and modifications can be made at this stage in the life cycle. Often this may not be possible or simply cannot be justified, on the grounds of economic costs of modifying the final product, the complexity of production which precludes making changes, and/or the attitudes of the users, who have certain expectations about how a product will function when used. Conversely, there are some situations that demand that the finished product undergoes modification if the safety of the users is placed at risk, e.g. some safety-critical systems.

User involvement can be employed, however, to assess if the product meets the end-users' requirements, as demonstrated in the study conducted by Bawa (1994), as well as being used to influence the next version of the design. Indeed, Nielsen (1993) concluded that the main purpose of usability work after product release is to gather data for the next version, and for new products. In order for this to happen, the results arising from end-user evaluations of the product need to feed back into the development process. In the life cycle model described by Dix *et al.* (1998), it was evident that the maintenance phase provided feedback to all of the preceding activities. However, in some instances, feeding back appropriate information may not be easy, for instance, in the case of commercial off-the-shelf (COTS) software packages, where the 'distance' of the end-users from the developers would make implementing feedback difficult. Admittedly, there are standard activities falling under the umbrella of 'passive evaluation', which provide the software developers with feedback, e.g. marketing studies on customer satisfaction, user complaints, modification requests, calls to help lines, etc. There is also 'active evaluation', where specific, experimentally-oriented evaluation studies are carried out to collect data from the end-users about the product, in the form of follow-up studies. Rubin viewed these as primarily for the collection of data for the next product release, and stated that 'structured follow-up studies are probably the truest and most accurate appraisals of usability, since the actual user, product, and environment are all in place and interacting with each other' (Rubin, 1994, p. 23).

As well as the type of user activities described by Rubin, there are occasions when it is necessary to involve the end-users, as with applications where there is a commensurate need for finished products to be assessed to determine their suitability for their intended purpose, which can only take place with the finished product (see Watkins *et al.*, 1995). Cohen *et al.* (1994) conducted an outcome-based evaluation of an educational software package to test students' conceptual understanding of some introductory statistics topics. They were assessing the statistical package against specific educational criteria, which would have been difficult, if not impossible, with the unfinished, incomplete package. In the educational arena, lecturers and teachers might need to know whether a software product will improve their teaching, or enhance students' learning, and a variety of advisors may be called upon to make recommendations on the use of such software (Hammond *et al.*, 1994). Furthermore, there may also be occasions when it is necessary to compare software products, or to assess them for different groups of end-users.

Throughout the Life Cycle . . .

Since it has been suggested that users should be involved throughout the life cycle, a logical step is to examine the nature and extent of the human factors activities in the design process. Page (1998) drew up the following table of the role and contributions of ergonomics in design, based on her own experiences working on the design and evaluation of products, and as such had a practical bias, but maintained the rigour of the scientific method.

It can be seen from Table 5.2 that Page included accidents as a design process stage. This may seem an anomaly at first, but she argues that by studying accidents, we can inform the design of future products and systems. Accident analyses often demonstrate exactly how users use the products, and not how they think they will when they are confronted with a new design during the development phase. Hence, they can provide a rich source of data. Although Table 5.2 highlights the ergonomics input, it does not provide any detail on how to do this. The different techniques are extensively covered in the next three chapters.

Table 5.2   Role and contribution of ergonomics in the design process. (Reprinted with the permission of Taylor and Francis.)

Design process stage	Ergonomics input
Initial concept or idea of the function of the product	*Data on: – human requirements – human needs – human shortcomings
Functional specification	*Data on: – human capabilities – human size – human strength – accidents
Design drawings and Pre-production prototypes	*Evaluation or appraisals *Recommended changes and modifications *Identification of potential hazards and mismatches
Production and marketed products	*Evaluations and appraisals *Anticipation of foreseeable misuse *Instructions and warnings
Accidents and complaints	*Accident investigations *Interactions with the environment and other products *Misuse

5.4   MODELLING ENGINEERING APPROACHES

This chapter has established that the involvement of users and their contributions to the product life cycle are often 'too little' and 'too late'. The typical involvement only at the evaluation stage of product and system development results in a poor realisation of their contributions (Walsh *et al.*, 1989), while the lateness of these contributions may make it more difficult to incorporate human factors requirements into the final design (Rosson, 1987). One generally recognised approach is to formalise the human factors input to the system design process, as suggested by Walsh *et al.*, who stated that 'human factors inputs to systems design would be more effectively achieved through the integration of software engineering and human factors methods' (Lim *et al.*, 1992, p. 1136). Thus several techniques have been developed that allow quantitative predictions of how well humans will carry out certain tasks. Some of the more common are considered here.

Software engineering relies on structured analysis and design methods (SADMs), which provide methodological support, and contrast with the more implicit and informal methods available to human factors engineering (see Downs *et al.*, 1988). Typically, SADMs reduce the development cycle to a number of stages, which are then given descriptive notations to represent the design at each phase, followed by procedures to facilitate the transformations of the design. A fairly recent development has extended the use of SADMs to support the human factors contributions in the design process (Lim *et al.*, 1991). This is contra the approach whereby software engineers are provided with user interface guidelines and tools, as a means to allow them to develop prototypes quickly. Criticisms of guidelines include the fact that they are often expressed in a form which is not necessarily compatible with design, while the provision of tools does not ensure that the methods used will support effective evaluation.

One approach might be to incorporate the SADMs used in software engineering into the system design process. There are two main benefits to doing this (see Walsh *et al.*, 1989):

1. The structured integration of human factors and software engineering help to ensure that the human factors component is explicitly represented in the overall design process.

2. The use of a common notation for the human factors and software engineering inputs will facilitate communications between experts in these two groups. This must be viewed positively, given that a lack of communication has been cited as one of the problems concerning the wider application of human factors knowledge, i.e. ergonomists do not always present their work in a coherent and comprehensive manner. However, it could be argued that this is partly due to the nature of the material with which they are working. For example, a user might talk about the 'feel of the keys on an ATM keypad'. The human factors specialist or ergonomist has to translate this into a language that the hardware engineer understands. In this example, a description of the force-displacement characteristics of the keys would be needed.

In terms of SADMs, two of the well known methodologies are SSADM (structured systems analysis and design method) and SSM (soft systems methodology). There are hosts of others; a comprehensive summary of participatory practices is given in the form of an appendix in Muller *et al.* (1997). Both SSADM and SSM are most appropriate for use in problem-type situations that arise during system design. For example, SSADM is used to overcome some of the problems encountered during the design process, such as overruns. It does this by involving users and thus ensuring that the system development is kept in touch with the 'real world'. The actual methodology for achieving this involves quality assurance reviews at a series of points in the design process (Longman, 1992). SSM, on the other hand, includes involving all the stakeholders in the final system (i.e. users, managers, developers) in its design and development, the aim being to provide a rich picture of the situation, taking into account possible effects (and problems) from a number of different perspectives, e.g. social, cultural and political implications. Initially, brainstorming activities might take place in order to locate possible problem areas. Hence, SSM has become a well-known general methodology for handling problem situations (Checkland, 1981).

Formal Methods

The use of formal methods allows a structured and precise description of the design requirements of the system to be generated, and this has stimulated their development and application in the design of interfaces (Johnson, 1992). However, although they continue to be used successfully in an engineering context, there are a number of problems associated with their use in interface design. The primary problem with adopting this approach in human–computer interaction is that it is generally difficult to specify user behaviour and/or performance in this way. There exists a degree of uncertainty about what information to collect, as well as the difficulties associated with how to elicit the relevant facts from the user population (see Chapter 2 on knowledge elicitation). This is particularly true for non-expert users, who often do not know or understand their own needs and requirements, let alone being able to express them to designers (Booth, 1989).

The umbrella term 'formal methods' refers to the notations used for describing some aspect of a system or user's behaviour. In essence, these analytical techniques provide a systematic approach to considering aspects of the human–machine interaction, breaking down user and system functions into manageable amounts; thus, allowing comparisons to be made between systems, and recommendations concerning improvements to be suggested. A common approach to classification of the set of formal methods is to divide them into two types: those which attempt to model the cognitive aspects of the user, and those which use notations derived from other fields and apply them to human–computer interaction. Examples of the first group include the GOMS model (goals, operators, methods and selection rules) (Card et al., 1980, 1983) and TAG (task-action grammar) (Payne and Green, 1986), while examples of the second group include the use of Backus Naur form grammar (BNF) (Reisner, 1981, 1984) and Z notation (Sufrin et al., 1985). However, the situation is slightly confused by the fact that Payne and Green developed their TAG model using a notation similar to BNF.

In terms of modelling the cognitive aspects of the user, there are a number of models available; the first one proposed was the GOMS model (Card et al., 1980), developed as an abstraction of human information processing in order to try and provide predictions of human behaviour at the interface. A GOMS model provides a description of the knowledge that a person must have in order to use the system. It is probably one of the best known of the modelling techniques, and consists of the following four components (Card *et al.*, 1983):

Goals: 'A goal is a symbolic structure that defines a state of affairs to be achieved, and determines a set of possible methods by which it may be accomplished.'

Operators: 'Operators are elementary motor or information-processing acts, whose execution is necessary to change any aspect of the user's memory or to affect the task environment.'

Methods: 'A method describes a procedure for accomplishing a goal. The description of the procedure is cast as a continual sequence of goals and operators, with conditional tests on the contents of the user's immediate memory and on the state of the task environment.'

Selection Rules: 'When a goal is attempted, there may be more than one method available to the user to accomplish the goal. The choice of method is governed by selection rules which depend upon the features of the task environment.'

A GOMS analysis comprises defining and then describing the goals, operators, methods and selection rules for a set of tasks in a formal notation. Kieras (1997) stated that identifying and defining the user's goals is often the most difficult part of the analysis, primarily because the task has to be examined in a lot of detail, which is often not particularly easy at this stage in development or in the case of a new system. In contrast, the operators and selection rules relating to the hardware and software are easier to define. Card *et al.* (1980) used GOMS to refer to a fairly simple model known as the keystroke-level model, in which task execution time is predicted by the total number of times that the keystroke actions are required to perform the task. In contrast, Kieras (1997) stated that one of the most complex uses of GOMS was developed by Gray *et al.* (1993), who mapped out the sequential dependencies between the user's perceptual, cognitive and motor processes in a schedule chart. A critical path analysis was used to predict the execution time. This model was known as CPM-GOMS (Gray *et al.*, 1993). A further example of development from a GOMS model was NGOMSL (natural GOMS language), where an attempt was made to devise a language that would allow GOMS models to be written down with a high degree of precision (Kieras, 1997).

Notations Derived From Other Fields

The 'cognitive dimensions' framework (Green, 1989, 1991) is a broad-brush description of devices and notations, designed to capture in easily understood terms the most important aspects of design. It purports to be applicable to any information artefact, but at present its main area of application has been to computer programming languages. Some glimpses of its application to grammar notations will be found in the following examples of grammar-based dialogue specification systems.

(i) Transition Networks

The transition network contains states (nodes) and arcs (edges), with each arc being associated with a set of tokens. Recognition proceeds by traversing the arcs between nodes, beginning at a start node and finishing at an end node.

In terms of cognitive dimensions, the basic system has no possibilities for abstraction at all, and when presented graphically has no hidden dependencies where one entity depends upon another. The dependencies are not made manifest in the representation, although its mode of operation can be dynamically displayed. The notation is quite viscous (where viscosity denotes 'resistance to change'). However, because the expressive power is quite low, there are serious difficulties of diffuseness. A more powerful system would include a sub-routine component; sub-routine calling reintroduces some hidden dependencies.

(ii) Backus-Naur Form (BNF)

BNF is a context-free phrase structure grammar, which contains rewrite rules, so that each non-terminal symbol is re-writable in terms of other non-terminals or terminals.

In terms of cognitive dimensions, this system has high viscosity (changing the structure is difficult because changing a rule often has knock-on effects). It has partially hidden dependencies (not always easy to see where a non-terminal symbol is used). It demands hard mental operations (note the recursive element); it has very little secondary notation or perceptual cueing; the level of abstraction is high, leading to distant mapping between problem domain and solution domain, and, depending on the editor system in use, it may cause premature commitment.

(iii) Regular Expression Grammars

Some text-processing tools, such as Unix grep and its derivatives, use a form of context-free phrase structure grammar in which non-terminals are not used; instead the structure is specified solely in terms of regular expressions over the terminal symbols. Complex regular expressions are notoriously hard to interpret, although some alleviation may be obtained by 'perceptual parsing' (Payne et al., 1984).

More Powerful Grammars

The three types of grammar listed above are too weak for many serious purposes, and there has been much research over the last decade into more powerful types of grammar, one of the most promising being the large class of feature grammars, in which parsing proceeds by unification (Shieber, 1986). Rules are associated with sets of structures of features and possibly with values of those features; parsing can only proceed by combining rules whose features can be unified. Besides being widely used for modelling natural language, unification parsing has also been shown to describe differences in 'parsability' of programming languages (Green and Borning, 1990). Some degree of semantic domain information may be included in the features, to guide interpretation of the rules, and unification parsing also has the useful property of being able to work on incomplete or partly erroneous input. Unfortunately, feature grammars in their visual environment have all the cognitive problems of BNF and other rule-based systems, compounded by the difficulty of visualising the unification process in operation. There may also be problems for most potential users in forming an analytic model of the domain suitable for guiding the operation of the parser.

5.5 CONCLUSIONS

One of the frequently cited criticisms of system life cycles is that they are far removed from 'real-life' system development. They represent an idealised set of steps, which probably provides little more than guidance on how systems should be designed. There are many explanations for this situation:

1. the nature of what life cycles are trying to portray is complex, i.e. a generic model of system (and product) development;
2. models are abstractions, and as such will inevitably be inaccurate;
3. the difficulties of accounting for the individual characteristics of specific systems are many.

They also tend to stop at product release, and the question of how the system will be used in the workplace, is often neglected. However, despite these limitations they do provide a starting point, as well as typifying other more complex life cycle models. As a general rule, all life cycle models represent a systematic and sequential approach to system development. They begin with specifications of requirements, moving through various design and testing stages to production, and end at the maintenance stage (in which the majority of systems and products spend their life). Hence, the standard technique for developing a product or system is based on iterative testing and revision with the involvement of the users, in order to identify and correct any problems. It is widely accepted that this approach (essentially one of applying human factors) will work when judiciously and carefully applied (Landauer, 1995). The 'costs' emanate around the fact that user testing and re-testing can be a slow and resource-hungry activity in the life cycle. Hence, the engineering modelling approaches such as GOMS have many advantages in product development, as these make it possible to test and retest designs much more rapidly. User testing would then take place once the design problems indicated by the engineering models have been addressed.

It is evident that there are many benefits from involving users throughout the development life cycle. Muller *et al.* (1997) stated that almost every part of the software life cycle could be improved through user participation. They gave three broad themes to support this. The first included the movement towards workplace democracy, stemming from the Scandinavian school of participatory design. The second was summarised in terms of epistemological effectiveness, where users enhance the design process on the premise that no individual or discipline has all the knowledge that is needed for system design. The third benefit concerns commitment, and the fact that users are more likely to 'accept' the product or system when actively involved in its development.

These perspectives on development can be grafted onto the four aspects of design that we have referred to throughout this text. The physical (including the psycho-physiological) would include the effects of human–computer interaction on (i) behaviour such as absenteeism; (ii) subjective experiences; (iii) physiological aspects, such as stress. The operational perspective is currently the dominant view in human factors when considering how to design the system, as demonstrated by the vast amount of work on the information processing aspects, dialogues, and the development of models such as GOMS. The need to have design specifications in order to ensure that products and systems are well designed for human use is generally recognised. For some time, cognitive psychologists have been taking what is known about human information processing and using it to develop guidelines for the designers of computer systems, in order to ensure that there is a good match between human capabilities and the system demands on the user (Karat, 1988). Guidelines encompassing the development of design procedures are numerous and generally available (see Smith and Mosier, 1986). However, there is a great deal not known or understood about human cognition, and subsequently difficulty in applying findings to design. Karat stated that what was missing was an overall framework to organise and bring together the principles which already existed. However, progress has been made on recognising the need to consider the whole system, and not just parts of the whole. This inter-disciplinary nature (and the need to communicate the designers' decisions to a whole raft of people) was recognised by Belotti (1989) and others, and encompassed the environmental and social aspects, in that design cannot take place in a vacuum. In terms of these perspectives, the human–machine interface could also be viewed as the interface to the organisation, where the system needs to be designed and evaluated in terms of how well criteria meet organisational criteria, e.g. the design of work practices and jobs.

The focus of this chapter has been on the system life cycle, although it becomes evident that it is not possible to consider this without reference to the different methodologies and human factors activities. Although a large number of different approaches are available, it has not been the aim here to suggest the adoption of a proprietary methodology in conjunction with a particular life cycle. This would be rather naïve, given that none of the approaches is applicable to all development environments or systems. There is also little in the way of empirical evidence to support the various efficiency claims of different analysis and design techniques. This point will be further exemplified in the following chapters.

5.6 SELECTED REFERENCES

William H Cushman and Daniel J Rosenberg, *Human Factors in Product Design*, Elsevier, The Netherlands, 1991.
This text was written to demonstrate how human factors can be effectively applied during the product design and development process. It also includes a couple of chapters specifically concerned with product safety. The book is a useful blend of theory, data, guidelines and practical advice.

Peter Johnson, *Human–Computer Interaction: Psychology, Task Analysis and Software Engineering*, McGraw-Hill, London, 1992.
This book takes the reader from the design idea at a user requirements' stage through the development process to the final product. The range of models developed in HCI is extensively covered, with detailed discussion relating to their various advantages and disadvantages. The topics of task analysis and task modelling are dealt with in some depth.

Steve Skidmore, *Introducing Systems Design*, Blackwell, Oxford, 1996.
This is the second of two texts on the development of computer systems. Although not primarily concerned with an ergonomic or human factors perspective, it presents a series of models and techniques that should help in the development, design and deployment of high-quality information systems.

Michael Muller, Jean Hallewell Haslwanter and Tom Dayton, 'Participatory practices in the software lifecycle' in Martin Helander, Thomas Landauer and Prasad Prabhu (eds.), *Handbook of Human–Computer Interaction*, Elsevier, The Netherlands, 1997.

The chapter defines participatory design and provides a taxonomy of participatory methods, and follows with an impressive appendix of 61 examples of participatory practices. These are presented under the headings 'abstract', 'object model', 'process model', 'participation model', 'results', 'phases of the life cycle', 'complementary formal methods', 'group sizes' and 'references'.

Neville Stanton (ed.), *Human Factors in Consumer Products*, Taylor and Francis, London, 1998.

The central theme of this book is to consider the application of human factors to the design of consumer products. It provides a number of case studies relating to everyday products (kettles, power tools, radio-cassettes to name but a few), as well as considering methods that might be used to evaluate these and similar products.

6

How Well Do the Users Think the System Works?

OBJECTIVES OF CHAPTER:

- To consider subjective methods of formative evaluation
- To overview these different approaches to system evaluation
- To indicate when each type of method can be used

HAVING READ THIS CHAPTER, THE READER WILL BE ABLE:

- To define the range of subjective methods which contribute to effective system evaluation
- To be able to select the most appropriate subjective method
- To understand how to use each method to best effect

6.1 THE NEED FOR METHODS

The importance of user involvement throughout the life cycle has already been discussed. To be able to do this in a reliable and valid way, there are a number of methods available that allow us to measure user opinion. Reliability, validity and ethical considerations have important implications for the success of these subjective methods. Reliability refers to the internal consistency of a measure, i.e. its repeatability and the probability of obtaining the same results if the measure was applied again and the study repeated. In contrast, validity is concerned with whether the method actually measures what it is purported to measure. It is possible to have a situation where a measure has high reliability and low validity, and vice versa. In the former, the overall outcome is not as good as when validity is high, whatever the level of reliability. Hence, some have argued that reliability is a precondition to validity (Noyes and Mills, 1998).

Reliability and validity are also influenced by bias. In all different types of evaluation, there will be many opportunities for bias, which can influence the outcome of the subjective evaluation. As an example, bias may arise through the choice of individuals to take part in the subjective evaluation, since they may have a vested interest in determining a particular outcome. This can apply to both participants and experimenters. Finally, ethical considerations are of the utmost importance in all work involving humans. A baseline in terms of ethics is that no individual should ever take part in a study and leave it in a worse position than when they started, in terms of either mental or physical health. In order to ensure this, many organisations have their own procedures relating to ethics, such as having approval from local ethics committees, and adhering to codes of practice. Anonymity and confidentially should be assured, and participants should be informed that they are free to withdraw from the study at any time.

6.2 SUBJECTIVE METHODS

Subjective methods for the formative evaluation of systems have a number of advantages over more objective methods, stemming from the fact that they are often what is referred to as 'quick and dirty', and can generally be carried out by informed non-experts. Some, however, would disagree with the extent to which this is possible in practice. However, one of the benefits of subjective methods is their ease of use by individuals with minimal training. In this sense, subjective methods are very adaptable. As always there are disadvantages, which arise primarily as a result of the advantages, such as the introduction of bias arising from the use of non-experts to carry out the subjective methods. Volunteer bias may arise where individuals available to organise the evaluation may have an invested interest in the outcome of the work. The term 'subjective methods' could also be queried, since these techniques are not always entirely subjective. There are occasions when a set of predefined criteria is used in order to guide the evaluation.

6.3 HEURISTICS

Heuristic evaluation is a systematic inspection of a user interface in order to find out about usability problems in the design (Nielsen and Molich, 1990). It typically involves a small group of people examining the interface, and checking the extent to which it meets recognised design principles, i.e. the heuristics.

A set of heuristics might include the following:

1. Simplicity – the design of the interface should remain as simple and as relevant to the required task as possible to avoid (or reduce) information overload of the human processing facilities.

2. Structure – humans excel at organising and classifying information in the environment; this in part helps reduce the complexity, thus reducing information overload. Hence, it is important that the information presented at the interface is structured to facilitate ease of handling.

3. Compatibility – when confronted with both new and known interfaces, humans draw on previous experience and knowledge. It is important, therefore, to ensure that the interface is designed in keeping with their expectations, e.g. the mode of operation of controls fits expectation. Likewise, population stereotypes should be adhered to.In the UK, the colour red tends to be used to signify 'keep away' or to alert someone to a potentially hazardous situation.

4. Control – it tends to be less stressful for humans when they have to maintain locus of control; they should therefore be allowed to proceed at their own pace when using the system (if appropriate). Computer systems, for example, which monitor user inputs in order to calculate piece-rate payments, have been found to be disliked and stress-inducing for the operator.

5. Adaptation – where public technology is being used, it is important to customise the interface to adapt to the user as far as possible. For example, library information databases could assess initially whether the user was novice or experienced, and adapt presentation of information accordingly by supplying the former with more introductory text and help.

6. Sutcliffe (1988) also listed: consistency, which helps reduce the processing load; economy, where tasks are completed in the minimum number of steps; predictability, where users are able to predict what to do next from the state of the system, and reversibility, where users are able to 'undo' their actions.

In terms of the heuristic evaluation, one of the initial steps is to decide which heuristics to use, and whether to base them on the characteristics of the product or the advice and knowledge of the discipline expert. Other decisions at an organisational level might include working out who is an expert and able to define the heuristics, and who is an appropriate user to become the evaluator. It is quite likely that the experimenter assumes the role of 'expert' and the users become the 'evaluators'. In fact, there may be little difference in the skill levels of either group; rather, it is probably a situation where whoever is driving the evaluation work becomes the expert. Nielsen (1992) considered this problem by carrying out a number of experimental studies. He defined three groups of evaluators:

1. 'novices' who knew about the computers, but with no specialist usability expertise;
2. 'single experts' who were usability experts, but with no knowledge of the interface;
3. 'double experts' who had knowledge of both the computer system and usability.

Analyses of performance in carrying out heuristic evaluations gave results as expected. There was a systematic group difference in the performance of the evaluators, with the double experts locating 60% of the usability problems, the single experts 41%, and the novices an average of 22%. Not surprisingly, the conclusion reached is that heuristic evaluation is best carried out by individuals with knowledge of usability engineering. Interestingly, this conflicts with the general recognition that heuristic evaluation is a 'discount usability engineering' method, i.e. it can be carried out by non-experts with good result. Although this is the case, it has to be concluded that heuristic evaluation can produce even better results when conducted by domain experts.

It is possible to carry out a heuristic evaluation with only one evaluator, but in order to reduce bias, it is safer to use a group of evaluators. Molich and Nielsen (1990) and Nielsen (1992) supported this in their analyses of six projects, where they found that single evaluator only located 35% of the usability problems associated with the interface. For non-critical applications, Nielsen recommended having five evaluators, with a minimum of three. In his analyses of the six studies, he found that five evaluators were locating 75% of the usability problems, but increasing this number had relatively little payoff, i.e. 15 evaluators were finding 90% of the problems. Virzi (1992) supported this finding by indicating that four or five evaluators usually highlight 80% of the usability problems of a product. In conclusion, the exact number of experts to be used in heuristic evaluations will need to be determined according to cost-benefit analyses, i.e. do the economic considerations justify using more evaluators? These additional considerations were reviewed by Lewis (1994). The one exception is where the usability of the interface is critical to the functioning of the system, perhaps on health and/or safety grounds.

Heuristic evaluations are generally carried out by each individual evaluating the interface on their own. This usually involves working through using the interface several times, and comparing its attributes with a list of recognised usability principles. A 'walkthrough' technique is often used (see, Lewis et al., 1990). Here, the user 'walks through' typical tasks carried out using the interface. The evaluator might perform a cognitive walkthrough, where s/he works through a series of tasks that have been designed by a cognitive psychologist in order to evaluate the interface in terms of how well it supports the user using certain psychological criteria. An extension of this is the pluralistic walkthrough, where the heuristic evaluation is carried out by usability experts, users and the system developers (Bias, 1991). A further point concerns the actual interface. Given that the evaluators are not using the interface to perform an actual task, it is possible to carry out a heuristic evaluation using 'pen and paper'. This might be appropriate for systems that are not yet developed. It also allows for heuristic evaluations to be carried out early in the life cycle.

When a number of evaluations have been completed, it is usual to collate these individual reports to produce a final overall picture of the evaluation. It is important that individual evaluators do not confer, since this may introduce bias. Reports are usually written, i.e. the evaluator uses the interface and records comments as they are experienced; alternatives are to write the report at the end of the evaluation or to have an observer record and compile information for the evaluation. The advantage of having an independent observer is that they can provide assistance if the evaluator is unfamiliar with the interface and needs certain aspects explained, or if he or she becomes embedded in a procedure and are unable to find the way out. If this happens, it should obviously be recorded as a usability problem!

In terms of time, a typical heuristic evaluation should take between one and two hours, depending on the application. If it is likely that the evaluation will take longer, it is probably preferable to consider aspects of the interface in a number of shorter sessions. Nielsen (1994b) suggested that the heuristic evaluation could be extended to include a debriefing session at the end, when everyone meets to discuss the interface design. The advantage here is that it allows good aspects of the design to be highlighted, as well as allowing some 'brainstorming' to consider how to address the major usability problems. The output from a heuristic evaluation is essentially a list of usability issues associated with the design of the interface; it does not provide solutions to these problems, but merely highlights them. However, as Nielsen (1993, p. 159) commented, 'many usability problems have fairly obvious fixes as soon as they have been identified'.

6.4 CHECKLISTS

In many respects, checklists are a sophisticated form of heuristic evaluation as the questions to be asked have already been researched and formed (Noyes and Mills, 1998). Checklists allow the experimenter to ask individuals to make judgements about whether or not the interface has certain favoured attributes and characteristics. Within this context of usability, Ravden and Johnson (1989) have made significant advances in the application of checklists as an evaluation method. The development of the checklist approach arose primarily from their work studying and developing user interfaces for systems in the late 1980s (Johnson, 1989; Johnson *et al.*, 1989). Hence, it was based on an iterative approach carried out in conjunction with industrial partners. One of the motivations for this early work on developing checklists was given by Johnson (1996). He stated the aim was to provide a technique which representative end-users could use relatively easily, in contrast to applying guidelines (as suggested by Smith and Mosier, 1986) and the heavily theoretical approach of some cognitive psychologists (see, Norman and Draper, 1986). Therefore, one of the main advantages of using checklists is that it provides a relatively straightforward 'off-the-shelf' method that is fairly easy to administer and can be used by the non-expert. In this way it shares many of the attributes of heuristic evaluations and self-report questionnaires, and indeed has been referred to as a hybrid of these techniques (Johnson, 1996). In order to sum up the attributes of the checklist method, it is useful to consider the outcome of Johnson's survey of checklist users, which generated the following table:

Meister (1986) also included amongst the negative aspects the fact that the items often require discrete responses, in contrast to many of the dimensions of the human–machine interface, which are continuous. Further, the relative value of each item in the checklist is unknown so it is not easy to arrive at a summative total that would, for example, allow comparison of interfaces. Following these criticisms, it has been suggested that checklists are more appropriate to use in the early stages

Table 6.1 Checklists: summary of attributes (adapted from Johnson, 1996)

Positive aspects
    Highly practical
    Visible to clients and evaluators in terms of its purpose
    Relatively quick to administer
    Relatively comprehensive
    Flexible
    Undemanding in analysis

Negative aspects
    Paper format
    Length in terms of time required when used fully
    Wording (which is often tailored to specific or local applications)
    Lack of a standard method of analysis

of the design life cycle. However, this may have been the case a decade or so ago, before the development of more sophisticated checklist measures.

These more recent developments have included the SUS (System Usability Scale) checklist (Brooke, 1985), the Questionnaire for User Interface Satisfaction (QUIS) by Chin *et al.* (1988), the Computer User Satisfaction Inventory (CUSI) by Kirakowski and Corbett (1988), and the Software Usability Measurement Inventory (SUMI), also by Kirakowski and Corbett (1993), which was developed as part of the ESPRIT project MUSiC (Measuring Usability of Systems in Context) (see, Bevan and Macleod, 1994; Macleod *et al.*, 1997; Rengger *et al.*, 1993). All these checklists assess the user's subjective perception of a system. They have also been designed according to psychometric principles, to surmount criticisms of earlier checklists with respect to validity and reliability. However, they are often quite simplistic when you consider what they are attempting to assess; for example, the QUIS assesses five factors (overall reaction to the system, the display screen, terminology and system information, learning, and system capabilities) through 27 items, the SUMI contains 50 items, whereas some have as many as nine factors, assessed through some 164 items. The SUS has ten items, with five-point Likert response scales providing a global view of the assessment of the usability of a system. The measure was deliberately meant to be straightforward, as it was developed in response to a need for a subjective usability measure that could be administered quickly at a number of customer sites (Brooke, 1996).

Questions covered in SUS and other checklists are (not surprisingly) similar to those areas addressed in heuristic evaluations. As an example, Johnson (1996) provided the following nine criteria to drive the development of the checklist:

- Visual clarity
- Consistency
- Compatibility
- Informative feedback
- Explicitness
- Appropriate functionality
- Flexibility and control
- Error prevention and correction
- User guidance and support

A characteristic of checklists is that the questions tend to be followed by standard four- or five-point response scales (e.g. 'always', 'most of the time', 'some of the time', 'never'). This is partly what makes them quick and easy to administer. Some also include open-ended questions towards the end of the checklist.

In summary, checklists for assessing the usability of human–machine interfaces have become more formalised over the last decade, and there are now a number of checklists commercially available.

6.5 QUESTIONNAIRES

Questionnaires, comprising a number of questions on aspects of the system, differ from checklists in that they usually include open-ended questions, and tend to be designed for a particular purpose that cannot be addressed by the more standardised approach evident with checklists. Further, the development of a questionnaire can be quite an arduous and involved process, especially for the individuals who are unfamiliar with questionnaire design techniques. Common difficulties include inaccurate expectations that it is a fast and easy task to develop, distribute and analyse a questionnaire, insufficient assessment of reliability and validity and control of bias, and difficulties with interpretation of the results of the data analyses. Questionnaires can often generate a huge amount of data that becomes difficult to make sense of when trying to refer back to the original research questions – a common problem with student project work!

When considering questionnaire development, Oppenheim provided the authoritative text on this topic (Oppenheim, 1992). He suggests a number of stages through which most questionnaires will need to go, and these are listed below.

1. Aims – the general aims of the overall study will need be compiled, changed into specific aims, then operational aims which can be addressed through the questionnaire.
2. Data gathering – review of relevant literature and discussions with relevant parties.
3. Conceptualisation of the study – more formal data gathering, perhaps based on interviews.
4. Finer design details – assessment of the feasibility of carrying out the questionnaire study.
5. Hypotheses formation – the development of operational hypotheses.
6. Questionnaire design – the actual development of the questionnaire or modification of existing scales, etc.
7. Pilot work – preliminary testing of the questionnaire, and making revisions as necessary.
8. Sample design – work on deciding and selecting the sample of individuals to be tested, taking into account representativeness, use of controls, follow-ups, non-response and missing data.
9. Field-work – the data collection process.

10. Data processing – preparation of the data for analyses; this often involves coding of responses, and entering data into the computer.

11. Statistical analyses – testing of the data for statistical significance.

12. The final report – compilation of the findings in relation to previous research, the original aims, and operational hypotheses.

Oppenheim suggested that it may be worth running through the stages of the questionnaire in reverse order, i.e. beginning with what issues will need to be addressed in the final report.

Questionnaires can be divided broadly into two types – descriptive and analytically. Descriptive surveys deal with locating the views and opinions of a parent population, based on the sample who completed the questionnaire, e.g. Davis's survey of over 2000 company car drivers (Davis, 1996). In this sense, the descriptive type of questionnaire is not intended to explain anything, or to show causal relationships between variables; it merely reports descriptive data from the sample, from which inferences concerning the parent population can be made. The analytical questionnaire, on the other hand, probes deeper, and attempts to explain causes and answer 'why' questions, e.g. the survey carried out by James and others on pilot attitudes to automation (James *et al.*, 1991).

Questionnaires are often administered by mail (i.e. self-administered), although on some occasions they will be group administered, taking place at the end of an experiment, when the experimenter will issue a questionnaire to participants. In this context, questionnaires are often used to provide subjective data to support the objective data collected during the experimental procedure. There are advantages and disadvantages associated with each mode of administration. The postal questionnaire has the primary advantage of providing an inexpensive means of locating a large and possibly geographically scattered population – in theory there is no reason why an entire user population could not be mailed a questionnaire. It also avoids experimenter bias, although this was disputed by Oppenheim (1992), who suggested that although there is no administrator present, the respondent may conjure up a ghost interviewer based on their stereotype of the organisation who sent the questionnaire. Consequently, they may complete the questions accordingly. The main disadvantage of the postal questionnaire concerns its low response rate; for some market research surveys this can be in the region of 2–4% return rate, which will perpetuate the problem of bias. However, not every postal survey has such a poor response rate: Armstrong and Lusk (1988) reported a study which had a 90% return rate when a prepaid envelope was enclosed (in contrast to 26% when one was not included). Sinclair (1975) provided a detailed set of remedies to overcome low response rates. Self and group-administered questionnaires are also subject to bias, but this time mainly in relation to the experimenter. Briefing of participants needs to be carried out very carefully and in a standardised manner, to reduce bias (which can often be unintentional as administrators 'help' the respondents answer questions either directly or indirectly). A final point concerns the medium of the questionnaire: postal questionnaires will inevitably be paper-based, while directly administered questionnaires can be either paper- or computer-based.

Data analyses of questionnaire items are usually undertaken with the use of a computer; there are many software packages to facilitate this. Data can either be analysed qualitatively (see, Dey, 1993; Silverman, 1993) or quantitatively, e.g. some spreadsheets and many database programs will provide summaries of descriptive statistics and carry out some inferential calculations (Drury, 1995). More detailed analyses may require the use of a specialist package such as SPSS-X (Statistical Packages for the Social Sciences) (Norusis, 1987). The important point here is to view the questionnaire analyses as merely another step in the procedure, and not to let the analysis dictate the design of the questionnaire.

To confirm reliability and validity, it is possible to have a number of external and internal checks within the questionnaire. For example, the reliability of answering factual questions can be assessed by acquiring the same information using questions presented in differing forms. Likewise, the validity of factual questions can be checked against external data from an independent source. In terms of ensuring the reliability and validity of attitude questions, reliability can be enhanced by using sets of questions to address an 'attitude', rather than adopting a single question approach. Assessment of validity is a more difficult problem, primarily because of the lack of criteria, i.e. what is needed is large groups of people with known attitudes, upon whom the questions could be tested in order to check their validity. An inherent difficulty is the tenuous link between attitudes and behaviour; locating a group of people with known behaviours does not necessarily guarantee homogeneity of attitudes.

In summary, questionnaires provide a useful measure when access to the opinions of a large population is required. They are particularly useful in finding out how users utilise systems, and their attitudes towards certain designs. In this sense, the cost benefits of this method are good value. As a caveat, we have found that people are not accurate at making opinions about interfaces that they have not used. Work in Bristol on pen-based systems found a difference between expectation questionnaires filled in before use of the handwriting recognition system, and the identical questionnaires completed afterwards on perceptions (Frankish et al., 1995). This supports the findings of Root and Draper (1983) and Karis and Zeigler (1989), and has important implications for using this method for unfamiliar and/or futuristic interfaces.

6.6 INTERVIEWS

Interviews and questionnaires are often discussed in the same context. Like questionnaires, interviews provide an indirect technique for finding out about users' reactions to the design of a system, and, not surprisingly, share many of the same advantages and disadvantages. However, one of the more obvious benefits of interviews is that you can overcome the difficulty of poor response rates found in many questionnaire surveys. This is on the proviso that you have access to a fairly large sample of participants. It is also possible to ask open-ended questions, to which the responses are recorded verbatim. This provides an opportunity for a rich supply of information from participants concerning the usability of the system to be accessed. A third benefit was highlighted by Oppenheim (1992). Being in conversation with the interviewee allows fuller explanations to be given than in a questionnaire, and Oppenheim suggested that the quality of the transaction would be greater, with participants more likely to spend time and effort and show commitment to an interview than a questionnaire.

Again, the disadvantages arise primarily as a result of the benefits. There are costs associated with tapping into such a rich data source. Interviews, like questionnaires, are resource-hungry, especially when conducted on a one-to-one basis, and/or involving time, effort, and travel to accommodate interviewees. The costs may not end here, as considerable work may be needed to complete the data processing stage. Further, validity may be difficult to assess if a non-standardised interview schedule is being followed, although there are statistical techniques for measuring reliability. Interviews may also suffer bias emanating from the interaction between the interviewer and the interviewee. Unlike questionnaire completion, user responses may be influenced by the attitude portrayed, the conversation and body language of the interviewer. One solution to this is to attempt to standardise interviewer behaviour through training, as well as ensuring that a strict adherence to the interview schedule is kept, in order to make sure that all interviewees are asked the same questions. There may be occasions, however, when this is not feasible.

Oppenheim summarised the main causes of interview bias, which have been adapted for presentation in Table 6.2.

The main objective of the interview is to collect data, but unlike the questionnaire, whose development, distribution, collation and analyses of responses often form the main part of a study, the interview is frequently one of many methods being used. It is often a step in the development of a questionnaire, or used to elucidate other findings.

Table 6.2 Main causes of interview bias

Before the interview:

the interviewer may digress from the quota of interviewees decided at the shortlisting stage;

the interviewer may engender fairly fixed perceptions about the candidates.

During the interview:

inadequate rapport and maintenance of it;

inappropriate prompting;

rephrasing of questions;

poor management of the interview;

asking biased or weighted questions;

asking questions out of the previously agreed sequence;

unreliable coding of answers, if a checklist;

biased recording of answers, that need to be taken down verbatim;

poor handling of 'problem' interviewees;

little regard paid to interviewing procedures.

In conclusion, interviews are preferable in some conditions and for some problems; often the choice will be made for extraneous reasons, such as costs or time pressure.

6.7 FOCUS GROUPS

Focus groups are sessions where several users (usually between six and ten) are brought together to consider various aspects of the design and use of a system. Although they appear to be unstructured, focus groups are in fact driven by one or two people, who act as moderators. They usually begin with an introduction to the concept or product under consideration (i.e. the focus), and then proceed to address a number of points and issues predetermined by the moderators (O'Donnell et al., 1991). In essence, they are controlled brainstorming sessions. Analysis might take the form of the moderators compiling a list of the key points made during the focus group and drawing various conclusions, or it might involve something more detailed, such as a content analysis of the discussion. The focus group might also be videotaped to allow a finer-grained analysis to be conducted. With reference to validity and reliability, there is little hard evidence upon which to draw conclusions. O'Donnell et al. (1991) gave an account of a focus group that discussed a videotape of a user's interaction with a product. Subsequent content analysis of the comments made during the discussion were shown to be predictive of the errors made be users, and corresponded to their ratings of task difficulty.

The advantages of the focus group approach are similar to the interview method, in that individuals are able to be spontaneous in their reactions and responses. Thus, the focus group is a little like a group interview, and as such can provide a rich source of data and information about the design of an interface, and the issues as perceived by the users. This can be done fairly expediently when lengthy analyses of the discussion content are not carried out. However, more detailed content analysis techniques are often time-consuming as well as needing to be set up by experts in both usability and data analysis techniques. Difficulties include keeping the discussion focused, and making sure it is not taken over by one or two individuals. Ideally, every participant should have an opportunity to offer opinions, etc. There will be occasions when it is necessary to run a number of successive focus groups. McClelland and Brigham (1990) described a case study where the focus group met on more than one occasion. The order of events was as follows:

1. A focus group was held with six users, who discussed their needs and problems with current tools and practices.
2. A design workshop was held with six experts, who over a two-day period, outlined five different design solutions to the problems highlighted by the focus group.
3. The focus group reconvened to consider the design proposals devised by the experts.
4. A more recent development in running focus groups has been to do this electronically, either through videoconferencing or the various computer networks that are now available. However, there are a number of problems with this approach. First, individuals partaking in computer-related activities are more likely to have an intrinsic interest in computing and computer technologies, and thus will not be representative of the user population. Interestingly, this may not be too much of a problem, since Von Hippel (1988) pointed out that this type of user ('lead users', as he referred to them) often experience usability problems well ahead of the rest of the user population. Hence, using these users in focus group activities can actually lead to locating usability issues well in advance. Second, it will be more difficult to control a 'remote' focus group, and the moderators may have to work hard to achieve a satisfactory outcome.

In conclusion, focus groups can provide a fairly swift method of finding out about the needs, requirements and subjective preferences of the design of a system. In their most basic form, they provide a quick and easy way to collect the opinions and views of a group of users. They also have scope for modification and tailoring to meet specific situations, and thus have many cost benefits, although their reliability, validity and opportunities for bias will need to be questioned.

6.8 CONCLUSIONS

The five subjective methods addressed in this chapter have a common theme in that they all attempt to assess the subjective preferences of the users concerning the design of system or interface. They are all techniques that comprise structured approaches, although the focus group may not appear to be a particularly structured method to the attendees. One main advantage is that they are often thought suitable for use by non-experts. In this context, they have been referred to as discount usability assessments. However, many would debate the extent to which they can be carried out successfully by inexperienced individuals. Heuristic evaluation, for example, presupposes knowledge of the relevant heuristics. This information would have to be located prior to conducting this type of subjective method of evaluation. In terms of ease of use, the checklist is probably the most appropriate for the informed non-expert. Also, some questionnaires that are already 'tried and tested' may be suitable, if you are fortunate to locate a standardised questionnaire tailored to your needs.

In conclusion, these methods are useful for finding out about users' likes and dislikes of a design, although their reliability and validity is questionable. The exception is the use of standardised questionnaires, whose reliability and validity have been formally assessed, and population norms collected. Checklist developers are also endeavouring to produce measures that have been subject to more rigorous reliability and validity testing. In terms of bias, the interview probably has the potential to be subject to the greatest bias. It also scores low on the

Table 6.3 Summary of attributes of subjective methods of formative evaluation

	Advantages	Disadvantages
Heuristic methods	Quick to run once set up	Need a local expert to define the heuristics
Checklists	Easy to administer Quick to analyse	Generally do not allow for different weighting of items
Questionnaires	Can access a large population	Need careful planning and extensive analyses
Interviews	Rich source of data and information	Resource-hungry
Focus groups	At their most basic, can provide a fast method of collecting subjective data	Information is mainly opinion – could be bias arising from more dominant group members

Table 6.4 Relative assessment of subjective methods of formative evaluation

	Reliability	Validity	Bias	Cost:benefits	Utility
Heuristics	✔	✔	+	+	+
Checklists	✔	✔	+	+	+
Questionnaires	–	✔	✔	✔	+
Interviews	–	–	–	–	✔
Focus groups	–	–	–	+	✔

+ = good, ✔ = neutral/OK, – = poor.

cost:benefits scale due to the amount of resource required for its successful execution. This is in contrast to heuristic evaluations, which can be expediently carried out by informed experts familiar with heuristic criteria. Finally, the utility of the various methods can vary, depending on the resources available. If experts are available, heuristics and focus groups can yield good results. If they are not available but there is sufficient resource in terms of time, money and personnel to support the exercise, questionnaires and interviews can be used to collect the relevant data. And if neither experts nor resources are present, the checklist is probably the most useful method to adopt.

6.9   EXERCISE 6

Exercise 6: Running a Focus Group
1. Prepare an agenda for the discussion:
- decide which topics are to be discussed, e.g. problems with current system, 'wishlist' for future systems, experience with other systems, etc.;
- define 'key points' for each topic. The key points will be used to prompt the focus group members in their discussion.
2. Recruit focus group members:
- select people who are typical of the range of users of the product;
- try to balance groups for factors such as experience, age, gender, etc.;
- try to use separate groups for each factor.
3. Run focus group:
- remember to set-up recording facilities, preferably video. If it is not possible to video the focus group, use a focus group rapporteur to record comments from the focus group members (identifying each comment with the member who made it);
- the focus group moderators should make sure that everyone in the focus group has a chance to speak on each of the topics, and should ensure that the focus group is not dominated by 'strong' individuals;

- it is often useful to provide models, prototypes or sketches of the product for the focus group, to help guide discussion and to ensure that people are talking about the same thing, rather than different ideas of the product.
4. Collate and analyse the data:
- it might be useful simply to use extracts from the video to play to the design team;

Alternatively, write the comments made for each topic, and consider the opinions expressed by the focus group, e.g. were all members in favour of a particular point of view, was there disagreement, did the focus group like the product or would they prefer changes?

6.10 SELECTED REFERENCES

A.N. Oppenheim, *Questionnaire Design, Interviewing and Attitude Measurement*, Pinter, London, 1992.
First published in 1966, and substantially revised in this second edition to include new chapters on research design and sampling, and chapters on interviewing, questionnaire planning, statistical analysis, and 'pilot work'.

Jakob Nielsen, *Usability Engineering*, Academic Press, London, 1993.
To quote from the preface of this book: 'its goal is to provide concrete advice and methods that can be systematically employed to ensure a high degree of usability in the final user interface'. Nielsen is one of the world authorities on usability, and has published extensively in this field. This book has a practical emphasis, focusing on software development providing information to improve user software interfaces. It also considers the economics of life cycle activities within the context of 'discount usability engineering'.

Patrick W. Jordan, Bruce Thomas, Bernard A. Weerdmeester and Ian L. McClelland (eds.), *Usability Evaluation in Industry*, Taylor and Francis, London, 1996.
This book arose from a seminar of 25 of Europe's leading human factors specialists in Eindhoven in September 1994. Subsequently, the text reflects the topics discussed and debated at this event, including standard methods of evaluation, new methods of evaluation, and issues specifically relating to usability evaluation.

John R. Wilson and E. Nigel Corlett (eds.), *Evaluation of Human Work: A Practical Ergonomics Methodology*, Taylor and Francis, London, 1995.
First published in 1990, with a second edition in 1995, this book provides a compendium of ergonomics methods and techniques in 38 chapters. These are compiled by experts from around the world, and the later edition includes new chapters on control room ergonomics, psychophysiological functions, ergonomics risk assessment, fieldwork, and participatory work design.

7 How Well Does the System Really Work?

OBJECTIVES OF CHAPTER:

- To consider objective methods of formative evaluation
- To overview these different approaches to system evaluation
- To indicate when each type of method can be used

HAVING READ THIS CHAPTER, THE READER WILL BE ABLE:

- To define the range of objective methods which contribute to effective system evaluation
- To be able to select the most appropriate subjective method
- To understand how to use each method to best effect

7.1 OBJECTIVE METHODS

Whereas subjective methods focus primarily on users' attitudes towards a system, objective measures, as the term suggests, provide an appraisal of the system based on measured data in a more controlled setting. Objective methodologies have the advantage of providing a systematic assessment of actual performance with the system, rather than relying on the more subjective views of the user or potential user population, hence providing a less biased assessment of the system. There are a number of difficulties associated with subjective methods, along with the advantages detailed in the previous chapter. They collect data in the form of user opinions. and so only reflect the views of the sample taken (particularly critical when considering the small samples which are possible and acceptable in heuristic evaluations and focus groups). In order to attain a truer representation of the actual situation, the experimental setting (and related variables) has to be more tightly controlled, which is what objective methods attempt to do.

7.2 OBSERVATION

When considering the design of systems, observation occurs at a number of levels. In an informal sense, it already plays a central role in system design in terms of observing people using products and interfaces, the observation of the design of other products, and the settings in which they are used. More formally, observation can be viewed as an objective method in the design of systems and products, and this is the approach we intend to review here.

The common message from all levels of observation is that there are many benefits from adopting this technique. This was summed up by Gould (1988, p. 764) whilst extolling the virtues of unstructured observation in the workplace:

'You may well learn that operators avoid changing tapes and ribbons or adding paper to machines; that secretaries avoid transferring calls for fear of making an error. You may learn that space is very limited, or that workstations must be shared, or that noone comes to training sessions, or that noone reads manuals . . . See what they have difficulty with, and what they dislike. You may learn that construction workers don't wear their reading glasses and don't want to press small keys, particularly whilst wearing heavy gloves; that office workers will not use an electronic mail system that automatically recognises their speech if they have to wait 30 seconds to activate it before each usage. . . . '

This was supported by Drury (1990), who stated that although walking around to see what is happening can hardly be called an observational method, he saw it as an important first step in finding out about the performance of a system.

As a method, observation is an important facet of designing systems, because it provides an indication of what people actually do, in direct contrast to the subjective methods, where people respond to the experimenter's questions, and there is no check that their responses mirror their actions. Observation is also an opportunity to discover the unexpected: Baber and Stanton (1996) cited the user of a ticket vending machine who was observed rolling up a five pound note, and attempting to insert it into the coin slot. It is unlikely that this use of public technology would have been located by a subjective method of assessment. Another example was given by Nielsen (1993). It was observed that users were overwriting their templates when editing electronic forms; subsequently, some word processing packages now specify templates as a special file category.

In its most basic form, observation involves looking at someone and recording what is seen. Baber and Stanton (1996) stated that it was not possible to separate recording from observing, regardless of whether it is done manually or electronically, for immediate or later use, by the observer or others. Observation studies may range from the informal observation of a single individual to a large-scale experiment with a number of people. In all the situations where observation is employed, it is vital that it does not interfere with the situation being observed, and the observer(s) needs to be as unobtrusive as possible. It could be argued, however, that the mere presence of an observer means that individuals will modify their behaviour (the so-called Hawthorne effect), possibly doing so without even knowing. For example, factory workers may use equipment in the way they have been trained, rather than adopting their usual shortcut methods. Similarly, placing people in a situation different from their normal setting, e.g. usability labs, might result in them modifying their behaviour. In order to overcome this, observation is carried out through the use of one-way mirrors or hidden cameras in some experimental settings, allowing the experimenters to observe proceedings, yet not be seen. An alternative approach is to engage a participant observer who participates in the study as a user. This may involve actually using a system, or perhaps sitting in on design meetings. The main drawback for the participant observer is the amount of training often necessary for full and beneficial participation. Observation studies thus have a high degree of face validity, i.e. actual live events can be recorded as they unfold, but a low degree of experimental control, i.e. the experimenter cannot change or modify the situation being studied.

As a general rule, observation methods can be classified according to the type of data that they produce. Inevitably, they are an abstraction, since it is impossible to record everything that is happening in the observation. Drury (1990) divided raw observation data into either events or states. Events are usually associated with particular points in time, e.g. observation of a person using an ATM might be broken down into events from the time they arrived at the machine to the time they removed their money and turned to move away. Event/time records are particularly useful for providing information about sequence and frequency of events, their duration, and spatial movements required for successful task completion. States, on the other hand, are usually descriptions of the system at predetermined times. For example, observation of the states of a number of ATMs would provide information about which ones were in use, and how many people were in the queue. The fundamental difference between event and state data collection is that the former is activity-driven, whereas the latter may record no action. It is also possible that collection of event data will allow deduction of state/time data during the time of observation. As Drury pointed out, the reverse is not true. Having collected the raw observation data, analysis is needed, although on some occasions the raw data is sufficient for the needs of the study.

Observations can involve the collection of quantitative data (i.e. numerical data, such as the overall time taken to complete a task, or the number of errors made) or qualitative data (i.e. descriptions of the different steps taken to complete a task). Quantitative techniques might focus on event frequencies, and Drury (1990) listed a number of different analyses, some of which are summarised in Table 7.1.

In many ways, the collection of qualitative data is similar to the objective methods such as task analysis, discussed in this chapter. Although qualitative studies can be relatively easy to conduct, they can very readily yield a wealth of data that is difficult to analyse fully and integrate appropriately. Hence, an inexperienced evaluator may have considerable difficulty extracting reliable objective information from the study. This is in contrast to quantitative methods, which offer a means of collecting objective performance data that can be more readily analysed. For example, Baber and Stanton (1996) estimated that one hour of video recording would take about 10 hours of qualitative analysis. However, there are a number of packages on the market specifically for the analysis of videotapes. Given that most content analyses of videotaped observations will focus on the frequency and duration of events, there is software available that will allow specified events to be time-stamped. This is facilitated through designated key presses, and allows analysis of the videotape to take place almost in real time.

The type of analysis is obviously going to depend on the nature of the observation, and this raises other questions concerning who or what to observe, when to observe, and the output from the observations. The issue of sampling arises in connection with determining who/what to observe and when. Common to all studies of human performance, it would probably be unrealistic to observe all events and states, therefore, a sample has to be observed. The question then arises of how to determine the sample; should it be a cross-section of the user population? Should it

Table 7.1 Activities for quantitative analysis of event frequencies

Activity	Brief description
Time study	Recording of times of activity
Process (Flow) charts	A layout of the process, showing movements of items
Gantt charts	A layout of the temporal aspects of a number of activities
Multiple activity charts	Modification of a Gantt chart
Link charts	Graphic representation of a number of activities, many of which are occurring simultaneously
Occurrence sampling	Observation of events at pre-determined times

focus on novices or experts or equal numbers of each? Should it take into account age, gender, frequency of use, optional versus compulsory usage, etc.? As a heuristic, the most logical rationale is to decide upon the sample for observation by referring back to the natural state of the system. This raises a further question of how often to sample. It is likely that time constraints, economic and practical considerations will determine this. For example, if novice users are going to be observed using a new computer system, it would seem logical to ensure that they are observed at start-up, rather than shut-down. Hence, it might be concluded that the nature of the task will be primary in determining the sampling rate. For example, a repetitive manual task such as packing on a production line is more likely to lend itself to infrequent sampling than observing a short task, such as an ATM transaction.

Observing people raises a number of ethical considerations, and as mentioned in Chapter 6, it is important to ensure that these are rigorously applied. The concern with the observation method is that there may be some occasions when people will not know they are being observed, e.g. observation of the flow of people through ticket barriers on public transport. Likewise, audio and videotapes of people at work may be used at a later date, to the detriment of the individuals involved. As with all research involving human participants, it is vital that ethics are observed. This means that prospective participants should be informed as to the objectives of the study, their rights to anonymity and confidentiality, and recognition that they can withdraw at any point. However, the one exception might be the example referred to above. Where it would be difficult, if not impossible, to ask individuals for consent, and where the observation is covert and does not seek to identify anyone, and will be used only for research purposes, it may be possible to relax the need to obtain permission.

One final point concerns the interpretation of the observations. Observations need to be taken at 'face value', since they tell us nothing about the reasons for the observed activities. For example, if a person begins to use an ATM and then walks away, there is nothing from this observation which provides any indication of why this event occurred. Hence, it is not possible to say whether this was due to the design of the interface, the individual or the situation. They may have found the machine difficult to operate, they may simply have changed their mind, they may have tried to process a stolen card, or forgotten their PIN, or the machine may have just closed – the list of possible explanations is endless. From observation alone, it is not possible even to speculate about causality. A solution to this is to run another method in parallel to the observation that does collect data about causes. Common techniques for this are verbal protocols as participants talk through (and walk through) their actions. These are discussed in detail in Chapter 9.

In conclusion, observation can provide a rich source of information concerning the use of a system. It should be noted that observation techniques have been used quite successfully for assessing the various aspects of the usability of computer systems, e.g. features such as ease-of-learning the systems (Wallace, 1986). This is regardless of whether the system is under development or the finished product. However, it should be noted that as a method, 'observation' is simply that; it does not tell us any more about the use of the system, or reasons as to why it is being used in a certain way. A supplementary method will be needed to locate this information. It is also very dependent upon robust reporting methods, which take careful account of the issues of sampling, ethics and analysis.

7.3   REQUIREMENTS' CAPTURE

The design process with respect to the system life cycle has been discussed at length in Chapter 5. When the design involves a large and/or complex system, it is usual to divide the process into more manageable sub-components. Although this provides a logical approach, it does raise the problem of successful integration of these units. The first step in the design process is to decompose the requirements of the system into a number of elements that the designer can address. Meister (1985) listed eight cognitive design elements appropriate to begin a requirements' analysis These included initial statement of the problem, design criteria (e.g. performance, reliability, cost, development time, etc.), constraints, design style (Nadler, 1985, categorised designers as inactivists, reactivists, preactivists and interactivists), designer's knowledge, designer's experience, designer's mental model, and fixed items in the design. From this, it is possible to begin the analysis of the design problem. The starting point for this is the mission analysis, which is essentially the development of a scenario or description of the sequential events in system operation (as described in Chapter 1). The mission analysis is a part of the requirements' capture, since it comprises a statement of how the system will be employed in its operational state, and usually includes a description of the whole system. However, as the design process develops, this will become more focused in terms of addressing the sub-systems. The mission analyses will reflect this. Meister suggested that at molecular levels, the scenario will describe physical processes, rather than observable events. The mission analysis is commonly written in narrative form, but may include graphical or pictorial models of the operations the product might be expected to perform. Chapanis (1995, p. 1269) suggested that the following questions might need to be addressed:

1. What will the product look like?
2. How will the product be used?
3. In what ways can the product be misused or abused?
4. What hardware and software will it require?
5. What will be the user-product interfaces?
6. For what kinds of users is the product designed?
7. How many users will be required to operate the product?
8. What skill levels must the users have?
9. What training must users have?
10. In what kinds of environments will the product be used?
11. How will the product be serviced and maintained?
12. What other constraints or special considerations apply to the product?

As already discussed, the output from the mission analysis is a statement of what the system and its components will be expected to do when operational. Hence, the outputs are the functions to be performed, with their various parameters and limitations. Some functions will be obvious and very explicit; others will need to be devised and clarified. Some of the functions and actions will be deduced from an analysis of similar products and systems. Likewise, some of the parameters will be clearer than others. Subsequently, the function analysis provides an overview of all the system functions. Functional flow analysis is a procedure for identifying the functions of the product and their sequence of operation (as discussed in Chapter 1).

Functional flow (or operational sequence) analysis was derived from engineering methods (Chapanis, 1995). It is essentially a graphical representation of the tasks the user has to carry out, based on events, actions and decisions. The representation will also take into account other users, and equipment needs. The advantage of the operational sequence analysis is that it is basically simulating the design of the whole system, but without the development of prototypes or mock-ups. Hence, it is an efficient way to generate a simulation. The disadvantage is that operational sequence analysis is a lengthy and complex procedure, because of the large amount of data that has to be collated.

7.4 TASK ANALYSIS

Task analysis has gained popularity in recent years in the development of systems, although it could be argued that as yet we have no agreed definition of a task, or accepted procedure for a task analysis (Stammers and Shepherd, 1995; Shepherd, 1998). In terms of definition, as the name suggests a task analysis is essentially a systematic analysis of tasks required by the user to attain the overall goals of the system. The overall aim of task analysis is to divide any work activity into a number of basic elements, each being directed towards a particular goal (Clegg *et al.*, 1988). The procedure usually begins by considering the overall activity, then dividing it into a number of main tasks which are then divided into sub-tasks. Clegg *et al.* suggested that although the top-level activity could be divided into any number of tasks, it is preferable to aim for between four and eight second-level elements. The analysis need not stop at this point, but in theory could continue dividing sub-tasks several times. The point at which to stop will be determined by the particular application, but the end-result is a pictorial representation of the hierarchy of task elements (Greif, 1991) and the points at which the human is concerned with the development of the system. This briefly overviews the main components of a hierarchical task analysis (HTA), as first described by Annett and Duncan in 1967 (see Figure 7.1). Task analysis is particularly useful for comparing tasks carried out on different systems having the same function, as the systematic breakdown of the tasks will provide interesting insights into how users will find using the system.

Task analysis usually follows the functional analysis, because at this point the functions to be allocated to humans will have been determined. Whenever possible, it should be based on actual observations of people carrying out the task, and supplemented by information of job descriptions, procedures, and accompanying documentation, perhaps even other techniques, such as walkthroughs and talkthroughs. Although the end-result often looks as if it has been easily achieved, for the inexperienced it is quite difficult to decompose tasks into sub-tasks, etc. Therefore, it is recommended that all task analyses are 'checked' for accuracy with the actual users. A useful approach is to consider task analysis as three stages of activity, as suggested by Stammers and Shepherd (1995), who divided task analysis into data collection, task description, and data analysis. It is pertinent to discriminate between task description and analysis, and a full task analysis (as the term implies) will follow through to actual analysis. Examples of questions to be asked at each stage of the task analysis might be:

1. What is the person doing?
2. Why is s/he doing that?
3. How is it being done?
4. What was the previous activity?
5. Are any activities being undertaken in parallel?
6. If so, how is priority decided?

As a method, task analysis can be applied during the development of new and existing systems to assess future task demands. It can also be used to compare task requirements for different systems, and in the evaluation of operational systems. Kirwan and Ainsworth (1992) also included the situation when a particular human–machine system performance problem had to be analysed and resolved. Indeed, it is a technique that has been successfully applied in a range of diverse applications and contexts, for example a display design project conducted at a number of industrial plants for coal preparation (Astley and Stammers, 1987).

Most task analyses use a hierarchical approach as described above; however, others have been developed in the context of human–computer interaction. One of these is TAKD (task analysis for knowledge description), which focuses on the cognitive rather than the physical aspects of the task (Diaper, 1989). TAKD provides an abstract description of the task and its components, as well as an abstract description of the knowledge required to perform the task. The latter is referred to as a 'grammar'. The intention of TAKD is not to be task specific; hence, it can be more widely applied in system design. Other examples include CLG (command language grammar) developed by Moran (1981), TAG (task action grammar) formulated by Payne and Green (1986), ETAG (extended task action grammar) (Trauber, 1990), and user action notation (Siochi and Hartson, 1989). The first three of these utilised language grammars, providing a description of the interface based on users' knowledge.

Time line analysis is a natural predecessor to task analysis, since the latter will have determined the times required for the various activities. In essence, the time line analysis will apply a logical order to the results of the task analysis. Thus, the time line indicates the temporal

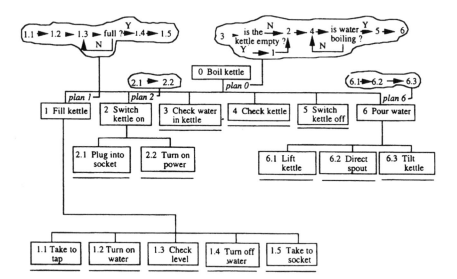

FIG. 7.1 Hierarchical task analysis example. (Reprinted with the permission of Taylor and Francis.)

relationships of the tasks, i.e. the times at which they should take place
and their duration. The advantage of this exercise is that incompatibility
amongst tasks can be identified. For example, two tasks may be
scheduled for the same time slot when insufficient resources are available
for both exercises.

Task analysis provides an extremely flexible approach to the design of
systems. It encompasses many other methods, as exemplified in Kirwan
and Ainsworth (1992), and it is not easy to specify drawbacks of the
method or to comment on its general validity and reliability, since it can
be adapted and modified for different situations and applications.
However, it is generally recognised that some expertise is needed before a
task analysis can be conducted effectively. Further, conducting a task
analysis also needs the support and co-operation of not only the users,
but also other staff involved in the system operation. Although this
strengthens the use of this method, it may generate practical problems, as
well as increasing overall costs.

7.5 ERROR IDENTIFICATION

Methods that fall under the umbrella of human error identification (HEI)
techniques have typically been used in the analysis of complex systems
where safety was paramount, e.g. the process control industries. This is
not surprising, given the prevalent role of the human in operating such
systems, and the tendency of humans to make errors. One commonly
cited occurrence of this is the cause given for aircraft accidents and
incidents; around two-thirds are generally attributed to human error
(Boeing, 1996) and more specifically, mistakes in decision-making
(Helmreich and Foushee, 1993). (Although it must be noted that this
does not provide the whole story in terms of either means of calculation
or reasons why it is sometimes 'convenient' to place the blame on the
human. However, it does give some idea of the magnitude and
importance of the human in the operation of advanced technologies.)

Error identification methods comprise a systematic analysis of the
operation of a product or system to indicate where errors are likely to
occur. Once the areas that are error-prone have been located, it is then
possible to take remedial actions to prevent/accommodate the human
making them. Many techniques for analysing errors have been
developed, e.g. THERP (technique for human error rate prediction;
Swain and Guttmann, 1983), HEART (human error assessment and
reduction technique; Williams, 1986), SHERPA (systematic human error
reduction and prediction approach; Embrey, 1986), PHECA (potential
human error cause analysis; Whalley, 1988), and PHEA (potential human
error analysis; Embrey, 1992).

One of the characteristics of the above error analysis techniques is their tendency to have been developed for use in complex, high-risk systems. Stanton and Baber (1996a) argued that this need not be the case, and provided an example where task analysis had been applied in error identification for domestic products. Their method was named TAFEI (task analysis for error identification) and is referenced in Stanton and Baber (1991, 1993, 1996a) and Baber and Stanton (1991, 1992, 1994). The technique differs from other error predicted methods, in that it explicitly analyses the interaction between humans and the system by mapping human activities onto machine states. A TAFEI analysis will consist of three basic components: HTA, state-space diagrams (SSDs) and transition matrices (TMs). In essence, the HTA is providing a description of human activity, the SSDs provide a description of machine activity, and the TMs provide an opportunity for determining erroneous activities through the interaction of the human and the system (Figure 7.2).

The TAFEI description is particularly appropriate for the assessment of consumer products, such as ticket and vending machines. Figure 7.3 illustrates the application of the TAFEI procedure to boiling a kettle. It also has the potential to contain information about hazards or by-products associated with particular states. Baber and Stanton are currently conducting research on its reliability and validity as an error identification technique, and results to date have been encouraging.

7.6 HUMAN RELIABILITY ASSESSMENT

Human error identification methods could be viewed as only the first step when considering the assessment of systems in order to reduce opportunities and incidences of human error. The next step, which constitutes part of the overall human reliability assessment (HRA), is to provide a more systematic means of preventing errors, by quantifying how often particular types of error occur. HRA techniques do this; they consider not only the probability of different types of errors, but also means of error reduction. If the latter is not possible, HRA will consider how the impact of the various errors can be minimised. A systematic methodology for HRA has been formulated by Kirwan and Ainsworth (1992), who outlined the following ten steps:

1. Problem definition – statement of problem and context.
2. Task analysis – explicit definition of tasks and sub-tasks, and factors affecting human performance.
3. Human error analysis – identification of human errors, and suggestions for recovery.

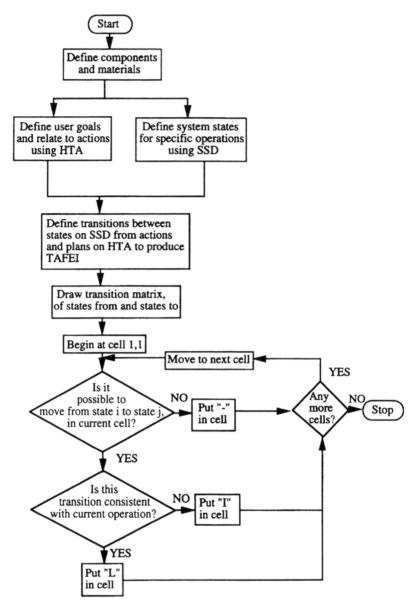

FIG. 7.2   TAFEI procedure. (Reprinted with the permission of Taylor and Francis.)

4. Representation – modelling of the errors and recovery paths, usually by means of a fault or event tree.

5. Screening – definition of the parameters needed for the error quantification.

6. Quantification – specification of human error probabilities and error recovery probabilities.

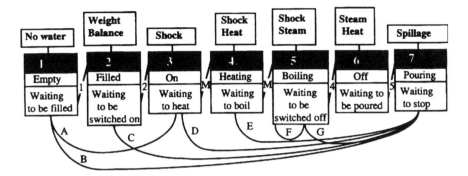

FIG. 7.3 TAFEI applied to boiling a kettle. (Reprinted with the permission of Taylor and Francis.)

7. Impact assessment – determination of acceptability of level of human reliability.

8. Error reduction – identification of error reduction mechanisms.

9. Quality assurance – check that system meets performance criteria.

10. Documentation – specification of all information relating to the HRA.

To summarise, HRA brings together some of the earlier objective methods discussed here. However, its development is still at a formative stage, and as Kirwan (1995, p. 964) stated 'it still has some way to go in the development of sound and theoretically and empirically valid methodologies'.

7.7 CONCLUSIONS

The five techniques discussed here differ from those in the preceding chapter in that they attempt to provide a more objective appraisal of individuals' use of the system, i.e. how users actually use the system, and not how they report they do. They are also techniques requiring considerable expertise in order to carry them out, primarily because they entail detailed data collection and analyses. These techniques tend to be more reliable than the subjective methods. However, this is really not surprising, given their nature. As already mentioned, observation has high face validity, but may be measuring observed rather than actual human behaviour, so bias may be a problem, in that the observers may be subjective in their recording of information. However, in terms of cost benefits and usefulness, observation can prove a beneficial technique, since it can considerably inform the design. The requirements' capture comprises a vital part of the life cycle and development of the system, so its reliability and validity needs to be high. Cost: benefits are long term,

Table 7.2 Relative assessment of subjective methods of formative evaluation

	Reliability	Validity	Bias	Cost:benefits	Utility
Observation	–	✔	–	+	+
Requirements' capture	+	+	+	✔	+
Task analysis	✔	+	+	✔	✔
Error identification	✔	–	+	✔	✔
Human reliability assessment	✔	–	+	✔	+

+ = good,   ✔ = neutral/OK,   – = poor.

i.e. carrying out a comprehensive requirements' capture can be an expensive procedure, and recuperation of these costs may not be realised in the short term. However, getting the design wrong can prove costly in terms of implementing changes late in the life cycle. The utility of this technique has to be viewed over the longer term. The remaining three methods have much in common in that they all involve systematic analysis of task components. This should enhance their reliability and validity. Due to their greater objectiveness, bias is less likely to be an issue in these techniques. Again, cost:benefits and utility will probably be realised in the longer term.

7.8   EXERCISE 7

Exercise 7: Task Analysis
Task 1: State the main stages to be carried out in conducting a task analysis.
Task 2: Apply this information to boiling a kettle.

Solutions
Task 1 (Figure 7.4)
Task 2
1. Data collection stage
   Familiarise yourself with the task; either attempt it yourself or watch others if you are not familiar with boiling a kettle.
2. Description stage
   Break down the task into its constituent units. Decide to what level you are going to go in terms of dividing the task.
3. Analysis stage
   This will involve grouping of the component tasks into an organised hierarchy, showing the clustering of the sub-tasks.

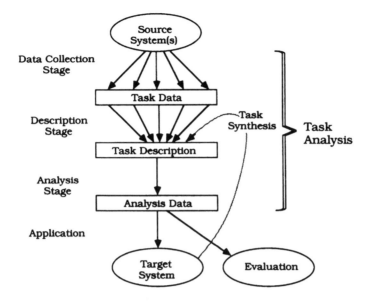

FIG. 7.4   The processes employed in task analysis. (Reprinted with the permission of Taylor and Francis.)

7.9   SELECTED REFERENCES

B. Kirwan and L.K. Ainsworth (eds.), *A Guide to Task Analysis*, Taylor and Francis, London, 1992.
This book comprehensively documents the application of task analyses techniques, and organises them into a practical user guide. It covers the task analysis process, task analysis techniques and case studies (the latter primarily from control room applications).

Erik Hollnagel, *Human Reliability Analysis: Context and Control*, Academic Press, London, 1993.
This book discusses how descriptions of human performance can be used to assess human reliability, i.e. identify erroneous actions and specify ways of preventing them from happening. Hence, the text focuses on how the modelling of human cognition can be applied to the analysis of human reliability and performance in complex technical domains.

Colin Drury, 'Methods for direct observation of performance' in John R. Wilson and E. Nigel Corlett (eds.), *Evaluation of Human Work: A Practical Ergonomics Methodology*, Taylor and Francis, London, 1995.
This excellent chapter on observation techniques provides lots of descriptions and examples of methods for collection and analysis of observation data. It also gives information on how to select methods.

Peter Johnson and Stephanie Wilson, *HCI 95 Tutorial Notes on Task-based User Interface Design*, British Computer Society, HCI Group.
An introduction to task-based design, presented in the form of OHP slides and notes, and a design case study. Some task analysis exercises are included. These tutorial notes provide a good introduction, with practical examples, to the topic of task analysis.

See also, J. Annett and N.A. Stanton (eds.), Task analysis, *Ergonomics* 1998, Volume 41, Number 11 (Special edition).

8 How Well Does the System Under Development Work?

OBJECTIVES OF CHAPTER:

- To consider empirical methods of formative evaluation
- To overview these different approaches to system evaluation
- To indicate when each type of method can be used

HAVING READ THIS CHAPTER, THE READER WILL BE ABLE:

- To define the range of empirical methods which contribute to effective systems evaluation
- To be able to select the most appropriate empirical method
- To understand how to use each method to best effect

8.1 EMPIRICAL METHODS

A third and final group of methods comprises the empirical techniques. These represent the most objective approach, in that the experimenter or investigator has more control over the variables and influences that may affect the outcome of the method. However, a price for this amount of control is paid in time, effort and resources, as empirical methods often incur substantial costs in their setting up, data collection and analysis. A further outcome of having this tight control concerns the ecological validity of the findings. Since the experimental study is being tightly controlled, it is questionable to what extent outcomes can be equated with the natural setting. This problem, of course, is not only specific to systems design, but applies to all experimental work conducted in a laboratory setting.

8.2   EXPERIMENTATION

Experimental design exemplifies the experimental method paradigm. Through careful design of an experiment, various hypotheses can be tested. These begin with the formation of a research question, to which a provisional answer will be given. In order to test the hypothesis, variables that may influence the experiment need to be taken into account. In general, there are two types of experimental variable: the dependent variable (DV) measured by the experimenter, and the independent variable (IV) manipulated by the experimenter. For example, in a reaction time experiment, the dependent variables might be response times and error scores, whilst the independent variables might be different types of keyboards or feedback. The independent variables are often investigated through a number of experimental conditions. In this example, condition 1 might be keyboard 1, condition 2 will be keyboard 2, and so on. The experimental hypothesis needs to be formulated, taking into account operational definitions (ODs). An operational definition is a standardised procedure for observing and measuring any observable event that is an appropriate indicator of an unobservable state or process. In all sciences, the raw materials are events that can be observed according to standardised procedures – this helps to ensure objectivity, and facilitates replication. The observed events are used to infer generalisations that deal with abstractions, e.g. memory, temperature, etc. This means that the events are the observable indicators of unobservable states or processes. Thus, a recognition test provides an OD for memory, and a thermometer provides an OD for temperature. In summary, an OD is a way of handling an abstraction, hence it may be necessary to rephrase the hypothesis using operational definitions. Once this is done, the controls need to be specified, i.e. the mode of selection and number of experimental participants, randomisation requirements, blocking and counterbalancing of experimental conditions, etc. The latter is often achieved through a 'repeated measures' experimental design, where every participant undergoes every condition. An alternative design is 'independent subjects', where individuals only undergo one condition. This often means that a much larger pool of participants is required, perhaps twice that of the equivalent repeated measures design. Once the number of 'levels' of each independent variable has been decided, the experimental design must now be checked to see if it is suitable for standard statistical analysis.

A further important distinction is to consider research methodology in the context of quantitative and qualitative approaches. Quantitative methods are based on quantity, and comprise a 'numbers' approach to explain the relationship between variables. Data will be analysed and evaluated using descriptive and/or inferential statistics. For example, in the reaction time experimental example, the emphasis will be on precise measurement of the DVs and control of the IVs in order to ensure against extraneous sources of error. The ultimate goal, of course, is to be able to infer a causal relationship between the variables of interest, i.e. by looking at the effect that IVs have on the DVs. In contrast, a quasi-experimental design compromises some of the rigour of the controlled experiment, but maintains the logic of experimental research. Qualitative methods focus on the quality of the data collected, and generally allow the researcher to be more flexible in studying variables in their natural environment. One major difference is that data are typically in the form of words as opposed to numbers, as more emphasis is placed on description and discovery, and less on hypothesis testing and verification. Favouring a holistic approach to research, qualitative will often involve the use of multiple sources of data, e.g. diary entries, field studies, interview notes, audio/video tapes of interactions. Consequently, qualitative methods typically involve the generation of a large amount of unrefined data that will require considerable effort to categorise and make sense of in terms of finding a coherent pattern.

The use of ODs in the hypothesis should indicate which materials and apparatus are appropriate. Once these have been prepared and checked, the experiment is ready to run. However, the experimenters should first carry out a 'dry-run' using themselves as experimental participants. The experimental detail should be altered accordingly as a result of this. Second, it is necessary to run a 'pilot' test, using a small number of experimental participants. This is the final check, and if everything runs smoothly, the experiment is ready to run.

In conclusion, this is a widely used method, especially in an academic setting. The reliability of studies, taking into account the above design details is usually high, and if carefully documented, replication is possible. Validity can be problematic, because the findings from the experimental study relate directly to the context in which the experiment was conducted, and it is dubious to what extent these results are applicable to other environments, especially the actual workplace. It could also be argued that this is an artificial setting, which does not exist outside of the experiment. In this sense the utility of experimental design is also questionable, although the use of this method in conjunction with other techniques increases this. Cost benefits tend to be on the high side, because of the amount of time, resources and expertise needed to run an experiment, ensuring experimental rigour.

8.3   USER TRIALLING

Advances in industrial product development in the 1970s brought the term 'user trialling' into popular usage (McClelland, 1995). As the term suggests, it allows users, potential users, or individuals representative of the user population to try out the system or product in a controlled setting. In this sense, the approach adheres to the experimental paradigm, allowing an assessment of participants' use of the system, taking into account the scientific method and experimental control, i.e. the application of IVs and DVs. However, user trialling differs from experimental design in that the process takes place within the context of the product environment. This has a number of implications. The components of the user trial will be the same as for an experimental study, but with the addition of having to take into account the location (site), and the individuals calling for the investigation.

One of the primary advantages of conducting user trials is the benefits which accrue from carrying out an empirical study in 'context'. An experimental study will often be conducted in a developer's laboratory or similar setting, which will not necessarily provide the same information as an evaluation carried out in the field, i.e. at the user's desk in their own workplace, or at home with their own tasks. Although it can be argued that the artificial setting of the laboratory can provide a more controlled environment, a field study generally overcomes the problems of differing individual and group needs, both within and between organisations. The case for context-sensitive research approaches was clearly stated by Whiteside et al. (1988), who concluded that 'understanding the usability of a product from the users' point of view necessitates developing data collection techniques that can access users' day-to-day life experience (Whiteside et al., p. 807). Since field-testing allows examination of the stable version of the product in the working environment, it can provide much insight that would not be available from laboratory studies. Furthermore, it has to be recognised that there will be some aspects of system and product design which are best studied in the field (e.g. installation) or in usage over a longer period of time (e.g. learning a new system) (Wiklund, 1994). In general, one of the most important features of a user trial must be that it obtains information from users in context; i.e. it assesses those aspects of the system or product that are relevant to individuals at that time.

In conclusion, user trials provide a method of implementing a systematic approach to system and product development in a naturalistic setting. In principle, they can be conducted at any stage in the life cycle, but it is expected that they would be carried out towards the end, with a near fully-designed system or product. Since they often take place in the field, they may incur organisational and practical difficulties that require negotiation when being set up. However, there may be a number of hidden benefits that result from exposing potential users to a system or product in a user trial. For example, they may then be more willing to accept the introduction of the technology, as they have a greater understanding of its functionality.

8.4 USER MODELLING

One of the characteristics of being human is that we continually construct and develop mental models. As pointed out by Neelamkavil (1987) mental modelling is a basic human activity that helps us to simplify our daily lives. As we build up knowledge about a product or system through training, experience, use of other devices, we modify our mental models accordingly. Hence, when designing systems, the phenomenon of the mental model is very important. Finding out about, and understanding what users know, should help designers build systems and products that are more suited to human use. This point was exemplified by Norman (1988), who stated that one of the explanations for poor design was the mismatch which occurred between the user's model of how the system worked and the designer's model. However, the assumption is being made here that users are aware of the design features they require, which is sometimes questionable. A further problem emanates from the exact definition of the term 'model'; does this refer to the actual physical interface, the task, or perhaps the software being used in a computer system? There is also the need to differentiate between what the user knows when using the system, and what the user should know.

In summary, models are mental representations of a system and its functionality. In this sense they are abstractions, as they try to explain activities that are not directly observable. Modelling may be particularly appropriate for allowing a system that is too large or too complex to be studied in operation. However, it is perfectly reasonable to develop a model of a physical activity that can be observed. Models have been classified into a number of different types. One such classification has been to divide them into 'surrogates', 'metaphors', and 'glass box machines'. Surrogates behave in the same way as the target systems, but the assumption is not made that they have the same internal workings (see Young, 1983). Thus, the construction of a surrogate is the production of an analogous system. However, this does not tell us anything about the causes of the underlying behaviour to help explain it. Metaphors are models that are already known to the user that they may employ when learning a new system (see Neale and Carroll, 1997). For example, Carroll and Thomas (1982) found that individuals referred to the test editor as a typewriter when learning to use the former. Metaphor models have been found to be frequently used and talked about by users. Unlike surrogate models, they do provide information to explain underlying behaviour, but are limited by their subjective nature, i.e. we tend to use metaphors emanating from other domains that may not be particularly meaningful or explicit to other people. Glass box models lie somewhere in between surrogates and metaphors; they are like surrogates in that they mimic the system, but like metaphors in that they provide some explanation of underlying behaviour (DuBoulay *et al.*, 1981). A fourth kind of model, 'a network', has been described as a combination of surrogate and glass box models. Briefly, they provide pictorial representations of the states of a system and the actions a user can carry out in order to change the system to another state. For further information, see the discussion by Kieras and Poulson (1985) of generalised transition networks (GTNs).

One of the more well known of the models for describing the cognitive processes of the user is GOMS (Card *et al.*, 1983). GOMS is appropriate for well-learned tasks, and focuses on what the user knows in order to complete a given task (see Chapter 5). To recap, the GOMS model was developed in the context of text processing. For example, if the user has to carry out some editing of a draft manuscript, this task could be broken down into goals, operators, methods and selection rules. If we began with the overall goal 'to edit a manuscript', this could be divided into a number of sub-goals, and likewise these could be sub-divided again and possibly again. At this level, it would be feasible to match a set of methods to the sub-goals in order to allow their satisfactory completion. This decision-making takes place within a framework of rules known to the user. Carroll and Olson (1988) concluded that a number of empirical studies had indicated that the GOMS model was reasonably accurate. They did suggest, however, that additional time parameters need to be specified, e.g. the time for users to choose between methods needs to be accounted. It also considers only performance that is error-free; this is a limitation because research has shown that even expert users spend a considerable amount of time making and recovering from errors.

In contrast to GOMS, command grammars analyse the same mental models, but use a different analytic representation. The examples given in Chapter 5 include the 'cognitive dimensions' framework described by Green (1989, 1991). Although we readily use the term 'mental models' both in this context and everyday life, there is a vast difference between the relatively simple measurements we are currently able to make, and the complexities and intricacies of human thinking. Mental representation and user modelling are still very much in an embryonic stage, and there is still much work to do on the practical aspects and implications of user modelling in the design of interfaces. Perhaps an appropriate

Table 8.1 Criteria of model effectiveness (Meister, 1995). (Reprinted with the permission of Taylor and Francis.)

Criterion	Definition
Validity	Agreement of model outputs with actual system performance
Utility	Model's ability to accomplish the objectives for which it was developed
Reliability	Ability of various users to apply the model with reasonable consistency and to achieve comparable results when applied to similar systems
Comprehensiveness	Applicability to various types of systems, to system devices, and stages of design
Objectivity	Requires as few subjective judgements as possible
Structure	Explicitly defined and described in detail
Ease of use	Ease with which analyst can readily prepare data, and apply and extract understandable results
Cost of development/use	Includes both time and money
Richness of output	Number and type of output variables and forms of presentation

starting point is Meister's comprehensive set of criteria for assessing the effectiveness of a model (see Table 8.1).

8.5 ANALYSES AND REPORTING

The writing of reports is an important facet of doing research, as it is this that helps convey the findings to other interested parties. It is common to all three types of methods, although the structure of research reports tends to be a fairly inflexible one, designed originally to reflect the process of empirical research itself. However, it is not intended that this structure should shackle the researcher, but rather provide a vehicle to make it easier for both writer and reader. Hence, a typical order of contents might be:

Abstract
Introduction
Method
    Design
    Experimental participants
    Materials/apparatus
    Procedure
    Data analyses
Results

Discussion

Conclusions

References

Appendices

Each of these will be considered in turn.

Abstract

This is a brief summary of the research. A reader should be able to tell enough from the abstract to decide whether the research is interesting and/or relevant to his or her work. It should be possible to understand the abstract without reference to any other part of the write-up.

Introduction

The introduction should offer background information relevant to the work being reported. It usually begins with some general statements about a topic, and then turns to a critical discussion of the research literature that has led to the particular investigation under consideration. The introduction should be structured so that a hypothesis, or research question, emerges from the discussion of background literature, and it must end with a clear statement of what is to be investigated. Often this is done by stating the experimental hypothesis; null hypotheses tend to be stated only when unusual.

Method

Sufficient information needs to be given in the method to allow replication of the study. In general, it should be divided into five (sometimes four) sub-sections: 'Design', 'Experimental participants', 'Materials (sometimes Apparatus)', and 'Procedure'.

Design

This section should report what kind of design was used for the experiment, i.e. independent subjects, repeated measures, questionnaire survey, correlational design, longitudinal study, etc.

Experimental participants

This includes a short description of all the experimental participants who took part in the study. Relevant descriptive information usually includes the number of participants, with data on age and sex. If it is relevant to the hypothesis, other data should be given, e.g. occupation, educational level, IQ, socio-economic status, etc.

Materials

All materials (and/or apparatus) used should be described in this section, e.g. questionnaires, paper and pencil tests, word lists, etc.

Procedure

Details of what was done in the actual experiment are given here. These should include the instructions given to participants, and if relevant, the number of trials of each condition, the order in which the trials were presented, how the performance of the experimental participants was measured, and how the results were recorded.

Results

This section usually includes: descriptive statistics (means and associated measures of variation, such as standard deviations or ranges) and inferential statistics (*t*-values, analysis of variance results, etc.). It is worth noting that some data may best be presented graphically, or in tabular form.

Discussion

The discussion section has three main purposes:

1. To discuss and elaborate upon the results presented in the above section in such a way as to draw conclusions about hypotheses stated in the introduction.
2. To discuss the findings from the investigation in the context of the background literature evaluated in the introduction, and to comment upon discrepancies or similarities between these experimental findings and those in the literature.
3. To indicate any hypothesis, or directions for future research, which the findings suggest.

At the end of the report a list of references should be provided. There are standardised procedures for presenting reference details, and these need to be followed, e.g. APA (American Psychological Association), Harvard, etc.

Appendices

Appendices should be used to present raw data, unpublished questionnaires/tests, computer programs (if relevant), details of stimuli, etc.

All appendices need to be appropriately labelled, and referred to in the relevant section of the report.

Reports should be written in an impersonal style, usually in the third person, and in gender-free language.

8.6   CONCLUSIONS

Some of the empirical methods are not new, and indeed some had their origins in work carried out over a century ago (Chapanis, 1995). Moreover, some are not exclusive to ergonomics and human factors psychology, having been borrowed from engineering. However, they did not come about by chance, but were all developed to accommodate specific needs, and have been 'tried and tested'. However, it has to be assumed that there will be a difference between subjective and objective measures, since people tend not to be good at assessing their own behaviour. The problem arises from the general belief that unless data has been collected objectively it is unreliable (Sinclair, 1975). Experimental evidence does not support this, as there are many instances when subjective judgements are quicker, more reliable and accurate than equivalent objective methods. Sinclair pointed out that perhaps the problems arise from the extrinsic factors associated with the data collection that can affect subjective methods. It may be that the solution is to use a combination of techniques that complement each other. For example, Root and Draper (1983) claimed that the use of checklists alone is not adequate, since they do not enable the user to specify what new features are needed. However, used in conjunction with user trialling, this information may be elicited.

In terms of reliability, the objective methods score high, since the experimental variables are tightly controlled. However, this does affect their validity, as such tight control of experimental settings means that their ecological validity is questionable. In other words, it is debatable to what extent parallels can be made with the actual system and its operation. The level of control also means that there are few opportunities for bias. However, there is a price to be paid for high

Table 8.2   Relative comparison of empirical methods

	Reliability	Validity	Bias	Cost:benefits	Utility
Experimentation	+	✔	–	✔	+
User modelling	✔	–	✔	+	+
User trialling	+	✔	✔	✔	+

+ = good,   ✔ = neutral/OK,   – = poor.

reliability and low bias, which is reflected in the cost benefits. Finally, the usefulness of the objective methods is high. Since they are particularly appropriate for research purposes, they have the capability to help us find out much about system and interface design. This is especially the case with experimental design.

8.7   EXERCISE 8

> **Exercise 8: Experimental Comparison of ATMs**
> Design an experiment to compare user performance on two different types of ATM.
> 1. State the experimental design.
> 2. List the IVs, the DVs, any ODs.
> 3. Who is your user group?
> 4. How will you select your participants?
> 5. What task will you ask them to carry out?
> 6. How will you measure user performance?
> 7. What type of data will you collect?
> 8. What conclusions will you be able to draw?

8.8   SELECTED REFERENCES

Some useful texts for research work and report writing include the following:

H.S. Becker, *Writing for Social Scientists: How to Start and Finish Your Thesis, Book, or Article*, University of Chicago Press, Chicago, 1986.

J. Bell, *Doing Your Research Project*, Open University Press, Milton Keynes, 1987.

J. Fitzpatrick, J. Secrist, and D.J. Wright, *Secrets for a Successful Dissertation*, Sage, London, 1998.

P. Harris, *Designing and Reporting Experiments*, Open University Press, Milton Keynes, 1986.

C. Hart, *Doing a Literature Review*, Sage, London, 1998.

K. Howard and J. Sharp, *The Management of a Student Research Project*, Gower Press, Aldershot, 1983.

K.E. Rudestam and R.R. Newton, *Surviving Your Dissertation*, Sage, California, 1992.

9 Can the System Be Improved?

OBJECTIVES OF CHAPTER:

- To consider methods of summative evaluation
- To overview these different approaches to system evaluation
- To indicate when each type of method can be used

HAVING READ THIS CHAPTER, THE READER WILL BE ABLE:

- To define the range of summative methods which contribute to effective system evaluation
- To be able to select the most appropriate method for evaluation of the system in order to improve it
- To understand how to use summative evaluation to best effect

9.1 SUMMATIVE EVALUATION

The preceding three chapters have focused on formative evaluation, the assessment of the system as part of the overall iterative design process (as described in Chapter 5). The main point of this evaluation is to find out about the design of the system during its development, in order to address those aspects that need modification and revision. This will allow changes to be made before product release. In contrast, summative evaluation takes place when the system or product has moved from being experimental to operational, and is usually carried out towards the end of the design life cycle. Consequently, the broad difference between formative and summative evaluation concerns the nature of the purpose. Formative evaluation (as implied by the term) is carried out to help the system designer refine and 'form' the design, while summative evaluation is concerned with the overall performance of the system. Hewett (1986) defines summative evaluation as follows: 'Summative evaluation involves assessing the impact, usability and effectiveness of the system – the overall performance of user and system.' Implicit here is the suggestion that the system or product is close to being launched.

9.2   PERFORMANCE MEASURES

Although it is open to debate at what point in the design process evaluation changed from being formative to summative, the assumption here is that summative evaluation takes place when the whole product exists as a working prototype. Dix *et al.* (1993, p. 364) identified three main goals for evaluation of particular relevance to summative evaluation. These were: (i) to assess the functionality of the product (or system); (ii) to measure the impact of the design on the user; (iii) to identify any specific problems that users have with the product. Functionality is important, because the design of the system must meet the requirements of the user, and allow them to complete the tasks they are required to do. Hence, user performance with the system needs to be ascertained and measured, in order to assess the effectiveness of the system in supporting the user. It is then necessary to measure the impact of the design on the user, e.g. how easy it is for the novice user to learn to use the system, how easy it is for the experienced user to operate, what their attitudes towards the system are – whether they like/want to use it, etc. One of the ultimate tests of a system might be whether people choose to use it, especially when they have opportunities for a viable alternative. The third goal is to locate specific problems associated with using the system; these should arise from the assessments relating to functionality and user performance with the system. It should be noted that summative evaluation of the user interface is not concerned with considering separate components, e.g. hardware, software and user interactions with them, but rather a combination of these elements. As Karat (1988, p. 891) concluded, 'evaluating "how good" any system is includes a consideration of all of these aspects'. This is an important point and endorses the approach taken here.

9.3   USABILITY

Usability is a term that has become popular in the last decade, both within the engineering and design communities and the wider population, via the media and advertisements. In many ways, it replaces the term 'user-friendly' often used in the 1980s, but notoriously non-objective and difficult to define. However, the inference could be said to be similar in terms of assessing the ease of using a system or product. Furthermore, an agreed operational definition of usability, like its predecessor, user-friendliness, remains elusive, because the meaning of usability conveys different things to different people. Stanton and Baber (1996a) provided a number of explanations for this, suggesting that some regard the term as a reincarnation of user-friendliness and not as a new concept, while others argue that usability is implicit in the 'user-centred design' approach, and does not warrant being dealt with separately. Given recent legislation relating to the legal aspects of ensuring usability in some products (ISO 9241, 1991), this situation would appear to need addressing urgently.

Many individuals have attempted to define usability (an ongoing debate, the implication being that until it can be satisfactorily defined, it cannot be successfully measured). One of the first definitions was by Shackel (1981), and refined five years later (Shackel, 1986). He suggested that for a system to be usable, it must satisfy the following criteria (subsequently given the acronym LEAF):

1. **Learnability** (i.e. users must be able to learn to use the system after a certain amount of training)

Measures:
- within some specified time from installation and start of user training
- based upon some specific amount of training and user support
- within some specified re-learning time (for intermittent users)

2. **Effectiveness** (i.e. a pre-dened proportion of target users must be able to use the system in a number of environments, within a certain time and error limits)

Measures:
- at better than some required level of performance (measured in terms of speed and errors)
- by some required percentage of the specified range of target users
- within some required proportion of the range of usage environments

3. **Attitude** (i.e. the engendering of positive attitudes towards using the system by the majority)

Measures:
- within acceptable levels of human cost in terms of tiredness, discomfort, frustration and personal effort

4. **Flexibility** (i.e. user performance must not degrade by more than a certain percentage across tasks and environments)

Measures:
- allowing adaptation to some specified percentage variation in tasks and/or environments beyond those first specified

(Shackel, *Ergonomics in Design for Usability*, 1986, Cambridge University Press. Reprinted with permission.)

Table 9.1 Amended set of criteria for usability. (From Booth, 1990.) (Reprinted with the permission of Psychology Press, Limited, Hove, UK and P.A. Booth.)

Usefulness
Effectiveness (or ease of use)
Learnability
Attitude (or likeability)

Shackel put forward the suggestion that usability can be measured through each of the above operational criteria, by giving them numerical values when the usability goals are set during the design process at the time of the requirements' specification. Thus, the approach taken by Shackel was to define usability in terms of evaluation that requires both operational definition and measurement. Although this approach is commendable, and made significant advances to the study and measurement of usability, there are a number of difficulties. One of the problems concerns the specification of the various levels of criteria, and the calculating of numerical scores. This was stated simply by Karat (1988), who referred to this difficulty as how to judge whether the system or product was good or bad. This is particularly true of 'flexibility', which would be inherently difficult to specify and then test, as stated above. Booth (1989) highlighted a further difficulty: the omission of 'usefulness', i.e. a system that helped users to achieve their goals. He argued that a system could achieve high ratings on learnability, effectiveness and attitude, but if it failed to allow a user to reach their chosen goals, it could

Table 9.2 Causal framework of usability. (From Eason, 1984.) (Reprinted with the permission of Taylor and Francis.)

Independent variables	*System functions* Task match Ease of use Ease of learning
User characteristics Knowledge Discretion Motivation	*Task characteristics* Frequency Openness
Dependent variables	*User reaction* Implicit cost/benefit analysis
Positive outcome Good task-system match Continued user learning	*Negative outcome* Restricted use Non-use Partial use Distant use

be deemed as 'useless'. Booth's conclusion was to amend Shackel's set of criteria to include usefulness and preclude flexibility.

Another milestone in reaching an agreed definition of usability was Eason's causal framework of usability, see Table 9.2.

The perspective taken by Eason was based on how systems are used in a work environment. He viewed usability in the context of the system, the user and the task, and to build on the characteristics of these three aspects of humans using systems. In his causal framework, the major system variables are learnability (ease of learning), usefulness (ease of use) and task match (the extent to which the system functions and characteristics 'match' the user needs). User variables include the knowledge and motivation levels of the user, and discretion (whether or not the user has any choice in using all or part of the system). Finally, task variables include frequency (the number of times a particular task is carried out) and openness (the extent to which a task can be modified). Eason (1984) placed great emphasis on discretion, arguing that the main indicator of usability is whether or not a system or function is used. This has methodological implications for usability testing, since it could be concluded that only 'natural' settings will allow a true indication of discretion. The increasing number of usability laboratories and usability booths could therefore be viewed as unfortunate.

A slightly different perspective was taken by Nielsen (1993), who viewed usability within the context of acceptability. He argued that usability was one aspect of a larger concern, namely the extent to which the system satisfied the needs and requirements of all the individuals involved. Thus, he extended the definition of usability (involving users) to acceptability (involving not only the users, but all the stakeholders, e.g. managers, clients of the user, etc.). Nielsen's model of acceptability encompassing usability is shown in Figure 9.1.

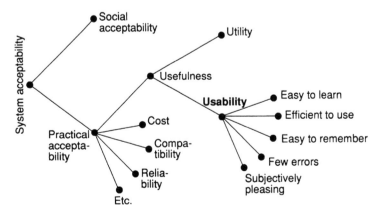

FIG. 9.1   A model of the system acceptability attributes. (Reprinted with the permission of Academic Press, Inc.)

Jordan *et al.* (1991) made the point that the usability of a system for a particular person will change over time as he or she becomes more experienced. To reflect the effects of practice, Jordan *et al.* (1991) devised a three-component model of usability, using guessability, learnability and experienced user performance (EUP). Guessability was associated with first-time use of a system, learnability was concerned with the number of task repetitions until an acceptable level of competence was reached, and EUP was the relatively stable level of performance that an experienced user attains. Jordan later extended this model to include the two additional components of system potential and re-usability (Jordan, 1994). System potential is concerned with the optimal performance attainable on specified tasks, while re-usability is the level of performance achieved when a user returns to the system after a period of non-use.

Despite the controversy surrounding the definition of usability, the International Standards Organisation (ISO) has proposed the following: 'The usability of a product is the degree to which specific users can achieve specific goals within a particular environment; effectively, efficiently, comfortably, and in an acceptable manner.' This is an interesting combination of work by Shackel (1981), Eason (1984) and Booth (1989), and the definition of the user-centred approach, as discussed in Chapter 1.

Having established in broad terms what usability is, the next stage is to consider how to measure it. In many ways, measurement is more important than definition, and there are numerous practical ways of measuring the various aspects comprising usability. Nielsen (1993) gave a list of performance measures for usability that should be readily quantifiable (Table 9.3).

Rather than deciding the level of acceptance for the various criteria, these performance measures can be readily applied. They tackle various aspects of the system or product design, and a general recommendation is not to rely too heavily on one measure, or to take a very narrow definition of the term usability (Stanton and Baber, 1996b). One of the most frequently used measures is the time taken to complete an action or task. Time usually needs to be considered in the context of errors, in order to combat the speed-accuracy trade-off. Whiteside *et al.* (1985) developed a work metric for assessing the usability of systems based on the time:

$$S = (1/T)PC$$

where S = the user's performance score; T = time spent on task; P = percentage of task completed; C = arbitrary constant based on the fastest possible task solution for an expert user.

Usability testing can involve any of the subjective, objective and empirical methods already discussed. For example, checklists such as SUS focus on assessing the complexity of the system (Brooke, 1996).

Table 9.3 Usability measurements. (From Nielsen, 1993, pp. 193–4.) (Reprinted with permission from Academic Press, Inc.)

The time users take to complete a specific task.

The number of tasks (or the proportion of a larger task) of various kinds that can be completed within a given time limit.

The ratio between successful interactions and errors.

The time spent recovering from errors.

The number of user errors.

The number of immediately subsequent erroneous actions.

The number of commands or other features that are utilised by the user.

The number of commands or other features that are never used by the user.

The number of system features the user can remember during a debriefing after the test.

The frequency of use of the manuals and/or the help system, and the time spent during these system elements.

How frequently the manual and/or help system solves the user's problem.

The proportion of user statements during the test that are positive versus critical toward the system.

The number of times the user expresses clear frustration (or clear joy!).

The proportion of users who say that they would prefer using the system over some specified competitor.

The number of times the user has to work around an unsolvable problem.

The proportion of users employing efficient working strategies, compared to those who use inefficient strategies (in case there are multiple ways of performing the tasks).

The amount of 'dead' time when the user is not interacting with the system. The system can be instrumented to distinguish between two kinds of dead time: response-time delays, where the user is waiting for the system, and thinking-time delays, where the system is waiting for the user. These two kinds of dead time should obviously be approached in different ways.

The number of times the user is side-tracked from focusing on the real task.

Observation could identify the ease with which users learn to use a system (see Wallace, 1986), and an experimental study with task scenarios may be constructed to indicate the boundaries of use for frequent and critical conditions (Booth, 1989).

In conclusion, usability is a global concept whose measurement encompasses all the methods reviewed in this book. It is also a paradox, posing a number of problems. On the one hand, it can be defined fairly satisfactorily, but unsatisfactorily in terms of the usability of its measurement. On the other hand, it has attained popular usage, entering the vocabulary of the masses and attracting the attention of a number of book authors, while some researchers in the area state that it is so vague and ambiguous as to be useless, and should be discarded. It is of central importance, given that systems and products designed for human use need to usable. But, within the context of summative evaluation, the implication is that the systems and products need to be utilised. However, It is unlikely that usability evaluation will lead to redesign of products. The final irony, of course, is the nature of the concept, and what it is purporting to measure!

9.4 MODELLING AND SIMULATIONS

It has been established in Chapter 8 that user modelling can be used to help match the facilities that a system has (or is intended to have) to the needs and requirements of the user. However, the focus here is on the modelling of the system, to allow summative evaluation to take place. Implicit in this term is the suggestion that the system or its components will be in the final stages of development, but this is not necessarily the case, as discussed below. Models of the system as outlined by Noyes and Mills (1998) might range from:

1. Paper-based prototypes – these include descriptions about functionality, usability characteristics and human interactions. This information is usually in hard copy form, as the term 'paper-based' suggests. The drawback, however, is that they are more open to interpretation than physical models.
2. Part prototypes – these include parts of the actual system or product, to allow some of the functions to be simulated. As McClelland (1995) pointed out, the part prototype may not resemble the full prototype or final product.
3. Full prototypes – these are models of the final system or product, with full equivalent functionality and appearance.
4. Complete system – on some occasions it may be possible to evaluate the final product. This may be when it is about to be released or when fully operational. Some COTS software packages would fall into the latter category, although surprisingly this area has attracted little interest (Smythe, 1992; Noyes and Harriman, 1995).

Each of these four system models could be used at any point in the life cycle. For example, a paper-based description might be developed in a comparative exercise conducted towards the end of the life cycle. Alternatively, the complete system might be employed in the early stages, to find out from users about its good or poorly-designed features for a future design; this was the approach taken by Noyes *et al.* (1996) during the design of their advanced warning system. The pros and cons of prototyping have been discussed in detail in Chapter 5.

The production of part or full prototypes is often demanding in terms of the time and effort that is needed to produce them. Moreover, it is sometimes difficult to justify building a model of a system that will eventually be discarded. In order to combat this, 'rapid prototyping' has been developed (see Wilson and Rosenberg, 1988, for an introduction to

Table 9.4   Pros and cons of prototyping

Pros

1. Tangible means of evaluating an interface design.

2. Improves the quality of feedback from the users.

3. Common reference point for all of the design team.

4. Opens up lines of communication.

5. More efficient development route than evaluating the finished system. (Cost savings have been reported; see, Boehm *et al.* 1984).

6. Improves the quality of the finished product.

7. Provides a flexible approach (see Beagley, 1996).

Cons

1. Not the real product.

2. Possible to sidestep some of the important design issues.

3. May create unrealistic expectations on the part of the users.

the topic). This involves the fast production and testing of prototypes, and there are a number of prototyping tools and techniques available to allow the system designer to generate an interface design, e.g. Richards *et al.* (1986). Historically, it is worth noting that there is a strong relationship between rapid prototyping techniques and the development of user interface management systems (UIMS).

A caveat is that there are few occasions that demand the production of the full prototype, because it is usually not necessary to have a complete system in order to test out a particular aspect.

Prototypes are a type of simulation, and there are some specific techniques that utilise this approach, e.g. slide shows, Wizard of Oz and the Café of Eve. These are considered in turn.

Slide shows involve the demonstration of parts of a system via presentation on a number of screens (slides). These are given in a predefined sequence in keeping with the function(s) of the system, e.g. the use of hyperlink in a software package under development. An alternative label for slide shows is 'storyboards' (the technique will sometimes be referred to as storyboarding). Advantages of this type of simulation include the fact that it can be developed quickly, as well as providing a means of representing the sketching and thinking activities of the designers.

The Wizard of Oz technique is a simulation of a system where the user does not know that there is another human providing the responses to their requests. (However, on some occasions there may be a machine responding to the user's input.) This technique is so called because of the scene in the film 'the Wizard of Oz' where the wizard is a large man with special powers and a deep voice, but in fact, is nothing more than a machine being operated by a human. Hence, the line 'pay no attention to the man behind the curtain . . . '. This type of simulation is particularly appropriate for use with immature technologies. For example, Baber and Stammers (1989) used this technique with an automatic speech recognition application. It is also useful when production of a fully working system is too costly. Further examples of the use of this technique are given in Beagley (1996) and Vermeeren (1996).

The Café of Eve is an innovative research and development environment for the design and evaluation of advanced office and business systems (Christie and Gardiner, 1992). The term 'CAFÉ OF EVE' is an acronym for 'controlled adaptive flexible experimental office of the future in an ecologically valid environment' (Gale and Christie, 1987). As the name suggests, it comprises a sophisticated simulation of an office environment in which to test out various experimental parameters. The advantages include high ecological validity, i.e. participants can be assessed working in a very realistic situation. However, it has been questioned whether this particular type of office might attract atypical workers, attracted to working in what is essentially an experimental setting. Further, the nature of the work is also likely to reflect the experimental and research aspects of the job, with a number of different projects being continually undertaken. Hence, it could be argued that the Café of Eve has high face validity. One of the disadvantages of this technique is expense: it is extremely costly to set up and run such an experimental environment.

In conclusion, modelling and simulation are techniques that can be used at any stage in the life cycle to enhance system and product development, but they are being considered here under the umbrella of summative evaluation. It should be noted, however, that models and simulations only provide a means by which designs can be evaluated; by themselves they do not provide the criteria for evaluation. Performance measures must be determined by other means.

9.5   MOCK-UPS, WALKTHROUGHS AND TALKTHROUGHS

Taken literally, a mock-up is a simulation of a system or a product. Several of the techniques already discussed could be classified as mock-ups. Mock-ups are considered here within the context of walkthroughs and talkthroughs, although the distinction is somewhat blurred.

Walkthroughs, as the name suggests, involve participants 'walking through' a task. They are quasi-rehearsals carried out by actual or prospective users, to provide information on the way in which the system or product will eventually be used. In terms of construction, a walkthrough will often consist of a static mock-up. This can range from the crude model of paper or cardboard, through to more sophisticated and refined dynamic mock-ups of the system, e.g. some advanced flight deck simulations in avionics applications. In the case of a rudimentary static mock-up, the user may have to be guided through its use, by being given descriptions of the tasks they need to execute. Often users are required to provide a verbal protocol of their interactions with the system, thus providing information on their perceptions of the difficulties of using the mock-up. The extent to which verbal data is collected for later analysis is dependent on the nature of the evaluation. Typically, walkthroughs collect data to feed into other evaluative procedures. (An example of a walkthrough is given by Marshall et al., 1990.) If they are not taking place in real time, it is possible to interrupt the task to find out more about the user's reactions and responses; hence, the concept of the 'interrupted walkthrough'. Further variations on the walkthrough described above are the 'cognitive walkthrough', which focuses on the cognitive aspects of the tasks carried out using the mock-up (see, Polson et al., 1992), and the 'pluralistic walkthrough' (Bias, 1991). The latter involves the designers as well as the users, with the former acting as 'living manuals' to allow users to ask them the questions they would look up in the accompanying documentation. A recent addition is the 'cognitive jogthrough' (Rowley and Rhoades, 1992). In order to make the walkthrough less time-consuming, Rowley and Rhoades introduced a means of recording the session, with an in-house software package that logged the significant events in real time.

Talkthroughs are a similar concept to walkthroughs in that participants 'talk though' carrying out a task, so that the tasks are verbalised rather than demonstrated (Meister, 1986). Since talkthroughs do not need the physical task environment, they have greater flexibility when being conducted, and do not require such extensive resources as walkthoughs. However, it is reasonable to assume that some props will be needed, if only pen and paper drawings of the proposed system. The possibility of being able to conduct a talkthrough with little physical resource means that they can be used early in the life cycle. It could be argued, however, that if carried out too early in the life cycle, there may be insufficient detail available about the system. In this case, it might be more suitable to conduct a table-top discussion (where a number of experienced users meet to discuss attributes of a system), or to run a focus group.

In conclusion, walkthroughs and talkthroughs can be effective demonstrations of carrying out a task. They can be set up and executed very quickly, with the minimum of resources. Furthermore, the investigator needs very little specialist training or experience of the method (Kirwan and Ainsworth, 1992), although extensive knowledge of the system or product under investigation is required. As walkthroughs and talkthroughs could be classed as a form of observation, the analyses referred to in Chapter 7 will apply.

9.6   VERBAL PROTOCOLS

Verbal protocols are records of the spoken reports generated when individuals 'think aloud' by talking through a task. Hence, they are closely related to the talkthrough method discussed in the preceding subsection. The main difference is that the former is more spontaneous, with individuals stating thoughts that have just occurred to them, rather than providing responses as prompted by questions about a task. As Nielsen (1993) pointed out, verbal protocols are typically the preserve of psychological research methods, but they are becoming increasingly used in the evaluation of system interfaces (see Denning *et al.*, 1990).

It hardly needs stating that we do not know what a person is thinking, and collecting verbal protocols is probably the closest way in which we can currently access this information. Some features of verbal protocols include the following:

1. They tend to contain mainly factual statements (Bainbridge and Sanderson, 1995).
2. Individuals can provide similar verbal reports when exhibiting quite different behaviours (Nisbett and Wilson, 1977).
3. They are particularly useful in providing information relating to the sequence in which task components are carried out.

The main advantage of verbal protocols is that they are fairly easy to collect. Like many methods however, there is a trade-off between speed and ease of data collection, and its analysis as they require time, resource and skill to analyse. One of the difficulties is that verbal reports do not lend themselves to most measures of performance. They are also open to bias, as individuals might not state their true feelings about a task or system, and/or may generate the responses that he or she thinks are expected, or comprise acceptable answers. Producing a verbal protocol also interrupts and disturbs carrying out the task. It often takes longer to complete a task when talking through it, but there have been benefits demonstrated in terms of enhancing problem-solving abilities. Wright and Converse (1992) found that users who were thinking aloud made approximately 20% of the errors made by users who were working silently on a file management task. Finally, some individuals may find this technique difficult, even embarrassing, and be reluctant to take part in a study that required them to 'think aloud'.

In conclusion, there are many aspects of collecting verbal protocols that can compromise their validity. Therefore, the information they provide must be considered in this light. They are also notoriously difficult and time-consuming to analyse (which is probably a reflection of the complexity of what they are trying to assess). Hence, it could be concluded that verbal protocols are not the easiest performance measure to execute.

9.7 'FITTING TRIALS' AND MANNEQUINS

Fitting trials allow the dimensions of the users of a system to be checked against the dimensions of the system or product. They have been defined as a type of psychophysical of the relationships between the anthropometric, biomechanical, and cognitive attributes of the human, and the system dimensions (e.g. workstation, workplace, environment) (Pheasant, 1995). In order to conduct a fitting trial, it is usually necessary to have some sort of prototype of the system that allows various dimensions of the human and the system to be used in the assessment of fit. There is also a subjective element in that participants might give their opinions with regard to comfort, ease of use, etc. The late Stephen Pheasant, who was the authoritative source on this topic, stated that the 'method of limits' can be used to establish final design recommendations. This is essentially a paper-based exercise, where the anthropometric data from imaginary users is used to determine the required dimensions (Woodworth and Schlosberg, 1954). However, this technique not does allow for collection of subjective data, which has now been established as an important adjunct to the successful outcome of a fitting trial.

An alternative to having a user check out the design of the actual system is to run a computer simulation. In the last couple of decades there has been a growth in CAD (computer-aided-design) engineering methods, which has extended to the development of CAD packages that model a human mannequin within a workspace setting. These screen-based simulations allow the various dimensions of the human component to be varied, e.g. limb lengths and reaches. More sophisticated systems allow postural, visual and comfort features to be taken into account. Although mannequins allow a large number of design possibilities to be readily and easily tried, they lack the subjective component of the fitting trial. Further, unlike the fitting trial (that could be carried out with a crude mock-up), they require sometimes costly computer packages, and personnel skilled in their use and operation. In conclusion, as design tools, the widespread use of these systems has met with limited success. Porter *et al.* (1995) pointed out that this could be because skilled personnel are needed to manipulate the mannequin successfully, and locating ergonomists with the requisite skills is not easy.

A number of commercially available packages exist; one of the more well-known UK mannequins is SAMMIE (System for Aiding Man–Machine Interaction Evaluation) (see Case and Porter, 1980; Porter *et al.*, 1996, 1998). SAMMIE is a versatile three-dimensional model, displayed as a set of 17 joints and 21 straight rigid links, that can be programmed to allow limb and joint movements to operate controls, e.g. pedals, doors, seats, etc. The postures selected are controlled by anthropometric and biomechanical databases, from which the operator can specify a precise population or individual. Viewing the resultant images of the mannequin allows the designer to draw conclusions about the programmed dimensions, e.g. tall drivers operating in those particular conditions would suffer neck discomfort. This would then allow modification of the design. SAMMIE is also useful in creating the 'worst case' design scenario, and this information can be used to inform the design. A two-dimensional mannequin of a short person (with short arms and legs), and likewise, a tall person (with long limbs), will not provide as much information about seat and steering wheel positions, and viewing angles and distances.

In conclusion, computer-based design has the obvious benefit over prototypes and mock-ups of being faster and easier to vary the dimensions. It can also be carried out early in the life cycle without

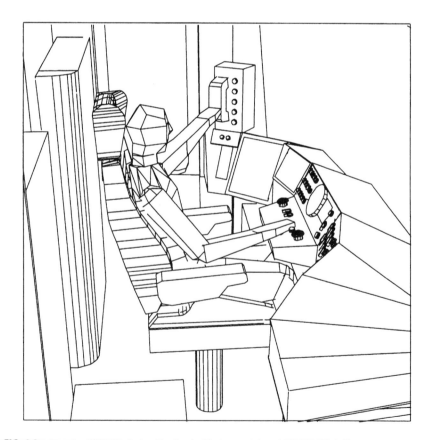

FIG. 9.2   Example of SAMMIE display. (Reprinted with the permission of SAMMIE CAD Ltd.)

user trials, and the accompanying problems associated with selecting and working with experimental participants. The costs incurred emanate from the need for experienced personnel to operate the system.

9.8   DATA COLLECTION AND RECORDING METHODS

There are a number of commonly used data collection and recording methods for all type of evaluation; these are briefly overviewed here.

The simplest way of collecting data is probably to use a pencil and paper. This might involve anything from collating a tally chart to more sophisticated pre-prepared data sheets involving the collection of written information. Written information could be in the form of user or experimenter reports. Although user reports are generally not as objective as investigator-based methods, they do offer an additional and valuable means of assessing users' attitudes to systems. However, they have not been without their critics. Typically, Chin *et al.* (1988) claimed that some measurement techniques show low validities (e.g. Gallagher, 1974); low reliabilities (e.g. Larcker and Lessig, 1980); response bias (e.g. Ives *et al.*, 1983); employ a small sample size, and a non-representative population (e.g. Bailey and Pearson, 1983). However, if the method lends itself to pen and paper recording, this can provide an economical and efficient means of data collection. It also has the advantage of being a 'hands-on' approach, so the actual physical recording usually facilitates the researcher's understanding. However, there will obviously be some occasions when pencil and paper will not suffice, e.g. some observation situations will not capture all the required data by using this medium. In these situations, pen and paper will need to be supplemented, or replaced by another technique.

If there is a lot of data to capture, as in walkthroughs and talkthroughs, some electronic means might be necessary, e.g. audio and video recording. (Chapter 7 discusses the use of video recording.) Electronic recording of information is usually fast, and allows 'data-rich' situations to be accessed more confidently in terms of completeness. However, the drawback concerns the amount of time and effort needed for analyses; basically, what you accrue from the recording, you spend on the analysis. In order to compensate for this, the solution would seem to lie in having automated analysis, and indeed, there are some packages on the market which carry out quick and efficient analyses of video data, e.g. the 'Observer' and the 'Drum'. These packages allow the analyst to control the rate at which the video is replayed, so that events of interest can be quickly located for analysis; basic statistical analysis of frequency and duration of these specified events can then be carried out automatically.

10 How Can the System Be Introduced Into a Workplace?

OBJECTIVES OF CHAPTER:

- To define the workplace within the context of the organisation
- To look at the reasons for introducing new (computer) technology to the workplace
- To consider some of the health and safety aspects of the use of computer technology
- To consider some of the more commonly cited reasons for project failure when systems are introduced to the workplace

HAVING READ THIS CHAPTER, THE READER WILL BE ABLE:

- To understand the reasons for introducing new technology
- To be familiar with some of the difficulties associated with the introduction of new computer systems
- To be aware of the health and safety aspects of using computer equipment

10.1 DEFINING THE WORKPLACE

Before attempting to define the workplace, it is necessary to consider the context (or organisation) in which it exists. However, defining the term 'organisation' is not easy, due to its diverse and complex nature, determined and exacerbated by the behaviour of the people who work in it. Arnold *et al.* (1995) made some observations about 'organisations' which provide a good starting point to inform the definition of the workplace:

1. Organisations are created and managed by humans, and ultimately they are the organisation rather than the buildings, equipment, etc.
2. The term 'organisation' does not only include the workplace, but also extends to other organised human activities, such as social clubs.
3. To some extent, people in organisations have common goals, but individuals may work towards their own specific set of goals.

It is difficult to capture the dynamic dimensions, the uniqueness and variability, of an organisation. One approach to combat this has been the use of systems theory for describing them (Cummings, 1980). The systems approach allows the organisation to be broken down into sub-units allowing for both the formal system, i.e. the formal structure of individuals in the organisation, and the social system, i.e. the interaction of individuals and groups with no reference to the formal structure. The sub-units within an organisation comprise a complex, interrelated network (Ackoff and Emery, 1972).

A good example of the interaction of formal and social (and technological) systems was provided by Trist and Bamforth (1951), emanating from their work examining the consequences of changing production methods in British coal mines. The traditional method of mining is known as the 'short-wall method' where small groups of 8–10 individuals work together as a team. However, post-war improvements in mining technology resulted in new mechanical coal cutting and removing systems being introduced (the so-called 'long-wall method'). This meant that the small groups had to be reorganised into much larger groups of 40–50 miners reporting to a single supervisor. The nature of their jobs changed, as they became more specialised, carrying out a limited range of tasks. This new method of mining was disliked by the workers and productivity fell. The solution put forward by Trist and Bamforth was a 'composite' long-wall method, where the new technology was used in conjunction with the older methods of working. This appeared to work: output increased while absenteeism decreased, with the composite method estimated to be working at 95% of its potential, compared with 78% on the conventional long-wall method.

In conclusion, consideration of what exactly comprises an organisation provides no clear-cut picture, other than the complex interrelation of a number of different elements arising from the formal (structural) organisation and the social aspects. This has important implications when considering the introduction of new technology.

10.2 NEW TECHNOLOGY

'New technology' applies to fairly recent developments in the use of computers in the workplace; it is the generic term given to computer-controlled equipment of various kinds (Arnold *et al.*, 1995), and is sometimes used interchangeably with the term 'information technology'. Within the last couple of decades, computer technology has been brought within easy reach of the majority of the population in Western society. In the UK, this is partly due to government edicts that have placed computers in every educational establishment, and to the dramatically falling costs of hardware and software. The development of computers with ever-increasing memory capacities has accompanied these changes, and the memory banks of the 1950s computers, which filled whole rooms, can now be etched onto single micro-chips. These advances in memory facilities have had enormous implications in terms of the amount of information that can be stored in computers, and its accessibility to users. Hence, increasing information processing capacities (i.e. faster access), coupled with decreasing costs, have resulted in a greater range of applications and take-up of computer technology, which has led to some heralding this era as experiencing the second industrial revolution (see Forester, 1985). Like all 'revolutions', it is not without its critics, and the move towards an information and technology-dominated society, and the need to be judicious in terms of exploitation and management has been questioned.

10.3 IMPLICATIONS FOR ORGANISATIONS

In general, organisations invest in new technology because it will yield one of a number of perceived benefits. Ewers *et al.* (1990) surveyed over 3000 organisations in Germany to determine whether they had invested in new technology, what benefits they had anticipated and whether the benefits accrued.

It is instructive to note that the expected benefits do not always occur immediately, and in a sizeable minority of cases they do not occur at all. Taking a simple approach to the statistics, it can be observed that the only benefit obtained immediately by a substantial number of organisations was the improvement in 'quality'. However, even this only represents half of the organisations, and if one goes further, the fact that quality is often defined 'in-house', i.e. rather than along the lines of an objective, standard definition, then it is surprising that not all organisations saw improvements in quality as soon as computers were introduced. Furthermore, even after a period of time, only around 50% of the organisations experienced any significant time savings. Given that one can relate time savings and quality of work to productivity, it is instructive to consider whether computers actually lead to gains in productivity.

In terms of changes in the organisations, most of them expected reduction in personnel requirements, increase in control and planning of work, and an increase in the perceptions of how interesting jobs were to perform. After all, having invested a significant portion of capital into the new technology, one might expect returns to begin as soon as possible. What are the productivity gains to be had from the use of computers? One would expect the gains to be very large; after all, most organisations have switched to computers, and they would not all waste their money. Most of us can probably think of aspects of our work that we could not do without computers. However, if we think beyond the number-crunching functions and ask how much more efficient and productive we are with computers, it is often difficult to find real evidence to support the initial assumption.

10.4 PRODUCTIVITY AND COMPUTERS

In recent years, a number of business analysts have begun to report a worrying trend in the relationship between productivity and computers. In very broad terms, as the amount of capital invested in computers increases, so the productivity falls. In other words, introducing computers is making organisations less rather than more effective. These results are so against 'common-sense' that they need to be explored in slightly more detail to appreciate what is going on.

Figure 10.1 presents one perspective on this argument. Roach (1992) compares the productivity of clerical workers with the amount of capital per worker invested in new technology. As Figure 10.1 illustrates, as investment increases productivity shows little change. These findings

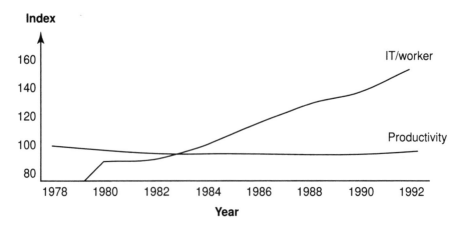

FIG. 10.1 IT investment for worker against productivity in office work. (From Franke, 1987.)

have been mirrored by other studies (Loveman, 1986; Franke, 1987), and raise several fundamental questions.

The first question, and one which critics of such data tend to advance, is that measuring productivity in office-work is very difficult. Thus, any analysis based on such measures is, by implication, spurious. However, one can counter this argument by saying that if one pursues the same measures in pre-and post-computerised versions of the same office, and finds a change in the measurement, then this change should be attributable to the process of computerisation. Notice that we use the word 'process' of computerisation; many management gurus have been pointing out that the benefits to be gained from the introduction of computers often relate as much to changes in the nature of the work being performed as in the technology used. Indeed, there is good evidence to consider redesign of the organisation first, and then automation. In many cases, computers are doing the 'wrong' tasks or sitting idle. For example, e-mail leads to a reduction in 'telephone tag', but an increase in trivial, junk messages. As a result, managers might have to change the workflow to realise the benefits of automation, i.e. simplify work practices before automation.

Furthermore, if one uses different measures to assess productivity and finds general agreement between the results of the measures, then one can have greater faith in the findings. Indeed, there are a variety of measures used in the research into the effects of computers on productivity, and a convergence in findings from these studies, i.e. the majority of the studies produced findings similar to those illustrated in Figure 10.1. Thus, while productivity is a difficult concept to measure in office work, there is enough evidence from different sources to suggest that, at present, computers are not paying for themselves in terms of productivity gains.

Given that there is such a poor level of payback, one needs to ask why this state of affairs has been allowed to continue, and how it came about. The first point is relatively easy to deal with; computers are seen as essential to modern business practices. We are so certain that computers have to be better than the 'old' systems, that we take their benefits for granted, even in the face of mounting evidence that they may not actually exist.

The second point comes back to the issues of system design and deployment. Recall that Table 10.1 indicated that organisations expect certain benefits to accrue from the use of computers, and that these benefits do not always happen immediately. This implies that either the benefits did not exist in the first place, e.g. perhaps the organisations were simply duped by successful marketing, or that the organisations themselves were not in a position to exploit the computers to maximum effect. Another more worrying explanation for the lack of productivity gains is that computers have not been adequately designed to allow people to use them effectively.

10.5 INTRODUCING NEW TECHNOLOGY

There are four broad reasons for introducing new technology:

1. to reduce production costs by reducing labour force or rent/rates, etc. by reducing space;
2. to increase efficiency by improving production scheduling and stock keeping;
3. to improve quality by automating inspection;
4. to improve managerial control by improving information about performance.

While many of these factors are assumed prior to the introduction of the technology, they are not all achieved immediately, and some of them may not be achieved at all. Thus, there are several instances where the implementation fails. Some of the more commonly cited reasons for project failure include:

1. Poor strategic planning.
2. Lack of awareness among key decision makers (i.e. top management).
3. Limited training of employees.
4. Inadequate employee consultation.
5. Lack of attention to human factors in procurement, and design of work environment.
6. Lack of attention to job design.

These problems can be categorised into four main areas: lack of awareness, lack of planning, lack of consultation, lack of human factors.

Lack of Awareness

A number of authors have argued that a key reason for failure of computer systems is lack of sufficient planning of the implementation. This is often left to the system engineers. While this can deal with the hardware problems, it does not take account of the organisational impact of the technology. As noted above, it is only when the computer is being used by people in an organisation that the system can be said to be fully operational.

The introduction of any form of technology will have an impact on the organisation into which it is introduced. Conversely, the nature of the organisation will also have a bearing on the uses to which the technology is to be put. Consequently, technology cannot be considered as a 'neutral' entity that simply fits into an organisation. Rather, the implementation of technology is a process of organisational change, by which the organisation adapts to fit the technology, and the technology is adapted to fit the organisation (Scarborough and Corbett, 1992). From this notion, it should be clear that proper groundwork and preparation will have a significant positive effect on the introduction of the computer system. It also follows that often the groundwork will be sufficient to produce changes in work practice and job design which will make the introduction of technology inappropriate.

There is a tendency to think that computers 'automatically' make processes more efficient and of higher quality. However, plugging a database into a disorganised and badly collated filing system might simply produce a disorganised and badly collated database, following the old adage of GIGO (garbage in–garbage out). If the filing system was organised and had a structure, there might not be a need for the computer system to file, although once the records had been organised, the computer could allow for expansion of operations pertaining to cross-referencing and production of records. One often finds that computer implementation projects begin with a process by which data is structured, collated, organised and prepared for the computer system. It would be interesting to see just how much effect this initial process had on the efficiency of the previous system, and how much more efficiency the use of the computer added. It is probable that the computer adds little beyond this initial productivity/efficiency gain. The benefits come from the range of extra functions that can be performed.

Of course, these extra functions also lead to the breakdown of efficiency. For instance, many writers note how much time is wasted 'prettying' documents using modem word processors. For example, a secretary of our acquaintance used to spend a disproportionate amount of time producing memos and notices; most of the production time was spent applying as many different font types, sizes and styles as possible to the memos, printing them and then modifying them until they looked 'nice'. Similar things happen with the word processing of documents, where a substantial amount of time can be spent tidying things up. Thus, computers offer functions that encourage perfection in document production. This will have an impact on productivity, as people may spend more time on production than when using older systems. In order to get the most effective return on the computer, therefore, it is necessary to know what it will be used for, how it will be used, and what constitutes acceptable levels of quality.

A further problem can arise when the decision makers involved in procurement and deployment of the computer systems do not know enough about the technology or about the work being performed. For example, the head of the design department of a manufacturer of gas cookers introduced a CAD system in 1989. Manual drafters were not consulted before the decision, but were given demonstrations and allowed to go to exhibitions of CAD. The head of design also went to the exhibition, and was shown a CAD system that could 'draw' cookers. On the assumption that the CAD package had templates for all types of cooker, which could be simply modified by the CAD users, the manager ordered five machines. When the machines arrived, some of the drafters received specialist training. This training did not, however, alter their pay or status. The management decided that, in order to allow 'fair' use of the CAD system, workers were only allowed to use it for one hour a day. During this hour, however, the usual run of interruptions occurred, e.g. calls from shop floor, etc. Drafters found that most of their work was being split between the board and CAD, with their 'hour' spent copying from board designs to CAD.

This example illustrates two key points concerning awareness of the technology. The first is that computers are often seen as tools for simplifying work (as opposed to making work more efficient). If we stay with CAD for the moment, a survey of CAD offices in Scotland found that managers tended to view the introduction of CAD in terms of deskilling drawing room staff (McLoughlin and Clark, 1988). This would have a number of 'benefits' for the management of the drawing offices: increased machine pacing to produce more work in the same time periods, and standardised, routine work in drawing pool, to maintain high volume. Thus, the notion of simplified, standard work was taken to an extreme by limiting the amount of time spent on the machines. While one would like to see this as an unusual aberration from the norm, there is much evidence to suggest that the introduction of computers is associated with the aim of standardising work, increasing production and maintaining strict control of the work activity. The implications of this state of affairs for job satisfaction should be apparent.

The second point is how easily the manager was led to believe that CAD was simply a matter of altering stored drawings. In some applications this state of affairs has already been reached (Cooley, 1981). In this example, the 'image' of the product was modified to fit certain expectations of how it would be used. This level of awareness (which can be manipulated through good marketing and advertising) is often underplayed, but can have a significant impact on procurement unless a structured approach is used, i.e. to follow an objective process rather than to rely on the assumptions and intuitions of a few people.

Lack of Planning

There have been many studies into the most effective approach to the introduction of technology. Not surprisingly, a common finding is that the best approach will depend on the nature of the technology, the organisation and the work being performed. However, it is possible to identify several 'types' of approach and to judge their relative pros and cons. Table 10.1 presents three 'models' of planning for the introduction of new technology.

Model 0 represents an appeal to the assumptions and intuitions of a few people, followed by a process of muddling through. As noted above, the 'image' of a product can be sufficient to sway the decision-makers, who then leave the installation of the equipment to the manufacturer, and are left with unanticipated problems after the installation. Not surprisingly, this approach can lead to technology which is not appropriate for the job, which can not be used by the people who are supposed to use it, and which creates more rather than less work. It would be nice to think that this does not represent the norm, but from speaking to people in a number of organisations, this is by no means an uncommon approach to procurement, especially when one considers small purchases, such as around ten PCs for an accounting office. Finally, the approach can be swayed by budget limitations, e.g. by assuming that there is a fixed amount of capital which can be invested and recouped as quickly as possible. Often the short-term accounting procedure is to see staff savings as justification for expenditure on computers. However, as several surveys have shown, job loss is not an inevitable consequence of the introduction of computer systems; indeed, it is possible that more

Table 10.1 Comparison of three models of planning (adapted from Blacker and Brown, 1987)

Phases	Model 0 (Muddle through)	Model 1 (Task-technology)	Model 2 (Human-centred)
1. Initial review	Awareness that some useful technologies are out there; defined budget.	Define operating conditions; top management led; see workers as cost.	Define operating conditions; consult all levels, with top management holding casting vote; see workers as asset.
2. Exploration and justification	Interest in technology; expect fast returns; look for short-term gains; managerial project.	Prescribe objectives; central coordination; expert-driven; look for up-to-date; consulting project.	General policy; decentralised; end-user driven; system development team group.
3. System design	Left to suppliers; fragmentation; needs-led; design engineers; technical advice.	Machine-led; enrichment; final design; design engineers; technical advice.	People-led; clean design; incremental process; human factors advice.
4. Implementation	Debugging and dealing with unanticipated problems.	Capability; minor mods.; one-off training; line managers.	User support; pilot and test; staff development; review of needs.

people could be needed in the computerised version. The point is that labour savings accrue when the work has been redesigned. The redesign of work requires planning and the specification of aims.

Clearly one would not embark on the design of a system without some notion of specifications, e.g. what will the system be used for, how will it be used, how will it function, etc. One could argue that the introduction of computers is a matter of system design. Imagine the organisation as a large system, and that the introduction of computers is a change to one part of the system. In any other system, one would anticipate that changes in one place would have knock-on effects throughout the system. In most engineering projects, the likely knock-on effects are considered during the design process, and modified during testing phases. It would seem sensible to adopt a similar approach when introducing computers, seeing the organisation–computer system as the object of investigation.

Rather than simply muddling through, many system development projects involve specifying clear technical and performance objectives. This approach is described by Model 1. While this represents an improvement on Model 0, it still leads to problems, normally related to organisational and human factors. For instance, the focus on technology in Model 1 implies that other factors will adapt themselves to the requirements of the technology. However, this is not always true. As noted above, the introduction of new technology can best be seen as a process by which both technical and organisational factors are tuned to maximise both (Klein, 1994).

Model 2, therefore, involves both a technical project and an organisational/human factors project. The aim is not to ignore technical factors, but to give equal weighting to organisational problems. This approach is often described by the term socio-technical systems, based on work conducted in the UK during the 1950s (Rice, 1958; Emery, 1959; Trist et al., 1963). In recent years, several authors have proposed methods by which socio-technics can be introduced into system development projects. One of the best known is the ETHICS (effective technical human introduction of computer systems) approach of Enid Mumford (Figure 10.2). The development project involves several stages by which end-users are consulted, their jobs examined and modified, prior to the introduction of computers. In this way, the system can be optimised to make best use of the computer system being introduced.

Lack of Employee Consultation

Many organisations are reluctant to include employees in the decision-making processes surrounding the procurement, design and deployment of computer systems. The main reasons given for this are that consultation is time-consuming and erodes management's 'right to

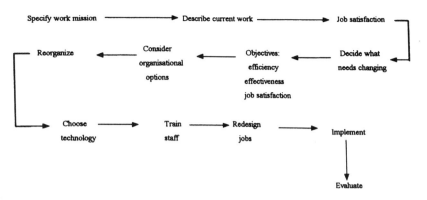

FIG. 10.2 The ETHICS approach. (Adapted from *Effective Systems Design and Requirements Analysis: The ETHICS Approach* by E. Mumford, 1995. Published by Macmillan Press Ltd.)

manage'. However, when successful implementation of computer systems is compared with failures, one finds that the successful organisations tend to exhibit high levels of consultation across all employees (Eason, 1988). It is obvious that, without effective human use of technology, the desired benefits will not be achieved. One could say that computers provide the potential for improved productivity, but that this potential needs to be realised by the computer's users. Furthermore, one reason why computer applications fail is because of employee reluctance to use them, either due to fears of job loss, or to erosion of skill. In a number of studies, consultation has been shown to alleviate many of these fears, and to foster a climate of acceptance of change.

Not only is the consultation directed at what sort of system to buy, but also what training is required, and how to supply it. Computers are often introduced on the assumption that they are easy to use, and that the manuals will provide all extra information required. However, it is clear that, while familiarisation with the software can allow users access to some of the features, it is normally essential to provide training to develop 'power users', i.e. people who can fully exploit the potential of the software. It is proposed that few companies aim to develop 'power users', which means that they are not exploiting the technology to its potential. By analogy, one could suggest that such an approach is akin to purchasing a fleet of company cars and not allowing drivers to leave the company's grounds. Not only does limited training reduce the exploitation of the technology, it also reduces the level of interest and control that people have in their work. This raises the important issue of human factors.

Lack of Human Factors

It has been so widely repeated that computers require changes in skill that most of us accept it without question. However, what exactly do these changes in skill requirements mean for work, and what do they mean for system design? Wall *et al.* (1987) investigated the design of jobs for both old and new technologies in a large electronics company. They found that one job involving old technology (bench assembly) and one with new technology (automatics) were superior in terms of perceived skill use, intrinsic job satisfaction and intrinsic job characteristics when compared to the other technologies, both old and new. The implementation of computers had removed the need for the workers to be dextrous, but had replaced this with new activities and responsibilities. It is interesting to note that the most commonly cited effects of introducing computers to the workplace appear to describe a paradox. On the one hand, the amount of work activity is generally reduced – this may include simple, repetitive, dangerous or physical work. On the other hand, the amount of monitoring and maintenance work is increased. The irony of automation was pointed out by Bainbridge (1983), who stated that computers create systems in which people are not supposed to intervene. However, they require people to intervene quickly and appropriately when things go wrong. In order to intervene appropriately, it is necessary for the users to 'know' the state of the computer and, in order to do this, it is necessary to not only monitor system states but also to assimilate intelligently the information that is displayed. Thus, one often finds the argument that computers lead to an increase in cognitive work, and a reduction in physical work.

From the replacement of physical work with cognitive work one might anticipate certain benefits relating to how interesting work is. However, computers are able to turn work into routines and procedures. Of course, this potential has been present in factory and office work for centuries. The aims of the various incarnations of scientific management have been to define simple tasks (requiring minimal skill and training) which can be ordered in an efficient manner (leading to greater predictability and control of performance), and which can be performed as quickly as possible. Historically, there has been a trend for jobs to be narrow and specialised; this is especially true of manufacturing industries, where the range of job tends to be closely prescribed. A classic example is work carried out on production lines, where workers repeat a single operation on a small part of a product at a pace determined by the machine. There is little scope in this activity for any discretion in how to carry out the job. The justification for this style of working is primarily economic, and based on keeping the unit cost of production as low as possible. This philosophy stems from the work of Adam Smith (1776) and Charles Babbage (1835) and their work on the 'division of labour', and was extended by Frederick Taylor (1911), from which the traditional approach to job design emanates. Taylor was an employee at an iron and steel works in Bethlehem, USA, and from his observations as a machine-shop foreman, he developed a number of suggestions for increasing productivity that became known as his principles of scientific management. Taylor had amassed a lot of information about machines and their production rates, but felt he knew little about people and their levels of efficiency. One of his first projects, therefore, was to consider the design of shovels, and to increase efficiency by altering the shape of the shovel according to what was being transported. He also provided training and higher wages for workers who increased their output. In essence, Taylor and his successor, Frank Gilbreth, were carrying out some of the first time and motion studies. The practical outcome from their work was to give specific production goals to each worker, and to ensure that they were closely supervised whilst working; this is evident in Taylor's first 'law'.

'. . . the average workman will work with the greatest satisfaction, both to himself and his employer, when he is given each day a definite task which he has to perform in a given time, and which constitutes a proper day's work for a good workman. This furnishes the workman with a clear-cut standard, by which he can throughout the day measure his own progress, and accomplishment of which affords him the greatest satisfaction' (Taylor, 1911).

Taylor's second law concerned the economic returns the individual received for the work. Since he assumed that humans worked primarily for money, he advocated payment by results, i.e. workers were at their best when assured of a large and permanent increase in pay. Today, we know that humans do not work primarily for money, although for many it is an important aspect (see Braus, 1992).

What is interesting about system designs is the number of times the designers attempt to produce an 'efficient' work system (usually without regard for real work practice), and end up designing a version of scientific management, which results in workers having mundane, repetitive, dull jobs to perform. In these instances, not only are the physical aspects of the work removed, so too are the cognitive aspects. It is at this point that the argument for tying system design and deployment together becomes most clear. In order to design something that people can use for work (or play), it is necessary to appreciate what the users' goals are, how they achieve those goals in their current work, and what the users require from the potential system. All this can be seen to differ from the conventional approach of designing to poorly-specified requirements that have been produced without consultation with the actual users of the product. Of course, for multi-purpose software, such as a word processing package, one might argue that it would be impossible to find the 'real' users; try telling that to the team that developed the Apple Lisa (which has transmuted into the standard 'wimp' interface).

Computers often seem to 'deskill' workers by removing the opportunity for making decisions using knowledge or judgement, so 'rationalising out' these skills. By programming efficient work activity, it is possible to remove the need for human skill, and remove control of the production process from the hands of workers. The 'alternative' to the deskilling hypothesis will vary as a result of the interrelationship between trade union, management and the market. This suggests that the introduction of computers is a matter of managerial choice.

10.6   JOB DESIGN

There has been much debate as to what constitutes a 'good' job (apart from salary). The current consensus of opinion is that jobs need to be designed to allow enlargement and enrichment in work activity. In the 1970s, job satisfaction was a fashionable topic. In the 1990s, the emphasis has shifted towards the issue of control (or autonomy). To increase individual discretion and control over work, there are several approaches to job design that can be employed. The most popular of these are job enlargement, job enrichment and group-based work

Job enlargement involves moving beyond the notions of simple task activity and 'one best way' to perform work. Rather than requiring individuals to perform simple activities, job enlargement requires people to perform a range of tasks, which often have different demands and requirements. In addition to allowing some discretion as to the order in which tasks are performed, job enlargement can also permit workers discretion as to how they wish to perform tasks. There are clear implications for software design from this perspective.

Job enrichment is, in effect, an extension of job enlargement. Basically, in addition to increased tasks, workers are given increased responsibility for work. For instance, a secretary could have a job involving the production of typed versions of dictated letters. In an enriched version of this job, the responsibility for formatting, checking and content of the letters could be left with the secretary. Not only will this expand the responsibility of the secretary, it will also reduce the amount of 'waste time' the boss spends on the letter production task, especially if the letters follow a standard format.

Automation leads to working groups being replaced by individuals with workstations (although maintenance is still in groups/teams). It is often felt that automation damages the social side of office work; there is less scope for conversation, and less need to move about and socialise (Argyle, 1989). Furthermore, in communication tasks a group of people using a computer tend to take longer than a face-to-face group, and individual group members make fewer remarks. However, the computer also permits greater feelings of equality, which means that individuals feel less inhibited and express views more freely (Kiesler *et al.*, 1984).

Contemporary computer systems are developed according to the notion of workstations, which involve people sitting in constrained postures performing actions with simple motions. This has led to an increase in reports of musculo-skeletal problems reported by office workers (Grandjean, 1987; Bergqvist *et al.*, 1995). In addition to the effect of computers on the content of work, it is important to consider the relationship between workstation and potential musculo-skeletal problems.

10.7   HEALTH AND SAFETY

As more and more people use computer workstations in the workplace, public concern has arisen about their effects on health, especially in the long-term. Awareness of the health hazards of computer workstations dates from the mid-1970s and is thought to have been precipitated by the move from electrical typewriters to electronic keyboards (Dainoff, 1982). This change in the nature of the technology had many effects on the type of user and their work role. On a macro level, we now have a large number of workers who use computer technology for a major portion of their working day, with no previous training in either keyboard skills or workstation ergonomics. Changes in the nature of jobs may result in workers spending more time using computers, and this may have adverse effects on job satisfaction. Low levels of job satisfaction, coupled with increasing levels of occupational stress, are likely to have a detrimental effect on the psychological well being of the worker. This, in turn, might lead the worker to see the computer as a significant factor in their ill health. The situation has also been compounded on a micro level. For example, the variety of movements carried out by the user has decreased, as there is no longer a need to feed in sheets of typing paper or stop to erase keying errors (Hünting *et al.*, 1980). Additionally, many keyboard users who acquired their typing skills on the old manual typewriters still pound the keys of modern, light-touch, keyboards, placing unnecessary physical stress on their hands, wrists and arms (Sauter, 1984). The computer workstation allows prolonged rapid keyboard activity and although less force is required, new demands are placed on delicate muscles; problems compounded by the lack of adequate rest breaks (Jeyaratnam *et al.*, 1989). Furthermore, some computer systems are able to monitor the minute-to-minute keying performance of the operator, and this may lead to piece-rate payments and increased psychological stress for keyboard operators. While this approach to job design is effectively outlawed under the regulations, several companies still use these work-monitoring capabilities.

Over the past few years, compensation for work-related injuries has risen dramatically in the USA, Australia and Europe. Recent court cases in the UK have involved 'blue chip' companies paying compensation running to many thousands of pounds to employees suffering the consequences of poor working conditions and practices. There are many more cases resulting in out of court settlements with non-disclosure clauses limiting their publicity. These cases illustrate the important point that work-related injuries are no longer considered to be solely confined to the factory, but can also occur in the office. In Australia in the 1980s, there was a dramatic increase in the number of reported cases of repetitive strain injury or RSI (Pearce, 1990), and these were responsible for a large percentage of the compensation claims paid to workers (Bammer and Martin, 1988). Although the term RSI originated in Australia, it has been widely adopted in the UK by the media and public at large. However, in scientific and medical circles, it has been widely depreciated to be replaced by the term 'work-related upper limb disorders' (Pheasant, 1992). Indeed, the Australian experience of repetitive strain injury suggests that the number of employees likely to be off work at any one time due to work-related problems is sufficient for the concept to merit serious consideration. In addition to problems arising from RSI, there is also a potential for difficulties to arise from injuries to the lower back; some 25% of work-related injuries in the UK stem from lumbar region problems (Health and Safety Executive, 1992). Typically, these back problems stem from the manual handling of materials, but there have been increasing reports of back problems caused by poor design and use of office furniture, leading to postural discomfort and strain. Ergonomics presents a means of assessing the level of risk posed by specific work environments with respect to these types of work-related injuries.

10.8 CONCLUSIONS

There are several organisational factors that can have a significant impact on the success or otherwise of a system design project. In broad terms, one can draw an analogy with any other form of engineering and state that computers can only be introduced when the conditions are right. It is important to supply the right equipment to the organisation, i.e. to ensure that the equipment performs the work the organisation requires. It is also necessary to ensure that the equipment has sufficient usability, i.e. that it can be used by the people for whom it is intended. Finally, the organisation needs to have been sufficiently modified to accommodate the computer system. Given the failure rate of computer systems, it is tempting to conclude that these relatively simple proposals are rarely adhered to.

10.9 SELECTED REFERENCES

Frank Blackler and David Oborne (eds.), *Information Technology and People: Designing for the Future*, British Psychological Society, Leicester, 1987.
A book that focuses on the human aspects of using information technology, and attempts to make recommendations for the design of future systems. Although a little dated now, this text still provides interesting reading about the human factors associated with the use of technology.

Ulf Bergqvist, 'Health-related aspects of VDT use' in J.A.J. Rouf (ed.), *The Man-Machine Interface, Vol. 15, Vision and Visual Dysfunction*, Macmillan Press, London, 1991.
This chapter covers potential and possible health complaints associated with working with computers, focusing on electromagnetic radiation and field types, as well as sound and ultrasound emission. Although a little dated now in view of recent developments in RSI (repetitive strain injuries) and computer usage, it provides a comprehensive overview of various physical emission factors from VDTs (visual display terminals).

John Arnold, Cary L. Cooper and Ivan T. Robertson, *Work Psychology: Understanding Human Behaviour in the Workplace*, Pitman, London, 1995.
This book looks at human behaviour in the workplace, and more specifically, at how people can be assessed, motivated, led, trained and developed at work. It is a combination of theory and practice covering personnel issues, such as selection and training, and organisational issues, such as decision-making.

Stephen Pheasant, *Bodyspace: Anthropometry, Ergonomics and the Design of Work*, Taylor and Francis, London, 1996.
A book that has been updated since its first edition over a decade ago, it is primarily concerned with the application of ergonomics in the workplace and the resulting benefits.

Marianne Rudisill, Clayton Lewis, Peter B. Polson and Timothy D. McKay (eds.), *Human–Computer Interface Design: Success Stories, Emerging Methods, and Real-world Context*, Morgan Kaufmann, San Francisco, CA, 1996.
As the title suggests, this considers HCI in the context of successful and emerging methods for designing and developing interfaces, and discusses how user interface design and development accommodates (or fails to accommodate) real-world organisational, commercial and practical requirements.

K.H.E. Kroemer and E. Grandjean, *Fitting the Task to the Human: A Textbook of Occupational Ergonomics*, Taylor and Francis, London, 1997.

A book, currently in its fifth edition, on the topic of occupational ergonomics. It has recently been updated to address the rapid and fundamental changes that have taken place in the workplace in the last few years. The text imparts basic knowledge of ergonomics relating to the design, management and safety of the workplace.

11 How Will the System Be Used in the Workplace?

OBJECTIVES OF CHAPTER:

- To consider the consequences of poor design
- To look at the actual operational use of the system
- To overview the role of human factors

HAVING READ THIS CHAPTER, THE READER WILL BE ABLE:

- To understand more about how poor design arises
- To distinguish between procedures and practice
- To know more about the multi-faceted nature of system design

11.1 AT THE END OF THE LIFE CYCLE

The design of a system does not stop when the finished product is ready to be shipped to the retailer or end-user; in fact, one could say that system design really begins when the user first encounters the product. This statement might appear confusing or misguided to many readers. However, if one remembers the assumption that a system comprises people and objects in a work domain, then it is possible to see some sense in it. Clearly any product (and the focus of this book has been on computers) functions in response to human activity. While computers are designed to support human activity in the pursuit of some goal, it is less likely that human activity will be performed to aid a computer in its pursuit of a goal. This latter statement is true, partly because computers cannot really be said to hold goals, and partly because of the avowed aim of software and computer engineering to allow users control over the interaction. Having said this, there are countless examples of computer systems that appear to require people to perform pointless, unnecessary or silly actions in order for the computer to function. In such cases, it often feels to users that they are responding to the demands of the computer and helping the computer to perform some work activity.

There are several consequences of this state of affairs. The first is simply increased frustration and lack of incentive amongst people to use the computer in the first place. If the users do not feel in control and think they are simply responding to the demands of the computer, or the computer is seen as running their lives, this will have an impact on job satisfaction (Clegg et al., 1988). One of the aims of introducing computers is to increase the efficiency with which work can be performed. However, one should be aware of the difference between making work more efficient and making work less demanding. The notion of simplification of work has been prevalent in Western job design since the industrial revolution. Although it is intuitively appealing to fragment tasks into short, simple cycles that allow greater control and predictability, there is ample evidence to suggest that such job designs lead to boring and unrewarding work. This could lead to unmotivated workers who lack the willingness and abilities to exhibit flexible, imaginative responses to changes in work requirements. Given the contemporary nature of work, with emphasis on quality and flexibility, it would appear that old-fashioned scientific management ideals are not producing the type of workforce that is needed (Klein, 1994). Rather than using computers to make work simpler, it makes more sense to see computers as offering the potential to make work more interesting and fulfilling. From this approach, one can see increases in flexibility and, potentially, of efficiency.

The second consequence is lack of awareness or willingness to learn the computer's functions. Under such situations, people will be likely to learn set procedure, rather than attempt to explore the full range of functions offered. It is clear that for many people the range of functions offered by the computer (or software package) is in excess of their requirements; it is also clear that many of the functions are either not used or not know by users. This is true of many 'white goods', VCRs (video cassette recorders), and doubly true of computers. It seems strange to produce functions that are not used; although given the fierce competitiveness of the market, one can appreciate the need to add more and more functions (or gimmicks). Far more useful would be products that offer exactly the functions that the user requires, in exactly the manner that the user expects and can easily use. Indeed, the well-designed product almost disappears from conscious awareness during use; one is not aware of using the product so much as performing the task.

The third consequence is the impact on work practices. Changing to computers will affect the way work is performed, organised and managed, with both negative and positive consequences. Often one's perception of whether the consequences are negative or positive relates to the particular perspective of the individual. For instance, it is possible to use a computer to record number of keystrokes, to ensure that people are working to speed. Is this a useful performance monitoring tool, a means of coercing workers to work faster, or simply a way of spying on people?

The consequences of computerisation are often dependent on the culture of the organisation in which they are used. This means that procurement and deployment becomes an important part of the design process. Interestingly, considering the development of a system in terms of the procurement process, i.e. the points at which payment should be made for reaching specific milestones, places a different (and more realistic) perspective on the design of life cycles. Designers may feel that their responsibility ends with the finished product. However, if people are unable to use the product due to lack of adequate training, or are being told to use the product for the wrong activities, then this has a bearing on the usability of the product. This may lead to users saying 'I won't buy from manufacturer X because their computer was hard to use'. The problem may not lie in the computer or product but in the deployment. Consequently, it is proposed that designers can sometimes consider the likely uses of the product or functions in the wrong way. From this, it is possible that the functions can be redescribed, or that manuals can be provided to spell out the appropriate use of the functions.

While there is an argument that deployment should feature in system design, it is a moot point as to whether one should expect designers to be doing this. After all, their work is sufficiently complicated by the demands of producing elegant software and hardware to meet specifications. Many systems fail on delivery and then require some modifications, and many systems fail to deliver the expected productivity benefits (see examples given by Nielsen, 1993). Moreover, many overrun their estimated costs of development. In one study, Lederer and Prasad (1992) found that 63% of large software projects significantly overran their estimates. Reasons included: (i) frequent requests for modifications by users; (ii) tasks that had been overlooked; (iii) lack of understanding by users of their requirements; and (iv) inadequate communication between the system developers and the users.

One could argue that this is probably due to the systems not being used properly in the first place. However, this raises the interesting question of what we mean by proper use. Presumably the proper use of a system is that for which it was designed by engineers. However, it is often unclear to what extent the engineers' idea of how to perform a task is commensurate with that of the end-user. It has been accepted for some time that designers hold a different 'model' of the system to users (Norman, 1988). The knowledge and experience of the system differ between these groups of people to such an extent that their perceptions of the technology and how to use it are radically different. Thus, rather than being an afternoon's work, the process of producing an engineer's report has been known by the authors to take the best part of a week, when parts of the report were written in such obscure word processing language that they actually had to be retyped by hand, rather than converted. What is striking about this state of affairs is the amount of extra work that computers required for this notational project, as compared with, say, having the reports hand-written (perhaps on pro-forma sheets) and typed. Of course, the benefits of the computer are apparent in the range of functions that can be performed, but should we still accept all the minor shortcomings and problems that they bring? Furthermore, what are the implications of these minor problems for productivity and organisational efficiency?

Returning to the topic of 'proper use' of systems, Degani and Wiener (1991) made some interesting observations. In their work with civil airline pilots, they looked at the extent to which SOPs (standard operating procedures) were followed. SOPs are intended to inform the crew how to proceed in various situations; violation of these procedures is frequently cited as a primary cause of incidents and accidents. However, procedures are often designed in a piecemeal fashion, rather than based on a sound philosophy of operations and policies, and as a result, crew will sometimes deviate from them. Degani and Wiener called this the '3 P's' (i.e. philosophy, policies, procedures) of flight deck operations, and suggested that the design of any procedure should first begin with an overall guiding philosophy of flight operations. This will allow policies to be generated that will lead to the procedures, i.e. how the tasks should be accomplished. More recently, Degani and Wiener have added a fourth 'P' to philosophy, policies and procedures; namely, practice. Practices differ from procedures in that they describe exactly what happens on the flight deck. Although this deviation may be trivial, it may also be significant; hence it must be the goal of organisations to minimise the difference between procedure and practice. This is especially the case on the flight deck and other safety critical situations. In order to do this however, it is necessary to find out what the actual practices are, i.e. how users actually use the system. Some of the methods discussed earlier – observation, self-report, experimental – will allow this information to be located. It should be noted that not all practice that differs from procedure is necessarily bad. There is a positive side to humans being able to generate their own individualistic practice, e.g. in the case of a situation arising where there is no procedure. Degani and Wiener's work highlighted a number of important points: (i) the extent to which the philosophy of the organisation influences procedures via policies; (ii) the fact that what people actually do differs from what they are supposed to do; (iii) the positive side of being able to carry out tasks that deviate from procedures, policies and philosophy.

11.2 ASSESSING EFFECTIVENESS

The underlying theme when considering human interactions with technology is performance, i.e. the extent to which the user is able to attain acceptable performance levels. However, when we talk about performance, there are a number of possible interpretations. The term 'performance' is multi-faceted, e.g. does it relate to performance of the whole system, user performance, or performance of the resultant interactions, or two or more combinations of these?

Performance could be considered according to the different perspectives taken in this book. For example, performance at a physical level might focus on the human–machine interactions in terms of physical design. Alternatively, the operational perspective will focus on performance in terms of the physical locale and ambience of the workplace. Social aspects will also affect human–machine interactions with regard to social relationships, individual lifestyles and cultural and ethnic factors. Further, the environment can be considered in the light of the various physical agents that act upon it. Common physical agents might include: kinetic (gravitational, vibrational, acoustic), thermal, radiant (ionising and non-ionising), and barametric agents. These will all affect performance, as chemical and biological agents will affect human performance. What becomes evident from this discussion is the importance of the operational environment, since this can be classified according to the physical environment, the psychosocial environment and the work environment (Fraser, 1989). One conclusion might be that it is extremely difficult to delimit the various perspectives to human–machine interaction, since they overlap and encompass each other. It could therefore be argued that any such division is contrived and of little use.

This discussion may be seen to detract from the importance of measuring performance. However, it could be argued that it also adds weight to the fact that performance measures are central to the design of systems, and their subsequent operational use. Performance in whatever sense relates directly to efficiency, reliability and safety. Given its importance and influence in the design of systems, its measurement has been extensively considered in the preceding chapters. However, designing systems in its broadest sense does not finish at product release, and it is important to consider how the system will actually be used in the workplace. The central question could thus be how can we best design tasks to support the system or product under consideration.

Task is a much used concept in human factors engineering, and in recent years task design has been favoured more by this community than interface design. This is because design is centred on the task and its characteristics, which in turn will determine the design of the interface, and it is easier to delimit the former. Further, task design is a more concrete concept than interface design. However, despite this prominence, there is little consensus on defining the term and its scope. Some common assumptions were put forward by Stammers and Shepherd (1995, p. 148). These included:

1. The term 'task' generally applies to a unit of activity within work situations.
2. A task may be given to, or imposed upon, an individual or alternatively carried out on the individual's own initiative and volition.
3. It is a unit of activity, requiring more than one simple physical or mental operation for its completion.
4. It is often used with the connotation of an activity that is non-trivial, or even onerous in nature.
5. It has a defined objective.

Hence, the components of a task would extend to include task requirements, task environment and task behaviour. Again, these components can be considered according to the physical, operational, environmental and social perspectives. For example, the design of a task might be greatly influenced by the physical design of the workplace and equipment.

11.3   ROLE OF ERGONOMICS

There are three principle reasons for considering human factors/ ergonomics in office, industrial and manufacturing environments. These are:

1. to produce safe working places;
2. to comply with legislation;
3. to maximise employee productivity and efficiency.

Safety

Humans make errors. However, most of these are of no consequence and are quickly forgotten. Some become positive events, in that the error nearly leads to an incident or accident (the so-called 'near miss' situation) and we actually learn a considerable amount that prevents us from making the same error in the future. Some compromise safety to such an extent that they precipitate an accident. In the 1960s and '70s, one approach to safety was to automate, i.e. take the person out of the loop, so that they could not make errors. However, the trend more recently has been to design to accommodate error, with the development of error-tolerant systems. We now know that we cannot prevent humans making errors; indeed some would argue that this would not be a desirable goal anyway (Rasmussen, 1987). In order to ensure safety, techniques are needed to manage our propensity to make errors. This could be at the level of ensuring human–machine interactions are designed with error management in mind, but really should extend to consider workplace, environmental and organisational influences. We know that accidents rarely arise from a single error, but are the result of a number of failures in the system encompassing management, operational, design, and organisational decisions and issues, e.g. lack of a safety culture within an organisation. Noyes and Stanton (1997) discussed this in detail in their work on accidents and their causes.

Legislation

There have been many attempts to regulate the safety of workplaces within legislation, with the Factories Act (1961), the Offices, Shops and Railway Premises Act (1963), and the Health and Safety at Work Act (1974) defining requirements in broad terms. Under the Health and Safety Act (1974) employers have a general duty to '. . . so far as is reasonably practicable, provide machinery, equipment and other plant that is safe and without risks to health and must maintain them in that condition. They must also ensure that, so far as is reasonably practicable, the systems of work are safe and without risks to health' (HASAW, 1974, Section 2[2][a]). If the organisation employs more than five people, then a health and safety policy, covering all aspects of health and safety relevant to the employment, must be drawn up. This requirement is expanded in the HSE Management of Health and Safety regulations. Furthermore, employers are obliged to provide adequate training, instruction and supervision to ensure that health and safety standards are maintained.

For many companies, health and safety is already managed effectively. However, legislation does not explicitly cover all aspects of health and safety at work, and recent Health and Safety Executive regulations have come into effect, based on European Community directives, to fill in the gaps. In a response to increases in reports of office-based, work-related injuries, governments and legislative bodies have been drafting statutes pertaining to safe working environments. In particular, regulations define requirements for health and safety in manual handling and in work with visual display terminals. While the health risks from manual handling may appear obvious, many people still find it difficult to accept that there might be health risks arising from the use of computers. Indeed, Health and Safety Executive regulations state that 'employers shall be obliged to perform an analysis of (computer) workstations in order to evaluate the safety and health conditions to which they give rise for their workers, particularly as regards possible risks to eyesight, physical problems and problems of mental stress'.

In recent years, a number of official ergonomic standards have been developed. Dul *et al.* (1996) cited 28 published standards, with a further 69 in preparation. These cover computer work, warnings, environmental parameters such as thermal stress, and manual materials handling.

Productivity

The measurement of productivity is not usually easy, and will vary according to exactly what is being measured. There is little evidence that introducing computers increases productivity, but this may reflect the difficulties in measurement. However, there is good evidence that well-designed workplaces lead to increases in worker productivity, while minimising detrimental health and safety consequences (Kragt, 1992). Dressel and Francis (1987) compared three office layouts over a 21-month period, and found significant gains in productivity (i.e. over 20%) for the 'ergonomically designed' workstation. If the gains in productivity are related to the costs of installing such equipment, then it is possible to show that the redesign pays for itself in a very short period of time. For example, Kleeman (1991) argued that even with a relatively small productivity gain of only 10%, an employee earning £15 000 per annum will produce a sufficient increase in productivity to pay for the changes in around six months – if the productivity increases are higher, then obviously the pay-back period will be even shorter.

11.4   A FINAL COMMENT

This book has attempted to consider the design of systems from a user-centred viewpoint. It has focused extensively on the use of methods, and although it might be argued that the categorisation of the techniques discussed here is just one of many, it does not detract from the usefulness and importance of methods in research and development. Human factors only exists in its application, and this needs to be structured via methods. There may not necessarily be one method, but a combination of techniques needed. Further, it is important to use appropriate methods, rather than those with which the reader feels comfortable. However, despite the growing interest and awareness of human factors, ergonomics and HCI, designers often do not use methods (Belotti, 1989; Mirza and Baber, 1994). Why is this the case?

One reason might relate to the mismatch between what are apparently still quite simple methods that we have for measuring the complexity and richness of human performance, e.g. the measurement of human personality using a pencil and paper. Other explanations may relate to the design process. Perhaps resistance on the part of designers is due to ignorance on their part of understanding what user-centred design is, and has to offer. In the past, perhaps there has been failure in communication between designers, engineers and human factors specialists, and when this interaction has taken place, thoughts have not been conveyed using a common language. For example, users may refer to a keyboard as having a 'proper feel', whereas an engineer might talk about high torques and the force-displacement characteristics of keys. Human factors information and data therefore have to be presented in a form that other members of the design team can readily access and use. Some may be bemused by the irony of this situation. Another reason for a reticence to employ methods concerns errors. The use of any method will be subject to errors. These are usually of two types: random errors, which need to be reduced in order to ensure greater overall accuracy, but should not bias the results in any particular direction, and systematic errors. The latter are more serious in that they may have a directional influence if committed on a regular basis, e.g. treating a particular type of user in a different way. The difficulty with systematic errors or bias is that they often go undetected, so it is difficult to make allowances for them. This is just one example of many that may dissuade individuals from using and applying methods.

Finally, taking into account the 'human' may be seen as the expendable bit of the design process. Whereas you cannot design a system or product without hardware, software, documentation, etc., you can attempt to design without consulting or taking into account the user. Indeed, in the short term, there may be cost: benefits in adopting this approach. All engineers are human, and a commonly heard proposition is that they do take the users into account, since they test and evaluate the designs on themselves. The fact that they comprise a special and completely atypical user group is overlooked. The end-result for the rest of us – a design that does not meet our needs and requirements, is difficult to use and maintain, and causes endless frustration and irritation.

11.5   SELECTED REFERENCES

Alphonse Chapanis wrote in 1965b (p. 124) that 'it would be ideal if the engineering psychologist could turn to handbooks of human data . . . much as an engineer can turn to the Handbook of Chemistry and Physics, the Radio Engineer's Handbook, or any of a dozen others'. Such books are listed here.

Mark Sanders and Ernest McCormick (eds.), *Human Factors in Engineering and Design*, McGraw-Hill, New York, 1993.
Although this is not a handbook as such, it is one of the key texts, currently in its seventh edition. It provides a very manageable overview and discussion of the main human factors topics in 790 pages.

Martin Helander, Thomas Landauer and Prasad Prabhus (eds.), *Handbook of Human-Computer Interaction*, Elsevier, Amsterdam, 1997.
This weighty tome was first published in 1988 and was completely revised in 1997. It covers all imaginable aspects of human–computer interaction in 62 chapters covering 1582 pages, with over 7000 references. This book has to be one of the primary information sources currently in this field.

Gavriel Salvendy (ed.), *Handbook of Human Factors and Ergonomics*, Wiley, New York, 1997.
This book first appeared in 1987, but has been revised as a second edition, and covers virtually all aspects of physical, cognitive and social ergonomics in 60 chapters, spanning 2137 pages. Like the *Handbook of Human-Computer Interaction*, this book must be one of the seminal texts in this area.

FORTHCOMING . . .

Waldemar Karwowski (ed.), *International Encyclopaedia of Ergonomics and Human Factors*, Taylor and Francis, London.

12 Bibliography

PERIODICALS

Applied Ergonomics. Butterworth-Heinemann, Oxford.
Behaviour and Information Technology. Taylor and Francis, London.
Cognitive Technology. Practical Memory Institute, Terre Haute, IN.
Ergonomics. Taylor and Francis, London.
Ergonomics Abstracts. Taylor and Francis, London.
Human-Computer Studies. Ablex, Norwood, NJ.
Human Factors. Human Factors and Ergonomics Society, Santa Monica, CA.
Interacting with Computers. Butterworth-Heinemann, Oxford.
International Journal of Cognitive Ergonomics. LEA, NJ.
International Journal of Human-Computer Studies (formerly *International Journal of Man-Machine Studies*). Academic Press, London.
International Journal of Industrial Ergonomics. Elsevier, Amsterdam.
International Journal of Human Factors in Manufacturing. Wiley, New York.

MAGAZINES AND BULLETINS

Ergonomics in Design: The Magazine of Human Factors Applications. Human Factors and Ergonomics Society, Santa Monica, CA.
Ergonomics International. International Ergonomics Association.
HFS Bulletin. US Human Factors Society.
The Ergonomist. Newsletter of the UK Ergonomics Society.

CONFERENCE PROCEEDINGS

Proceedings of the Annual Congress of the International Ergonomics Association. Taylor and Francis, London.
Proceedings of the Annual Ergonomics Society (published as *Contemporary Ergonomics*). Taylor and Francis, London.
Proceedings of the Annual Meeting of the Human Factors Association of Canada/ACE. HFAC/ACE, Mississauga, Ontario.
Proceedings of the Australian Conference on Computer-Human Interaction.
Proceedings of British Computer Society HCI Group.

Proceedings of CHI. ACM Press, New York.

Proceedings of the Human Factors Society Annual Meeting. Human Factors and Ergonomics Society, Santa Monica, CA.

Proceedings of International Conference on Cognitive Ergonomics and Engineering Psychology.

Proceedings of 'People in Control' Conference. IEE, London.

13 References

A

Ackoff R.L. and Emery F.E. On *Purposeful Systems*. Tavistock, London, 1972.

Alavi M. An assessment of the prototyping approach to information systems development, *Communications of the ACM*, 27, 6, 1984.

Alden D.G., Daniels R.W. and Kanarick A.F. Keyboard design and operation: a review of the major issues, *Human Factors*, 14, 275–93, 1972.

Annett J. and Duncan K.D. Task analysis and training design, *Occupational Psychology*, 41, 211–21, 1967.

Annett J. and Stanton N.A. Special issue on task analysis, *Ergonomics*, 41(11), 1998.

Anshel J. *Visual Ergonomics in the Workplace*. Taylor and Francis, London, 1998.

Argyle M. *The Social Psychology of Work*. Penguin, London, 1989.

Armstrong J.S. and Lusk E.J. Return postage in mail surveys, *Public Opinion Quarterly*, 51, 233–48, 1988.

Arnold J., Cooper C.L. and Robertson I.T. *Work Psychology: Understanding Human Behaviour in the Workplace*, 2nd edn. Pitman, London, 1995.

Astley J.A. and Stammers R.B. Adapting hierarchical task analysis for user-system interface design, in Wilson J.R., Corlett E.N. and Manenica I. (eds) *New Methods in Applied Ergonomics*. Taylor and Francis, London, 175–84, 1987.

B

Babbage C. *On the Economy of Machinery and Manufacturers*. Charles Knight, London, 1835.

Baber C. *Speech Technology in Control Room Systems: A Human Factors Perspective*. Ellis Horwood, Chichester, 1991.

Baber C. *Beyond the Desktop: Designing and Using Interaction Devices*. Academic Press, London, 1997.

Baber C. and Noyes J.M. Speech recognition in adverse environments, *Human Factors*, 38, 142–55, 1996.

Baber C. and Stammers R.B. Is it natural to talk to computers: an experiment using the Wizard of Oz technique, in Megaw E.D. (ed) *Contemporary Ergonomics*. Taylor and Francis, London, 1989.

Baber C. and Stanton N.A. Task analysis for error identification: towards a methodology for identifying human error, in Lovesey E.J. (ed) *Contemporary Ergonomics*. Taylor and Francis, London, 1991.

Baber C. and Stanton N.A. Defining problems in VCR use, in Lovesey E.J. (ed) *Contemporary Ergonomics*. Taylor and Francis, London, 1992.

Baber C. and Stanton N.A. Task analysis for error identification: a methodology for designing error-tolerant consumer products, *Ergonomics*, 37, 1923–41, 1994.

Baber C. and Stanton N.A. Human error identification techniques applied to public technology: predictions compared with observed use, *Applied Ergonomics*, 27, 119–31, 1996.

Baber C. and Wankling J. An experimental comparison of text and symbols for in-car reconfigurable displays, *Applied Ergonomics*, 23, 255–62, 1992.

Baber C., Usher D.M., Stammers R.B. and Taylor R.G. Feedback requirements for automatic speech recognition in the process control room, *International Journal of Man–Machine Studies*, 37, 703–719, 1992.

Bailey J.E. and Pearson S.W. Development of a tool for measuring and analysing computer user satisfaction, *Management Science*, 29, 530–545, 1983.

Bainbridge L. Ironies of automation, *Automatica*, 19, 775–779, 1983.

Bainbridge L. and Sanderson P. Verbal protocol analysis, in Wilson J.R. and Corlett E.N. (eds) *Evaluation of Human Work*. Taylor and Francis, London, 169–201, 1995.

Bammer G. and Martin B. The arguments about RSI: an examination, *Community Health Studies*, XII, 348–358, 1988.

Basili V. and Turner A. Iterative enhancement: a practical technique for software development, *IEEE Tutorial: Structured Programming*, No. 7CH1089-6, 1975.

Bawa J. Comparative usability measurement: the role of the usability lab in PC Magazine UK and PC/Computing, *Behaviour and Information Technology*, 13, 17–19, 1994.

Beagley N.I. Fieldbased prototyping, in Jordan P.W., Thomas B., Weerdmeester B.A. and McClelland I.L. (eds) *Usability Evaluation in Industry*. Taylor and Francis, London, 95–104, 1996.

Becker H.S. *Writing for Social Scientists: How to Start and Finish Your Thesis, Book, or Article*. University of Chicago Press, Chicago, 1986.

Bell J. *Doing Your Research Project*. Open University Press, Milton Keynes, 1987.

Belotti V.M.E. Implications of the current design practice for the use of HCI techniques, in Jones D.M. and Winder R. (eds) People and Computers IV, *Proceedings of HCI* 1988, Cambridge University Press, Cambridge, 1989.

Bergqvist U. Health-related aspects of VDT use, in Rouf J.A.J. (ed) *The Man-Machine Interface*, Vol. 15. Macmillan Press, London, 1991.

Bergqvist U., Wolgast E., Nilsson B. and Voss M. Musculo-skeletal disorder among visual display terminal workers: individual ergonomic and work organizational factors, *Ergonomics*, 38, 763–776, 1995.

Berry D.C. Involving users in expert system development, *Expert Systems*, 11, 23–28, 1994.

Bevan N. and Macleod M. Usability measurement in context, *Behaviour and Information Technology*, 13, 132–145, 1994.

Bias R. Walkthroughs: efficient collaborative testing. *IEEE Software*, 8, 94–95, 1991.

Blacker F. and Brown C. Management, organizations and the new technologies, in Blackler F. and Oborne D.J. (eds) *Information Technology and People: Designing for the Future*. British Psychological Society, Leicester, 1987.

Boehm B.W., Gray T.E. and Seewaldt T. Prototyping versus specifying: a multi-project experiment, *IEEE Transactions Software Engineering*, 10, 290–303, 1984.

Boehm-Davis D.A. Knowledge elicitation and representation, in Elkind J.I., Card S.K., Hochberg J. and Huey B.M. (eds). *Human Performance Models for Computer-aided Engineering*. National Academy Press, Washington DC, 291–298, 1989.

Boeing Airplane Company. Table of all accidents - world-wide commercial jet fleet, *Flight Deck*, 21, 57, 1996.

Booth P.A. *An Introduction to Human–Computer Interaction*. LEA, Hove, 1989.

Booth P.A. Identifying and interpreting design areas, *International Journal of Human–Computer Interaction*, 4, 307–332, 1990.

Bradford J.H., Murray W.D. and Carey T.T. What kind of errors do unix users make? in *Proceedings of IFIP INTERACT, Conference on Human–Computer Interaction*. Cambridge, 43–46, 1990.

Braus P. What workers want, *American Demographics*, 14, 30–37, 1992.

Bricklin D. Jot defines electronic ink, *Byte*, Oct Issue, 110, 1993.

Bridger R.S. *Introduction to Ergonomics*. McGraw-Hill, New York, 1995.

Bristow G. *Electronic Speech Recognition*. Collins, London, 1986.

Brooke J. *System Usability Scale*. Digital Equipment Corporation, 1985.

Brooke J. SUS: A quick and dirty usability scale, in Jordan P.W., Thomas B., Weerdmeester B.A. and McClelland I.L. (eds) *Usability Evaluation in Industry*. Taylor and Francis, London, 189–194, 1996.

Brown C.M.L. *Human–Computer Interface Design Guidelines*. Ablex Publishing Corporation, Norwood NJ, 1988.

Brüel and Kjaer. *Noise Control: Principles and Practice*. (Adaptation from a publication of the Swedish Workers; Protection Fund - Arbetarskyddsfonden), Naerun, Denmark, 1982.

BS 5959. *Specifications for Key Numbering System and Layout Charts for Keyboards on Office Machines*. British Standards Institute, London, 1980.

Buell B. and Brandt R. The pen: computing's next big leap, *Business Week*, 128–129, 14 May 1990.

C

Cakir A., Hart D.J. and Stewart T.F.M. *Visual Display Terminals*. IFRA, Darmstadt, Germany, 1979 (published in 1980 by Wiley).

Card S., Moran T.P. and Newell A. Computer text-editing: An information-processing analysis of a routine cognitive skill, *Cognitive Psychology*, 12, 32–74, 1980.

Card S., Moran T.P. and Newell A. *The Psychology of Human–Computer Interaction*. LEA, Hillsdale, NJ, 1983.

Carpenter R.H.S. *Neurophysiology: Physiological Principles in Medicine*. Edward Arnold, London, 1987.

Carroll J.M. *What's In a Name?* Freeman, New York, 1985.

Carroll J.M. (ed) *Scenario-based Design: Envisioning Work and Technology in System Development*. Wiley, New York, 1995.

Carroll J.M. and Olson J.R. Mental models in human–computer interaction, in Helander M. (ed) *Handbook of Human–Computer Interaction*. Elsevier, Amsterdam, 45–65, 1988.

Carroll J.M. and Thomas J.C. Metaphor and the cognitive representation of computing systems, *IEEE Transactions: Systems, Man, and Cybernetics*, SMC-12, 107–116, 1982.

Case K. and Porter J.M. SAMMIE: a computer aided ergonomics design system, *Engineering*, 220, 21–25, 1980.

Chapanis A. On the allocation of functions between men and machines, *Occupational Psychology*, 39, 1–11, 1965a.

Chapanis A. *Man–Machine Engineering*. Wadsworth, Belmont, CA, 1965b.

Chapanis A. National and cultural variables in ergonomics, *Ergonomics*, 17, 153–175, 1974.

Chapanis A. Should you believe what the new ANSI/HFS standard says about numeric keypad layouts? No, *Human Factors Society Bulletin*, 31, 6–9, 1988.

Chapanis A. Ergonomics in product development: a personal view, *Ergonomics*, 38, 1625–1638, 1995.

Chapanis A. and Lindenbaum L.E. A reaction time study of four control-display linkages, *Human Factors*, 1(4), 1–7, 1959.

Checkland P. *Systems Thinking, Systems Practice*. Wiley, New York, 1981.

Chin J.P., Diehl V.A. and Norman K.L. Development of an instrument measuring user satisfaction of the human–computer interface, in *Proceedings of CHI 1988*, 213–218.

Christ R.E. Review and analysis of colour coding research for visual displays, *Human Factors*, 17, 542–570, 1978.

Christie B. and Gardiner M.M. Evaluation of the human–computer interface, in Wilson J.R. and Corlett E.N. (eds) *Evaluation of Human Work*. Taylor and Francis, London, 271–320, 1992.

Christie B., Stone R. and Collyer J. Evaluation of human–computer interaction at the user interface to advanced IT systems, in Wilson J.R. and Corlett E.N. (eds) *Evaluation of Human Work*. Taylor and Francis, London, 310–356, 1995.

Clegg C., Warr P., Green T., Monk A.F., Kemp N., Allison G., Lansdale M., Potts C., Sell R. and Cole I. *People and Computers: How to Evaluate Your Company's New Technology*. Ellis Horwood, Chichester, 1988.

Cohen S., Chechile R., Smith G., Tsai F. and Burns G. A method for evaluating the effectiveness of educational software, *Behavior Research Methods, Instruments & Computers*, 26, 236–241, 1994.

Conrad R. and Hull A.J. The preferred layout for numeral data-entry keysets, *Ergonomics*, 11, 165–173, 1968.

Cooley M. The social implications of CAD, in Mermet J. (ed) *CAD in Medium-sized and Small Industries*. North Holland, Amsterdam, 1981.

Cordingley E.S. Knowledge elicitation techniques for knowledge-based systems, in Diaper D. (ed) *Knowledge Elicitation*. Ellis Horwood, Chichester, 1989.

Cox K. and Walker D. *User Interface Design*. Prentice Hall, Singapore, 1993.

Cummings T. *Systems Theory for Organisational Development*. Wiley, Chichester, 1980.

Cushman W.H. and Rosenberg D.J. *Human Factors in Product Design*. Elsevier, Amsterdam, 1991.

D

Dainoff M.J. Occupational stress factors in visual display terminal (VDT) operation: a review of empirical research, *Behaviour and Information Technology*, 1, 141–176, 1982.

Davidson J., Coles D., Noyes P. and Terrell C.D. Using computer-delivered natural speech to assist in the teaching of reading, *British Journal of Educational Technology*, 22, 110–118, 1991.

Davies D.R. and Jones D.M. Hearing and noise, in Singleton W.T. (ed) *The Body at Work*. Cambridge University Press, Cambridge, 1982.

Davies D.R. and Parasuraman R. *The Psychology of Vigilance*. Academic Press, London, 1980.

Davis G. Effective informal methods, in Jordan P.W., Thomas B., Weerdmeester B.A. and McClelland I.L. (eds) *Usability Evaluation in Industry*. Taylor and Francis, London, 115–119, 1996.

Davis M.R. and Ellis T.O. The RAND tablet: a man-machine graphical communication device, in *Proceedings of the Fall Joint Computing Conference*, 325–331, 1964.

Degani A. and Wiener E.L. Philosophy, policies, and procedures: the three Ps of flight-deck operations, in *Proceedings of the 6th International Symposium on Aviation Psychology*, Columbus OH, 8 p, 1991.

de Keyser V. Les interactions hommes–machine: caracteristiques et utilisations des different supports d'information par les operateurs, *Rapport Politique Scientifique/FAST* n8. Psychologie du Travail, Universite de l'Etat a Liege, 1986.

De Montmollin M. and Bainbridge L. Ergonomics or human factors? *Human Factors Society Bulletin*, 28, 1–3, 1985.

Denning S., Hoiem D., Simpson M. and Sullivan K. The value of thinking-aloud protocols in industry: a case study at Microsoft Corporation, in *Proceedings of the Human Factors Society 34th Annual Meeting*, 1285–1289. Human Factors Society, Santa Monica, CA, 1990.

Dey I. *Qualitative Data Analysis: A User-Friendly Guide for Social Scientists*. Routledge, London, 1993.

Diaper D. (ed) *Task Analysis for Human–Computer Interaction*. Ellis Horwood, Chichester, 1989.

Diaper D. Task analysis for knowledge descriptions (TAKD): the method and an example, in Diaper D. (ed) *Task Analysis for Human–Computer Interaction*. Ellis Horwood, Chichester, 23–27, 1989.

Dieli M., Dye K., McClinstock M. and Simpson M. The Microsoft Corporation usability group, in Wiklund M.E. (ed) *Usability In Practice: How Companies Develop User-friendly Products*. Academic Press, London, 327–358, 1994.

Dimond T.L. Devices for reading handwritten characters, in *Proceedings of the Eastern Joint Computing Conference*, 232–237, 1957.

Dix A., Findlay J., Abowd G. and Beale R. *Human–Computer Interaction* (1st edn). Prentice-Hall, Hemel Hempstead, 1993.

Dix A., Findlay J., Abowd G. and Beale R. *Human–Computer Interaction* (2nd edn). Prentice-Hall, Hemel Hempstead, 1998.

Downs E., Clare P. and Coe P. *Structured Systems Analysis and Design Methods: Application and Context.* Prentice-Hall, London, 1988.

Dressel D. and Francis J. Office productivity: contributions of the workstation, *Behaviour and Information Technology*, 18, 15–26, 1987.

Drury C. Methods for direct observation of performance, in Wilson J.R. and Corlett E.N. (eds) *Evaluation of Human Work: A Practical Ergonomics Methodology* (1st edn). Taylor and Francis, London, 35–57, 1990.

Drury C. Designing ergonomics studies and experiments, in Wilson J.R. and Corlett E.N. (eds) *Evaluation of Human Work: A Practical Ergonomics Methodology* (2nd edn). Taylor and Francis, London, 113–140, 1995.

DuBoulay B., O'Shea T. and Monk J. The black box inside the glass box: presenting computing concepts to novices, *International Journal of Man-Machine Studies*, 14, 237–249, 1981.

Dul J., de Vlaming P.M. and Munnik M.J. A review of ISO and CEN standards on ergonomics, *International Journal of Industrial Ergonomics*, 17, 291–297, 1996.

Dul J. and Weerdmeester B.A. *Ergonomics for Beginners.* Taylor and Francis, London, 1993.

Dvorak A. *Typewriter Keyboard.* US Patent No. 2 040 248, 1936.

E

Eason K.D. Towards the experimental study of usability, *Behaviour and Information Technology*, 3, 133–143, 1984.

Eason K.D. *Information Technology and Organisational Change.* Taylor and Francis, London, 1988.

Eason K.D. User-centred design: for users or by users? *Ergonomics*, 38, 1667–1673, 1995.

Edwards A.D.N. *Speech Synthesis: Technology for Disabled People.* Chapman, London, 1991.

Edworthy J. The design and implementation of non-verbal auditory warnings, *Applied Ergonomics*, 25, 202–210, 1994.

Edworthy J. and Adams A. *Warnings Design: A Research Prospective.* Taylor and Francis, London, 1996.

Ellis J. and Dewar R. Rapid comprehension of verbal and symbolic traffic sign messages, *Human Factors*, 21, 161–168, 1979.

Embrey D.E. SHERPA: a systematic human error reduction and prediction approach, in *Proceedings of the International Topical Meeting on Advances in Human Factors in Nuclear Power Systems.* Knoxville, TN, 1986.

Embrey D.E. Quantitative and qualitative prediction of human error in safety assessments, *IChemE Symposium Series No. 130.* IChemE, London, 1992.

Emery F.E. The characteristics of a socio-technical system. *Tavistock Institute Document* 527, London, 1959.

England R. Sensory-motor systems in virtual manipulations, in Carr K. and England R. (eds) *Simulated and Virtual Realities Elements of Perception.* Taylor and Francis, London, 113–130, 1995.

Enterkin P. Voice versus manual techniques for airborne data entry tasks, in Lovesey E.J. (ed) *Contemporary Ergonomics*, Taylor and Francis, London, 131–136, 1991.

European Directive (90/270/EEC) Work with display screen equipment, implemented in UK through *Health & Safety, Display screen equipment, L26 Guidance on Regulations*. HMSO, London, 1992.

Ewers H.-J., Becker C. and Fritsch O. The effects of the use of computer-aided technology in industrial enterprises: it's context that counts, in Schettkat R. and Wagner M. (eds) *Technological Change and Employment: Innovation in the German Economy*. Avebury, Aldershot, 1990.

F

Fitts P.M. Human engineering for an effective air navigation and traffic control system, *Ohio State University Research Foundation Rept*. Columbia OH, 1951.

Fitts P.M. and Jones R.E. Analysis of factors contributing to 460 'pilot error' experiences in operating aircraft controls, Aeromedical Laboratory Report AMRL-TSEAA-694-12, in Sinaiko W. (ed) *Selected Papers in the Design and Use of Control Systems*. Dover, New York, 1961.

Fitzpatrick J., Secrist J. and Wright D.J. *Secrets for a Successful Dissertation*. Sage, London, 1998.

Forester T. *The Information Technology Revolution: The Complete Guide*. Blackwell, Oxford, 1985.

Fracker M.L. and Wickens C.D. Resources, confusions and compatibility in dual axis tracking: displays, controls and dynamics, *Journal of Experimental Psychology: Human Perception and Performance*, 15, 80–96, 1989.

Franke R.H. Technological revolution and productivity decline: computer introduction in the financial industry, *Technology Forecasting and Social Change*, 31, 143–145, 1987.

Frankish C.R. Pen-based computing, in Noyes J.M. and Cook M.J. (eds) *Interface Technology: The Leading Edge*. Research Studies Press Ltd., Baldock, Herts, 61–74, 1999.

Frankish C.R., Hull R. and Morgan P.S. Recognition acccuracy and user acceptance of pen interfaces, in *Proceedings of CHI 95*. ACM, New York, 503–510, 1995.

Frankish C.R., Morgan P.S. and Noyes J.M. Pen computing: some human factors issues, in *Proceedings of Colloquium Handwriting and Pen-based Input*, IEE, London, Digest No. 1994/065, 1994.

Fraser T.M. *The Worker and Work*. Taylor and Francis, London, 1989.

G

Gaines B.R. An overview of knowledge acquisition and transfer, *International Journal of Man–Machine Studies*, 26, 453–472, 1987.

Gale A. and Christie B. (eds) *Psychophysiology and the Electronic Workplace*. Wiley, Chichester, 1987.

Galitz W.O. *It's Time to Clean Your Windows: Designing GUIs That Work*. Wiley, New York, 1994.

Gallagher C.A. Perceptions of the value of a management information system, *Academy of Management Journal*, 17, 46–55, 1974.

Garg-Janardan C. and Salvendy G. A structured knowledge elicitation methodology for building expert systems, *International Journal of Man-Machine Studies*, 29, 377–406, 1988.

Gaver W.W. Auditory icons: using sound in computer interfaces, *Human-Computer Interaction*, 2, 167–177, 1986.

Gaver W.W. The sonicFinder: an interface that uses auditory icons, *Human-Computer Interaction*, 4, 67–94, 1989.

Geer C. *Human Engineering Procedures Guide*, AFAMRL-TR-81-35. Aerospace Medical Research Lab., Wright-Patterson Air Force Base, OH, 1981.

Gerard M.J., Jones S.K., Smith L.A., Thomas R.E. and Wang T. An ergonomic assessment of the Kinesis ergonomic computer keyboard, *Ergonomics*, 37, 1661–1669, 1994.

Gibson J.J. *The Senses Considered As Perceptual Systems*. Houghton Mifflin, Boston, MA, 1966.

Gould J.D. and Lewis C. Designing for usability: key principles and what designers think, *Communications of the ACM*, 28, 300–311, 1985.

Grandjean E. *Ergonomics in Computerised Offices*. Taylor and Francis, London, 1987.

Gray W.D., John B.E. and Atwood M.E. Project Ernestine: a validation of GOMS for prediction and explanation of real-world task performance, *Human-Computer Interaction*, 8, 237–309, 1993.

Green T.R.G. Cognitive dimensions of notations, in Sutcliffe A and Macaulay L (eds) *People and Computers V*. University Press, Cambridge, 1989.

Green T.R.G. Describing information artefacts with cognitive dimensions and structure maps, in Diaper D. and Hammond N.V. (eds) *HCI 91: Usability Now*. University Press, Cambridge, 1991.

Green T.R.G. and Borning A. The generalised unification parser: modelling the parsing of notations, in Diaper D., Gilmore D., Cockton G. and Shackel B. (eds) *Human-Computer interaction - INTERACT '90*. Elsevier Press, North-Holland, 1990.

Greenstein J.S. and Muto W.H. Keyboards, in Sherr A. (ed) *Input Devices*. Academic Press, Boston, 1988.

Gregory R.L. and Colman A.M. *Sensation and Perception*. Longman, Harlow, 1995.

Greif S. Organisational issues and task analysis, in Shackel B. and Richardson S.A. (eds) *Human Factors for Informatics Usability*. University Press, Cambridge, 247–266, 1991.

Gremillion L. and Pyburn P. *Breaking the Systems Development Bottleneck*. Harvard Business Review, 01C2, 133, 1983.

Grieco A. Sitting posture: An old problem and a new one, *Ergonomics*, 29, 345–372, 1986.

H

Hackos J.T. *Managing Your Documentation Projects*. Wiley, New York, 1994.

Hammond N.V., Trapp A.L. and McKendree J. Evaluating educational software: a suitable case for analysis, *Psychology Software News*, 5, 46, 1994.

Harris P. *Designing and Reporting Experiments*. Open University Press, Milton Keynes, 1986.

Hart C. *Doing a Literature Review*. Sage, London, 1998.

Hartley J. Return to sender: why written communications fail, *The Psychologist*, 11, 477–480, 1998.

Harvey R. and Peper E. Surface electromyography and mouse use in position, *Ergonomics*, 40, 781–789, 1997.

Health and Safety Executive. *Display Screen Equipment Work*. HMSO, London, 1992.

Hedge A. and Powers J.R. Wrist postures while keyboarding: effects of a negative slope keyboard system and full motion forearm supports, *Ergonomics*, 38, 508–517, 1995.

Helander M., Landauer T. and Prabhu P. *Handbook of Human-Computer Interaction* (2nd ed). Elsevier, Amsterdam, 1997.

Helmreich R.L. and Foushee H.L. Why crew resource management? Empirical and theoretical bases of human factors training in aviation, in Wiener E.L., Kanki B.G. and Helmreich R.L. (eds) *Cockpit Resource Management*. Academic Press, San Diego, 1993.

Henderson G., Dixon A.T. and Ellender J.H. Speech recognition as an aid to productivity in word processing, in *Proceedings of the 1st International Conference on Speech Technology*, Brighton, 203–213, 1984.

Hettinger L.J. and Riccio G.E. Visually induced motion sickness in virtual reality system: Implications for training and mission rehearsal, in *Proceedings of the Interagency Conference on Visual Issues in Training and Simulation*, Armstrong Laboratory, Aircrew Training Research Division, Williams Air Force Base AZ, 1991.

Hewett T.T. The role of interative evaluation in designing systems for usability, in Harrison M.D. and Monk A.F. (eds) People and Computers: Designing for Usability, *Proceedings of the 2nd Conference of the BCS HCI Specialist Group*, University Press, Cambridge, 1986.

Hobday S.W. The maltron keyboards, in *Proceedings of the IEE Colloquium 'Interfaces - The Leading Edge'*, Digest 96/126, 8/1–8/10, 1996.

Hoffman R.R., Shadbolt N.R., Burton A.M. and Klein G. Eliciting knowledge from experts: a methodological analysis, *Organizational Behavior and Human Decision Processes*, 62, 129–158, 1995.

Hollnagel E. *Human Reliability Analysis: Context and Control*. Academic Press, London, 1993.

Howard K. and Sharp J. *The Management of a Student Research Project*. Gower Press, Aldershot, 1983.

Howarth C.I. The relationship between objective risk, subjective risk, and behaviour, *Ergonomics*, 31, 527–535, 1988.

Hünting W., Läubli Th. and Grandjean E. Constrained postures of VDU operators, in Grandjean E. and Vigliani E. (eds) *Ergonomic Aspects of Visual Display Terminals*. Taylor and Francis, London, 1980.

I

IEC Draft Standard 1508. *Functional Safety of Electrical/Electronic/Programmable Electronic Safety-related Systems.* IEC, 1997.

International Organisation for Standardisation. *Office Machines - Keyboards - Keynumbering System and Layout Charts.* ISO 4169, Geneva, 1979.

International Organisation for Standardisation. *Ergonomic Requirements for Office Work with Visual Display Terminals. Part 4: Keyboard requirements.* ISO 9241, Geneva, 1991.

International Organisation for Standardisation. *Guidance on Usability.* International Standard (Draft) ISO 9241, Part 11, 24 pp, 1994.

Ives B., Olson M.H. and Baroud J.J. The measurement of user information satisfaction, *Communications of the ACM*, 26, 785–793, 1983.

J

James M., McClumpha A., Green R., Wilson P. and Belyavin A. Pilot attitudes to automation, in *Proceedings of the 6th International Symposium on Aviation Psychology*, 192–197, 1991.

Jeyaratnam J., Ong C.N., Kee W.C., Lee J. and Koh D. Musculoskeletal symptoms among VDU operators, in Smith J. and Salvendy G. (eds) *Work with Computers: Organisational, Management, Stress and Health Aspects.* Elsevier, Amsterdam, 1989.

Johnson G.I. The user's side of the computer interface, *Applied Ergonomics*, 20, 158–159, 1989.

Johnson G.I. The usability checklist approach revisited, in Jordan P.W., Thomas B., Weerdmeester B.A. and McClelland I.L. (eds) *Usability Evaluation in Industry.* Taylor and Francis, London, 179–188, 1996.

Johnson G.I., Clegg C.W. and Ravden S.J. Towards a practical method of user interface evaluation, *Applied Ergonomics*, 20, 255–260, 1989.

Johnson P. *Human–Computer Interaction: Psychology, Task Analysis and Software Engineering.* McGraw-Hill, London, 1992.

Johnson P. and Wilson S. *HCI 95 Tutorial Notes on Task-based User Interface Design*, British Computer Society, HCI Group, 1995.

Jordan P.W. What is usability? in Robertson S.A. (ed) *Contemporary Ergonomics 94*, Taylor and Francis, London, 454–458, 1994.

Jordan P.W. *An Introduction to Usability.* Taylor and Francis, London, 1998.

Jordan P.W., Draper S.W., MacFarlane K.K. and McNulty S.A. Guessability, learnability and experienced user performance, in Diaper D. and Hammond N. (eds) *People and Computers VI.* University Press, Cambridge, 237–245, 1991.

Jordan P.W., Thomas B., Weerdmeester B.A. and McClelland I.L. *Usability Evaluation in Industry.* Taylor and Francis, London, 1996.

K

Kantowitz B.H. Mental workload, in Hancock P.A. (ed) *Human Factors Psychology.* North-Holland, New York, 1987.

Karat J. Software evaluation methodologies, in Helander M. (ed) *Handbook of Human–Computer Interaction*. Elsevier, North-Holland, 891–903, 1988.

Karis D. and Zeigler B.L. Evaluation of mobile telecommunication systems, in *Proceedings of the Human Factors Society 33rd Annual Meeting*, Human Factors Society, Santa Monica, CA, 205–209, 1989.

Karlqvist L., Hagberg M. and Selin K. Variation in upper limb posture and movement during word processing with and without mouse use, *Ergonomics*, 37, 1261–1267, 1994.

Karwowski W. *International Encyclopaedia of Ergonomics and Human Factors*. Taylor and Francis, London, in press.

Kieras D. A guide to GOMS model usability evaluation using NGOMSL, in Helander M.G., Landauer T.K. and Prabhu P.V. (eds) *Handbook of Human–Computer Interaction*. Elsevier, North-Holland, 733–766, 1997.

Kieras D.E. and Poulson P.G. An approach to the formal analysis of user complexity, *International Journal of Man–Machine Studies*, 22, 365–394, 1985.

Kiesler S., Siegel J. and McQuire T.W. Social psychological aspects of computer-mediated communication, *American Psychologist*, 39, 1123–1134, 1984.

Kirakowski J. and Corbett M. Measuring user satisfaction, in Jones D.M. and Winder R. (eds) *People and Computers IV*. University Press, Cambridge, 329–430, 1988.

Kirakowski J. and Corbett M. SUMI: the software usability measurement inventory, *British Journal of Educational Technology*, 24, 210–214, 1993.

Kirwan B. Human reliability assessment, in Wilson J.R. and Corlett E.N. (eds) *Evaluation of Human Work: A Practical Ergonomics Methodology* (2nd edn). Taylor and Francis, London, 921–968, 1995.

Kirwan B. and Ainsworth L.K. *A Guide to Task Analysis*. Taylor and Francis, London, 1992.

Kleeman W.B. *Interior Design of the Electronic Office: The Comfort and Productivity Payoff*. Van Nostrand Reinhold, New York, 1991.

Klein L. Socio-technical/organizational design, in Karwowski W. and Salvendy G. (eds) *Organization and Management of Advanced Manufacturing*. John Wiley, New York, 1994.

Klockenberg E.A. *Rationalisierung der Schreibmaschine und ihrer Bedienung*. Springer-Verlag, Berlin, 1926.

Kragt H. *Enhancing Industrial Performance*. Taylor and Francis, London, 1992.

Kreifeldt, J.G. and Hill P.H. The integration of human factors and industrial design for consumer products, in *Proceedings of the 6th Congress of the International Ergonomics Association*, Human Factors Society, Santa Monica CA, 108–112, 1976.

Kroemer K.H. E. and Grandjean E. *Fitting the Task to the Human: A Textbook of Occupational Ergonomics* (5th edn). Taylor and Francis, London, 1997.

L

Lam S.-T. and Greenstein J.S. The effects of input medium and task allocation strategy on the performance of a human computer system, in *Proceedings of the Interact 84*, North-Holland, Amsterdam, 458–463, 1984.

Landauer T.K. *The Trouble with Computers: Usefulness, Usability and Productivity.* MIT Press, Cambridge MA, 1995.

Lantz K. *The Prototyping Methodology.* Prentice-Hall, London, 1984.

Larcker D.F. and Lessig V.P. Perceived usefulness of information: a psychometric examination, *Decision Science*, 11, 121–134, 1980.

Lea W.A. Speech recognition: past, present and future, in Simon J.C. (ed) *Trends in Speech Recognition.* Reidel, Dordrecht, 397–412, 1980.

Lederer A.L. and Prasad J. Nine management guidelines for better cost estimating, *Communications of the ACM*, 35, 51–59, 1992.

Leedham G.C. Historical perspective of handwriting recognition, in *Proceedings of the Colloquium Handwriting and pen-based input*, IEE, London, Digest No. 1994/065, 1994.

Lewis C., Polson P., Wharton C. and Rieman J. Testing a walkthrough methodology for theory-based design of walk-up-and-use interface, in Chew J.C. and Whiteside J. (eds) *Proceedings of CHI 90*, Addison-Wesley, Reading, MA, 235–242, 1990.

Lewis J.R. Sample sizes for usability studies: additional considerations, *Human Factors*, 36, 368–378, 1994.

Lienard J.-S. An overview of speech synthesis, In Simon J.C. (ed) *Spoken Language Generation and Understanding.* Reidel, Dordrecht, 397–412, 1980.

Lim K.Y., Long J.B. and Silcock N. Case-study illustration of a structured method for user interface design, in Lovesey E.J. (ed) *Contemporary Ergonomics.* Taylor and Francis, London, 335–342, 1991.

Lim K.Y., Long J.B. and Silcock N. Integrating human factors with the Jackson System Development method: an illustrated overview, *Ergonomics*, 35, 1135–1161, 1992.

Longman G. *A User's Guide to SSADM (Version 4).* Blackwell, Oxford, 1992.

Loveman G.W. The productivity of information technology capital: an economic analysis, *Massachussetts Institute of Technology Report*, 21 January 1986.

Luce P.A., Feustel T.C. and Pisoni D.B. Capacity demands in short-term memory for synthetic and natural speech, *Human Factors* 25, 17–32, 1983.

Lutz M.C. and Chapanis A. Expected locations of digits and letters on ten-button keysets, *Journal of Applied Psychology*, 39, 314–317, 1955.

M

Macauley L. *Human–Computer Interaction for Software Designers.* Thomson Computer Press, London, 1995.

Macleod M., Bowden R., Bevan N. and Curson I. The MUSiC performance measurement method, *Behaviour and Information Technology*, 16, 279–293, 1997.

Malt L.G. Keyboard design in the electronics era, in *Proceedings of the PIRA Symposium on Developments in Data Capture and Photocomposition*, PIRA (Printing Industry Research Association), London, 1977.

Marlin Brown C. *Human–Computer Interface Design Guidelines.* Ablex, Norwood, NJ, 1988.

Marshall C., McManus B. and Gardiner M.M. Usability of product X – lessons from a real product, *Behaviour and Information Technology*, 9, 243–253, 1990.

Martin T.B. Practical applications of voice input to machines, *Proceedings of the IEEE*, 64, 487–501, 1976.

McClelland I.L. and Brigham F.R. Marketing ergonomics – how should ergonomics be packaged? *Ergonomics*, 33, 519–526, 1990.

McClelland I.L. Product assessment and user trials, in Wilson J.R. and Corlett E.N. (eds) *Evaluation of human work: a practical ergonomics methodology* Taylor and Francis, London, 249–284, 1995.

McLoughlin I. and Clark J. *Technological Change at Work*. OUP, Milton Keynes, 1988.

Mechan J.E. and Porter M.L. Stereophotogrammetry – A three-dimensional posture measuring tool, in Robertson S.A. (ed) *Contemporary Ergonomics*. Taylor and Francis, London, 455–460, 1997.

Meister D. *Human Factors, Theory and Practice*. Wiley, New York, 1971.

Meister D. *Behavioral Analysis and Measurement Methods*. Wiley, New York, 1985.

Meister D. *Human Factors Testing and Evaluation*. Elsevier, New York, 1986.

Meister D. Simulation and modelling, in Wilson J.R. and Corlett E.N. (eds) *Evaluation of Human Work: A Practical Ergonomics Methodology*. Taylor and Francis, London, 202–228, 1995.

Mezick D. Pen computing catches on, *Byte*, 105–112, Oct 1993.

Mirza M. and Baber C. The role of ergonomics in the testing and evaluation of consumer products, in *Proceedings of EUROLAB 94*, Milan, Italy, 1994.

Molich R. and Nielsen J. Improving a human–computer dialogue, *Communications of the ACM*, 33, 338–348, 1990.

Monk A.F., Wright P.C., Haber J. and Davenport L. *Improving Your Human–Computer Interface: A Practical Technique*. Prentice Hall, London, 1993.

Moran T.P. The command language grammar: a representation for the user interface of interactive computer systems, *International Journal of Man-Machine Studies*, 15, 3–50, 1981.

Morris M.E., Plant T.A. and Hughes P.T. CoOpLab: practical experience with evaluating a multi-user system, in Monk A., Diaper D. and Harrison M.D. (eds) *Proceedings of the HCI 92, People and Computers VII*. University Press, Cambridge, 355–368, 1992.

Muller M.J., Haslwanter J.H. and Dayton T. Participatory practices in the software life cycle, in Helander M.G., Landauer T.K. and Prabhu P.V. (eds) *Handbook of Human-Computer Interaction*. Elsevier, North-Holland, 255–297, 1997.

Mumford E. *Effective Systems Design and Requirements' Analysis: The ETHICS Approach*. Macmillan, London, 1995.

Myers B.A. and Rosson M.B. Survey on user interface programming, in Bauersfeld R., Bennett J. and Lynch G. (eds) *Proceedings of CHI 92*, ACM Press, New York, 195–202, 1992.

N

Nadler G. Systems methodology and design. *IEEE Transactions on Systems, Man, and Cybernetics*, SMC-15(6), 685–697, 1985.

Naumann J.D. and Jenkins A.M. Prototyping: the new paradigm for systems development, *MIS Quarterly*, September 1982.

Neelamkavil F. *Computer Simulation and Modelling*. Wiley, Chichester, 1987.

Nielsen J. *Hypertext and Hypermedia*. Academic Press, Boston MA, 1990.

Nielsen J. Finding usability problems through heuristic evaluation, in *Proceedings of CHI 92*, ACM Press, New York, 373–380, 1992.

Nielsen J. *Usability Engineering*. Academic Press, London, 1993.

Nielsen J. Usability laboratories, *Behaviour and Information Technology*, 13, 3–8, 1994a.

Nielsen J. Heuristic evaluation, in Nielsen J. and Mack R.L. (eds) *Usability Inspection Methods*. Wiley, New York, 1994b.

Nielsen J. and Molich R. Heuristic evaluation of user interfaces, in *Proceedings of CHI 90*, ACM Press, New York, 249–256, 1990.

Nisbett R.E. and Wilson T.D. Telling more than we can know: verbal reports on mental processes, *Psychological Review*, 84, 231–259, 1977.

Norman D.A. *The Psychology of Everyday Things*. Basic Books, New York, 1988.

Norman D.A. and Draper S. *User-centred Systems Design: New Perspectives on Human–Computer Interaction*. LEA, Hillsdale, NJ, 1986.

Norman D.A. and Fisher D. Why alphabetic keyboards are not easy to use: keyboard layout doesn't much matter, *Human Factors*, 24, 509–519, 1982.

Norusis M.J. *The SPSS Guide to Data Analysis*. SPSS, Chicago IL, 1987.

Noyes J.M. The QWERTY keyboard: a review, *International Journal of Man–Machine Studies*, 18, 265–281, 1983a.

Noyes J.M. Chord keyboards, *Applied Ergonomics*, 14, 55–59, 1983b.

Noyes J.M. Speech technology in the future, in Baber C. and Noyes J.M. (eds) *Interactive Speech Technology: Human Factors Issues in the Application of Speech Input/Output to Computers*. Taylor and Francis, London, 189–208, 1993.

Noyes J.M. QWERTY – the immortal keyboard, *Computing and Control Engineering Journal* 9, 117–122, 1998.

Noyes J.M. and Frankish C.R. A review of speech recognition applications in the office, *Behaviour and Information Technology*, 8, 475–486, 1989.

Noyes J.M., Frankish C.R. and Morgan P.S. Pen-based computing: some human factors issues, in Thomas P.J. (ed) *Personal Information Systems: Business Applications*. Stanley Thorne, Cheltenham, 65–81, 1995.

Noyes J.M., Haigh R. and Starr A.F. Automatic speech recognition for disabled people, *Applied Ergonomics* 20, 293–298, 1989.

Noyes J.M. and Harriman J.C. User involvement in the design process: A case for end user evaluation of software packages, in *Proceedings of the IEE Colloquium 'Human Centred Automation'*, Digest 95/141. Institution of Electrical Engineers, London, 1995.

Noyes J.M. and Mills S. *Display Design for Human–Computer Interaction*. Cheltenham and Gloucester CHE, Cheltenham, 1998.

Noyes J.M. and Stanton N.A. Engineering psychology: contribution to system safety, *Computing and Control Engineering Journal*, 8, 107–112, 1997.

Noyes J.M., Starr A.F. and Frankish C.R. User involvement in the early stages of the development of an aircraft warning system, *Behaviour and Information Technology*, 15, 67–75, 1996.

O

Oborne D.J. Ergonomics at Work: *Human Factors in Design and Development* (3rd edn). John Wiley, Chichester, 1995.

O'Donnell P., Scobie G. and Baxter I. The use of focus groups as an evaluation technique in HCI, in Diaper D. and Hammond N. (eds) *People and Computers VI*. University Press, Cambridge, 211–224, 1991.

Oppenheim A.N. *Questionnaire Design, Interviewing and Attitude Measurement* (2nd edn). Pinter, London, 1992.

P

Page M. Consumer products – more by accident than design? in Stanton N.A. (ed) *Human Factors in Consumer Products*. Taylor and Francis, London, 127–146, 1998.

Palmer M.T., Abbott K.H., Schutte P.C. and Ricks W.R. An evaluation of a real-time fault diagnosis expert system for aircraft application, in *Proceedings of the 26th IEEE Conference on Decision and Control*, 1987.

Payne S.J. and Green T.R.G. Task-action grammars: A model of the mental representation of task languages, *Human–Computer Interaction* 2, 93–133, 1986.

Payne S.J., Sime M.E. and Green T.R.G. Perceptual structure cueing in a simple command language, *International Journal of Man–Machine Studies*, 21, 19–29, 1984.

Pearce B.G. Upper limb disorders of keyboard users, *Occupational Health Review*, 8–10, Feb/March 1990.

Perlman G. Software tools for user interface development, in Helander M. (ed) *Handbook of Human–Computer Interaction*. Elsevier, North-Holland, 819–833, 1988.

Petropoulos H. and Brebner J. Stereotypes for direction-of-movement of rotary controls associated with linear displays: the effects of scale presence and position of pointer direction, and distances between the control and the display, *Ergonomics*, 24, 143–151, 1981.

Pheasant S.T. Does RSI exist? *Occupational Medicine*, 42, 167–168, 1992.

Pheasant S.T. Anthropometry and the design of workspaces, in Wilson J.R. and Corlett E.N. (eds) *Evaluation of Human Work: A Practical Ergonomics Methodology*. Taylor and Francis, London, 557–573, 1995.

Pheasant S.T. *Bodyspace: Anthropometry, Ergonomics and the Design of Work* (2nd edn). Taylor and Francis, London, 1996.

Polson P.G., Lewis C., Rieman J. and Wharton C. Cognitive walkthroughs: a method for theory-based evaluation of user interfaces, *International Journal of Man–Machine Studies*, 36, 741–773, 1992.

Porter J.M., Case K. and Freer M. SAMMIE: a 3D human modelling computer aided ergonomics design system, *Co-design Journal*, s2 07, 68–75, 1996.

Porter J.M., Case K. and Freer M. Computer-aided design and human models, in Karwowski W. and Marras W. (eds) *Handbook of Industrial Ergonomics*. CRC Press, LLC, Florida, US, 1998.

Porter J.M., Freer M., Case K. and Bonney M.C. Computer-aided ergonomics and workspace design, in Wilson J.R. and Corlett E.N. (eds) *Evaluation of Human Work: A Practical Ergonomics Methodology*. Taylor and Francis, London, 574–620, 1995.

Pressman R.S. *Software Engineering*. (2nd edn). McGraw-Hill, London, 1987.

Price H.E. The allocation of function in systems, *Human Factors*, 27, 33–45, 1985.

R

Rasmussen J. *Information Processing and Human–Machine Interaction: An Approach to Cognitive Engineering*. Elsevier, New York, 1986.

Rasmussen J. The definition of human error and a taxonomy for technical system design, in Rasmussen J., Duncan K. and Leplat J. (eds) *New Technology and Human Error*. Wiley, Chichester, 1987.

Ravden S. and Johnson G. *Evaluating Usability of Human–Computer Interfaces*. Ellis Horwood, Chichester, 1989.

Reisner P. Formal grammar and human factors design of an interactive graphics system, *IEEE Transactions Software Engineering*, SE7-2, 229–240, 1981.

Reisner P. Formal grammar as a tool for analysing ease of use: some fundamental concepts, in Thomas J. and Schneider M. (eds) *Human Factors in Computing Systems*. Ablex, Norwood, NJ, 1984.

Rengger R., Macleod M., Bowden R., Drynan A. and Blaney M. *MUSiC Performance Measurement Handbook*. National Physical Laboratory, DITC, Teddington, UK, 1993.

Rhyne J.R. and Wolf C.G. Paperlike user interfaces, *IBM Technical Research Report* RC 17271, 1991.

Rhyne J.R. and Wolf C.G. Recognition based user interfaces, *IBM Technical Research Report* RC 17637, 1992.

Richards J.T., Boies S.J. and Gould J.D. Rapid prototyping and system development: examination of an interface toolkit for voice and telephony applications, in Mantei M. and Orbeton P. (eds) *Proceedings of CHI 86*, Elsevier, Amsterdam, 1986.

Rideout T. Changing your methods from the inside, *IEEE Software* 8, 99–100, and 111, 1991.

Roach S.S. *Technology Imperatives*. Morgan Stanley, New York, 1992.

ROBUST. *ROBUST Safety Methodology Handbook, Part 2, ROB/SRC/WP490/SMH/3*. UK Robotics, Manchester, 1996.

Rogers Y. Icons at the interface: their usefulness, *Interacting with Computers*, 1, 105–117, 1989.

Root R.W. and Draper S. Questionnaires as a software evaluation tool, in *Proceedings of CHI 83*, ACM Press, New York, 83–87, 1983.

Rosson M.B. Real world design, *SIGCHI Bulletin* 19, 61–62, 1987.

Rouf J.A.J. *Vision and Visual Dysfunction*. Macmillan Press, London, 1991.

Rowley D.E. and Rhoades D.G. The cognitive jogthrough: a fast-paced user interface evaluation procedure, in *Proceedings of CHI 92*, ACM Press, New York, 389–395, 1992.

Rubin J. *Handbook of Usability Testing: How to Plan, Design, and Conduct Effective Tests*. Wiley, New York, 1994.

Rubinstein R. and Hersh H. *The Human Factor: Designing Computer Systems for People*. Digital Press, Burlington, MA, 1984.

Rudestam K.E. and Newton R.R. *Surviving Your Dissertation*. Sage, California, 1992.

Rudisill M., Lewis C., Polson P.B. and McKay T.D. *Human–Computer Interface Design: Success Stories, Emerging Methods, and Real-world Context*. Morgan Kaufmann Publishers, San Francisco, CA, 1996.

S

Salvendy G. *Handbook of Human Factors and Ergonomics* (2nd edn). Wiley, New York, 1997.

Sanders M. and McCormick E.J. *Human factors in engineering and design* (7th edn). McGraw-Hill, New York, 1993.

Sarno K.J. and Wickens C.D. Role of multiple resources in predicting time-sharing efficiency: evaluation of three workload models in a multiple-task setting, *International Journal of Aviation Psychology*, 5, 107–130, 1995.

Sauter S.L. Predictions of strain in VDU users and traditional office workers, in Grandjean E. (ed) *Ergonomics and Health in Modern Offices*. Taylor and Francis, London, 1984.

Scarborough H. and Corbett M.J. *Technology and Organisations*. Routledge, London, 1992.

Schalk T.B., Frantz G.A. and Woodson L. Voice synthesis and recognition, *Mini-micro Systems*, 15, 147–160, 1982.

Schiepers C.W.J. Response latency and accuracy in visual word recognition, *Perception and Psychophysics*, 27, 71–81, 1980.

Sclater N. *Introduction to Electronic Speech Synthesis*. Howard W Sams, Indiana, USA, 1982.

Senay H. and Stabler E.P. Online help system usage: an empirical investigation, in *Abridged Proceedings of the 2nd International Conference on Human-Computer Interaction*, Honolulu, HI, 244, 1987.

Shackel B. The concept of usability, in *Proceedings of IBM Software and Information Usability Symposium*. Ploughkeepsie, New York, 1–30, 1981.

Shackel B. Ergonomics in design for usability, in Harrison M.D. and Monk A.F. (eds) People and Computers: Designing for Usability, *Proceedings of the 2nd Conference of the BCS HCI Specialist Group*. University Press, Cambridge, 1986.

Shadbolt N. and Burton M. Knowledge elicitation: a systematic approach, in Wilson J.R. and Corlett E.N. (eds) *Evaluation of Human Work: A Practical Ergonomics Methodology*. Taylor and Francis, London, 406–440, 1995.

Shepherd A. HTA as a framework for task analysis. *Ergonomics*, 41, 1537–1552, 1998.

Shieber S.M. *An Introduction to Unification-based Approaches to Grammar*. Center for the Study of Language and Information, Stanford, CA, 1986.

Sholes C.L., Glidden C. and Soulé S.W. *Improvement in Type Writing Machines*. US Patent No 79,868, 1868.

Siochi A.C. and Hartson H.R. Task-oriented representation of asynchronous user interfaces, in *Proceedings of CHI 89*, ACM Press, New York, 183–188, 1989.

Silverman D. *Interpretating Qualitative Data: Methods for Analysing Talk, Text and Interaction.* Sage, London, 1993.

Simpson C.A., McCauley M.E., Roland E.F., Ruth J.C. and Williges B.H. System design for speech recognition and generation, *Human Factors*, 27, 115–141, 1985.

Sinclair M.A. Questionnaire design, *Applied Ergonomics*, 6, 73–80, 1975.

Skidmore S. *Introducing Systems Design* (2nd edn). Macmillan, Basingstoke, 1996.

Smith A. *On the Wealth of Nations.* Penguin, Harmondsworth, 1776.

Smith S.L. and Mosier J.N. *Design Guidelines for User–System Interface Software, Report MTR-9420*, Mitre Corporation, Bedford, MA, 1986.

Smithies C.P.K. The handwritten signature in pen computing, in *Proceedings of Colloquium Handwriting and pen-based input*, IEE, London, Digest No. 1994/065, 1994.

Smythe J.A. Evaluating software packages: a case study, in Lovesey E.J. (ed) *Contemporary Ergonomics 92.* Taylor and Francis, London, 385–390, 1992.

Sommerville I. *Software Engineering.* (5th edn.) Addison-Wesley, Wokingham, UK, 1996.

Stammers R.B. and Hoffman J. Transfer between icon sets and ratings of icon concreteness and appropriateness, in *Proceedings of the Human Factors Society 35th Annual Meeting*, Human Factors Society, Santa Monica, CA, 354–358, 1991.

Stammers R.B. and Shepherd A. Task analysis, in Wilson J.R. and Corlett E.N. (eds) *Evaluation of Human Work: A Practical Ergonomics Methodology.* Taylor and Francis, London, 144–168, 1995.

Stanton N.A. Alarm initiated activities, in Stanton N.A. (ed) *Human Factors in Alarm Design.* Taylor and Francis, London, 93–118, 1994.

Stanton N.A. *Human Factors in Consumer Products.* Taylor and Francis, London, 1998.

Stanton N.A. and Baber C. A comparison of two word processors using task analysis for error identification, in *Proceedings of HCI 91*, University Press, Cambridge, 1991.

Stanton N.A. and Baber C. Task analysis for error identification, in *Proceedings of the MRC/RNPRC/APRC Workshop on Task Analysis*, University of Warwick, 1993.

Stanton N.A. and Baber C. Alarm-initiated activities: an analysis of alarm handling by operators using text-based alarm systems in supervisory control systems, *Ergonomics* 38, 2414–2431, 1995.

Stanton N.A. and Baber C. Factors affecting the selection of methods and techniques prior to conducting a usability evaluation, in Jordan P.W., Thomas B., Weerdmeester B.A. and McClelland I.L. (eds) *Usability Evaluation in Industry.* Taylor and Francis, London, 39–48, 1996a.

Stanton N.A. and Baber C. A systems approach to human error identification, *Safety Science*, 22, 215–228, 1996b.

Steiner B.A. and Camacho M.J. Situation awareness: icons *vs* alphanumerics, in *Proceedings of the Human Factors Society 33rd Annual Meeting*, Human Factors Society, Santa Monica, CA, 28–32, 1989.

Stewart T.F.M. and Miles P.D. *Improvements In or Relating to Keyboards.* Patent Specification 1,492,538 (23 Nov 1977).

Straub H.R. and Granaas M.M. Task-specific preference for numeric keypads, *Applied Ergonomics*, 24, 289–290, 1993.

Sufrin B.A., Morgan C.C., Sorensen I. and Hayes I.J. *Notes for a Z Handbook: Part 1, The Mathematical Language.* Programming Research Group, Oxford, 1985.

Sutcliffe A.G. *Human-Computer Interface Design.* Macmillan, London, 1988.

Swain A.D. and Guttmann H.E. *A Handbook of Human Reliability Analysis with Emphasis on Nuclear Power Plant Applications.* Nureg/CR-1278, USNRC, Washington, DC, 1983.

T

Taylor F.W. *The Principles of Scientific Management.* Harper, New York, 1911.

Taylor R.H., Lavallée S., Burdea G.C. and Mösges R. *Computer-integrated Surgery: Technology and Clinical Applications.* MIT Press, Cambridge, MA, 1996.

Trauber M. ETAG: Extended Task Action Grammar – A language for the description of the user's task language, in Diaper D., Gilmore D., Cockton G. and Shackel B. (eds) *Proceedings of INTERACT 90*, North Holland, 163–174, 1990.

Travis D. *Effective Color Displays: Theory and Practice.* Academic Press, London, 1991.

Trimble G. Knowledge elicitation – some practical issues, in Diaper D. (ed) *Knowledge Elicitation.* Ellis Horwood, Chichester, 223–234, 1989.

Trist E.L. and Bamforth K.W. Some social and psychological consequences of the long-wall method of coal getting, *Human Relations*, 4, 3–38, 1951.

Trist E.L., Higgin G.W., Murray H. and Pollock A.B. *Organisational Choice.* Tavistock, London, 1963.

V

Virzi R.A. Refining the test phase of usability evaluation: how many subjects is enough? *Human Factors*, 34, 457–468, 1992.

Von Bertalanffy L. The theory of open systems in physics and biology, *Science*, 111, 23–29, 1950.

Von Hippel E. *The Sources of Innovation.* Oxford University Press, New York, 1988.

W

Wall T.D., Clegg C.W., Davies R.T., Kemp N.J. and Mueller W.S. Advanced manufacturing and work simplification: an empirical study, *Journal of Occupational Psychology*, 8, 233–250, 1987.

Wallace F.L. Learning to use SPSS, BMDP, SAS and NTSL: A comparison, in *Proceedings of 2nd South Texas Symposium on Human Factors and Ergonomics*, 1986.

Walsh P., Lim K.Y. and Long J. Jackson System Development and the design of user interface software, *Ergonomics*, 32, 1483–1498, 1989.

Wason P.C. and Johnson-Laird P.N. *Psychology of Reasoning: Structure and Content*. Batsford, London, 1972.

Waterworth J.A. and Thomas C.M. Why is synthetic speech harder to remember than natural speech? in *Proceedings of CHI 85, Human Factors in Computing Systems*, ACM Press, New York, 1985.

Watkins J., Davies J., Calverley G. and Cartwright T. Evaluation of a physics multi-media resource, *Computers in Education*, 24, 83–88, 1995.

Weisberg L.L. and Lanzetta T.M. Incorporating end user input into the design process, in *Proceedings of Interface 91, 7th Symposium on Human Factors and Industrial Design in Consumer Products*, Dayton, OH, 36–41, 1991.

Whalley S.P. Minimising the cause of human error, in Libberton, G.P. (ed) *10th Advances in Reliability Technology 10th Symposium*, Elsevier, London, 1988.

White J. and Hutchinson A. STINGRAY: The development of an ergonomic keypad for use with computerised aptitude tests, in Robertson S.A. (ed) *Contemporary Ergonomics 94*, Taylor and Francis, London, 507–512, 1996.

Whitefield A., Wilson F. and Dowell J. A framework for human factors evaluation, *Behaviour and Information Technology*, 10, 65–79, 1991.

Whiteside J., Bennett J. and Holtzblatt K. Usability engineering: our experience and evolution, in Helander M. (ed) *Handbook of Human–Computer Interaction*. Elsevier, North-Holland, 791–817, 1988.

Whiteside J., Jones S., Levy P.S. and Wixon D. User performance with command, menu and iconic interfaces, in Borman L. and Curtis W. (eds) *Proceedings of CHI 85, Human Factors in Computer Systems Conference*, North-Holland, Amsterdam, 1985.

Wickens C.D. Processing resources and attention, in Damos D.L. (ed) *Multiple Task Performance*. Taylor and Francis, New York, 1991.

Wickens C.D. *Engineering Psychology and Human Performance* (2nd edn). Harper Collins, New York, 1992.

Wiklund M.E. *Usability in Practice: How Companies Develop User-friendly Products*. Academic Press, London, 1994.

Williams J.C. HEART – a proposed method of assessing and reducing human error, in *Proceedings of the 9th Advances in Reliability Technology Symposium*, University of Bradford, 1986.

Wilson J. and Rosenberg D. Rapid protoyping for user interface design, in *Handbook of Human–Computer Interaction*. Elsevier, Amsterdam, 859–875, 1988.

Wilson J.R. and Corlett E.N. (eds) *Evaluation of Human Work* (1st edn). Taylor and Francis, London, 1990.

Wilson J.R. and Corlett E.N. (eds) *Evaluation of Human Work* (2nd edn). Taylor and Francis, London, 1995.

Wolf C.G., Rhyne J.R. and Ellozy H. The paper like interface, in Salvendy G. and Smith M.J. (eds) *Interfaces and Knowledge-based Systems*. Elsevier, Amsterdam, 494–501, 1989.

Woodworth R.S. and Schlosberg H. *Experimental Psychology* (3rd edn). Methuen, London, 1954.

Wright P.C. and Converse S.A. Method bias and concurrent verbal protocol in software usability testing, in *Proceedings of Human Factors Society 36th Annual Meeting*, 1220–1224, 1992.

Y

Young R.M. Surrogates and mappings: two kinds of conceptual models for interactive devices, in Gentner D. and Stevens A. (eds) *Mental Models*. Erlbaum, Hillsdale, NJ, 1983.

Younge P.D. Pyrex measures up: the redesign of a classic product, in *Proceedings of the 4th Symposium on Human Factors and Industrial Design in Consumer Products Interface 85*, Human Factors Society, Santa Monica, CA, 17–21, 1985.

Yourdon E. Whatever happened to structured analysis? *Datamation*, 133–138, 1 June 1986.

Z

Zimbardo P., McDermott M., Jansz J. and Metaal N. *Psychology: A European Text*. Harper Collins, London, 1995.

Zuboff S. *In the Age of the Smart Machine: The Future of Work and Power*. Basic Books, New York, 1988.

Index